CALL IT NORTH COUNTRY

GREAT LAKES BOOKS

CALL IT
North Country

The Story of Upper Michigan

BY

JOHN BARTLOW MARTIN

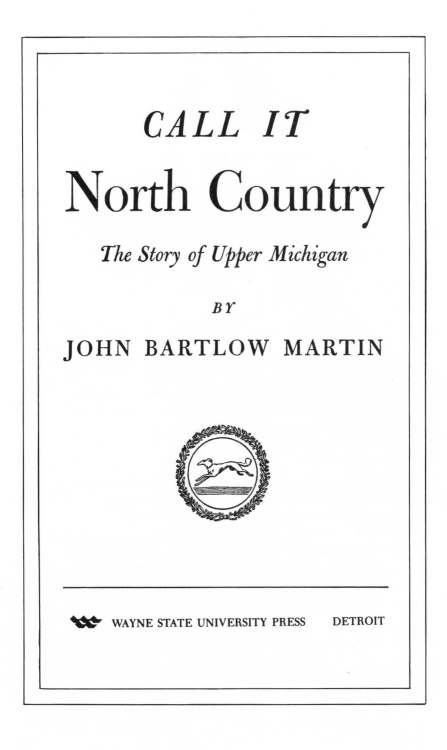

WAYNE STATE UNIVERSITY PRESS   DETROIT

03   02   01   00   99   9   8   7   6   5

Library of Congress Cataloging-in-Publication Data

Martin, John Bartlow, 1915–
    Call it north country.

    (Great Lakes books)
    Bibliography: p.
    Includes index.
    1. Upper Peninsula (Mich.)—History.   2. Upper
Peninsula (Mich.)—Social life and customs.   I. Title.
II. Series.
F572.N8M3   1986   977.4′9   86–15922
ISBN 0–8143–1868–1
ISBN 0–8143–1869–X (pbk.)

CONTENTS

ℰ

Call It North Country was, I now realize, what has come to be called social history—how the American people dressed, talked, worked, and behaved at various times in our history. When social history attempts to deal with the whole history of a nation, it is terribly inadequate, for it omits military, diplomatic, and political history. But I suppose it's all right for a small area, as here. At times, however, I went further and even lapsed into what television now calls "docudrama" technique. Some scenes never happened—at least they are not based on any written documents or eye-witness accounts. They are scenes that simply *ought to* have happened or *must* have happened. I have never written another book in this way. Yet few of my books have sold better, relatively, than *Call It North Country*.

We still, forty-six years later, go up to the Upper Peninsula in the summer. Twenty years ago we bought an empty piece of land far out in the woods, no road to it, no house within twelve and a half miles, and built there a log camp. When we can, we spend the whole summer there, and each morning with the July sunlight glancing off the lake below us through the pines, each deer we see, and each loon we hear, is like the first.

I know we share this feeling with many others. People born and raised in the Upper Peninsula never really leave it. This is why so many times in other people's camps up there, or in their houses in town, I've found copies of *Call It North Country* that are almost read literally to pieces, the spine cracked, pages loose, pages pencil-marked and with coffee spilled on them, books that have really been read. This is the readership an author appreciates.

What merit *Call It North Country* has, I think, derives from its having been written from interviews. Nearly everybody whose recollections of the old days are entombed here is himself entombed. It wasn't a bad idea to get them down on paper for our children. So it is not inappropriate that this book is being reprinted in the sesquicentennial year of Michigan's statehood, for it is, after all, a link to the remembered past.

John Bartlow Martin
June 5, 1986

CALL IT NORTH COUNTRY

To CAL OLSON

§ I §

THREE-FOOTED PEGGY

PETER MOORE—nobody ever called him Pete—stood apart at the bar, and his heavy shoulders drooped and even his full gray beard looked sad. Down at the end of the bar a bunch of miners, money in their fists, and their clothes red with iron ore, were punishing a bottle of George Voelker's best tanglefoot; this was payday in the mines and tonight the boys would lower the boom in Ishpeming. But not Peter Moore. He leaned over the bar alone and frowned at his liquor and scuffed his hobnailed Chippewa boots savagely on the iron plate that protected the floor at the bar. The country was going to hell.

It wasn't that trapping wasn't good; Peter had toted in a good-sized pile of beaver hides when he came in from the woods. It wasn't that Peter Moore needed money; he had plenty of money, though nobody ever knew where he kept it hid. No, it just plain was getting too crowded up at the Mulligan. Peter Moore was beset with neighbors. And he, who had followed the pine all the way from Maine and the Maritime Provinces, who could fall a tree so true it'd drive a nail, he, Peter Moore, was getting pushed around by men who called themselves lumberjacks. Lumberjacks! They wouldn't have made good swampers in the pine days of the eighties and nineties. Why, they were cutting stuff and calling it timber that a real lumberjack wouldn't use to build a fire. Hemlock, birch, tamarack, cedar, balsam, spruce—what kind of wood was that? What were they trying to do—skin it out right

3

down to the sand? Before long the woods that Peter Moore called
home would look like a city park. And it would be crowded as a
picnic ground on Sunday afternoon. The loggers were moving
in, a fresh generation of young squirts cutting her over a second
time, taking what the departed great men had scorned; they were
moving in on Peter Moore's domain, pushing him farther and
farther up into the woods.

Already they had forced him to move twice. But what good
did it do? You moved a few miles up into the woods and what
happened? Pretty soon the young squirts were logging the scrub
cedar ten feet from your privy. It was a new century, the
twentieth, the pine was gone, the white-water men who drove
her down the Big Dead River were all gone. Peter Moore spat
and thumped the bar gently for another drink. The country was
going to hell fast.

He was not a big man, but he was powerful. Short, heavy-built,
he had shoulders like a box car, and though he was past fifty, he
could hoist a two-hundred-pound half-barrel of beer to his back
like a gallon jug. You couldn't have guessed his age; with that
gray, full-flowing beard, he could have been seventy. Yet his
cheeks were pink and his blue eyes, deep-set in outdoor wrinkles,
shone bright as ever. Year in, year out, his dress did not change—
in the summer, cotton work shirt crisscrossed with suspenders
and a pair of lightweight pants rolled up over Chippewa boots;
in the winter, macmillan wool pants and a checkered shirt; and
always that lumberjack's fedora, dirty and soft and gray and inevitably with a turned-up brim front and back.

Scotch-Irish, he had been born in eastern Canada (but nobody
ever called him a Canuck to his face) and he had followed the
pine all the way from Nova Scotia to Maine to lower Michigan
along the Saginaw and then on up here to the Upper Peninsula
of Michigan, and here he had remained. He had cut the pine up
around Silver Lake and he had driven it from Silver Lake down
the river that the old French had named Rivière des Morts and
he had driven it down the cascading Yellow Dog to Lake Superior.
And when the pine was gone and the loggers moved on west in
the nineties, Peter Moore stayed. He liked it up in the Silver
Lake country north of Ishpeming; he stayed there, alone in the

woods, trapping and, now, watching dam.

His was the loneliest job of all, and he liked it that way. The city of Marquette's power company had taken over an old logging dam at the outlet of Silver Lake where it spills out to form the Big Dead River; the company had bolstered the dam to form a reservoir and now needed someone to watch the dam; Peter Moore was the only man who lived out that way any more; so he took the job for about thirty-five dollars a month. He stayed a year or two at the Dead River Farm and ran a trap line twelve miles up to the dam, walking the twelve miles almost daily.

But that camp at the farm was only about ten miles north of Ishpeming, which was too close to town for Peter Moore; and besides, now at the turn of the century, a new lumbering company came in to clean up the short stuff. It got too crowded; Peter Moore moved, moved up to old Camp Three, the abandoned headquarters camp of the Dead River Milling Company near the forks of Mulligan Creek and the Big Dead River. This was like coming home; he'd logged out of here. Now the place was deserted, a ghost-haunted sepulcher, but Peter patched up the tar-paper roof and the log walls and put out his traps and settled down here deep in the woods, miles from any other human; settled down and lived here alone—except for three-footed Peggy.

Peggy was not a woman (Peter Moore didn't like women, wouldn't allow them in camp); Peggy was a cat. She had belonged to a lumber camp; when the loggers moved on, she stayed, like Peter Moore. He adopted her. Before she had been long with him, she caught her foot in a coyote trap of Peter's. Peter Moore operated by the light of a kerosene lamp up there in the woods; he nursed her back to health and now they understood each other, Peter and Peggy. Like him, she needed no coddling; despite her infirmity, she hunted in the woods like a tiger-striped wild cat, killing her own food, prowling with grotesque agility through the timber, and at night lying in the cabin beside Peter's bed, arching her back and spitting wildly when a bear came too close to the back door. Peggy could stand on her own three feet.

Peter wished that she were here now, in George Voelker's saloon on Main Street in Ishpeming. He was lonesome. Alone in the woods, Peter Moore never was lonesome. But here in town he felt lost among the hurrying people of the new century, among the crowds of miners with their strange tongues from Finland and Italy and Sweden. He only came in three times a year, to get his chuck and bring out his skins and maybe see the circus, and he dreaded the trip. He missed Peggy, more than ever today. Maybe next time he'd bring her in. But he hated to. People stared at her. Damn it all, anyway.

The old man was putting down another drink when he heard someone say: "Peter" in that quiet voice and he knew without turning that Tommy Wilson had come back. Tommy was Peter Moore's partner if ever any man truly was. Tommy stayed up in the woods with Peter for long stretches. But Tommy, restless for the bright lights, would go away with the circus for maybe a year, maybe two years.

But why was he here now? Just the day before, when the Ringling Brothers circus paraded through Ishpeming, Tommy Wilson, all decked out in red with golden spangles, had driven the eight-horse team that pulled the animal cage, just like he always did. Time was when Peter had watched proudly the way Tommy handled those eight horses. But yesterday Peter Moore had turned his back on Tommy Wilson and his circus and he hadn't even said good-by when Tommy left with the circus to go down below. Now, unaccountably, Tommy Wilson had reappeared. He stepped up beside Peter Moore, ordered a drink, and drank it without saying anything; then, still without looking at Peter, he said he guessed he'd come back because he got lonesome for Silver Lake. And besides, he had an idea. Why not build a camp right up there at the lake?

Peter Moore shook his head and spoke bitterly in that high-pitched squeaky voice which suited so ill his powerful frame. What good would it do? He'd moved from the Dead River Farm to old Camp Three at the forks of the Mulligan and the Dead; the loggers had chased him out of there and he'd moved on to the old clearing three miles up the Mulligan where he'd thought he'd be safe from them forever. But they were coming closer now all the time; before the snow was flying, they'd be up there, hot-logging for all they were worth, stump to mill from dawn to dusk, not decking the giant logs along the rivers all winter, and then in the spring, when the river got a driving head on, breaking the rollways and sending the logs roaring into the white water where the river-hogs rode her down to the mill high, wide, and handsome—no, not logging properly, but just sawing down little sticks of trees summer or winter and snaking 'em out with a team and hauling 'em down to the mills all in one day. Hot-logging, stump to mill, dawn to dusk. They'd cut over the Dead River basin till there was nothing left but sand and brush; now they were crowding in on the Mulligan; pretty soon they'd be up at Silver Lake. Why go to all the trouble of building a camp up there for a year or two? Let 'em cut her. To hell with it.

But Tommy Wilson was persistent. And he had the answer: Induce the city of Marquette to buy a forty or so up at Silver Lake. Build your camp on that. Then you could tell 'em all to go to hell. Why not? The big companies were grabbing all the land everywhere. Why not get a piece for yourself?

And he won the argument. The city bought the land for Peter Moore and, hardly believing it was really coming true, the old man went up to camp on the Mulligan with Tommy Wilson. There he chucked three-footed Peggy under the chin and had a couple of drinks of good liquor to celebrate—not just plain whisky but whisky fixed up right so it wouldn't hurt you: you take beaver castors and you put 'em into a whisky bottle and fill the bottle and let it sit a good long time; and then, Peter Moore claimed, you could drink till your hair came out and the liquor wouldn't hurt you one bit.

And after they had their drink, they got to work. All during June month and July month they were busy falling the trees and peeling them and decking them out to dry. In the mists of dawn they'd walk up through the hardwood, over the rough hills where the gold and silver and iron ore still are locked in rock; they'd work all day in the woods as Peter loved to work; and just before dark, they'd walk back to the camp at the Mulligan. What matter if, when they went into town for chuck, they saw the puny little loggers moving closer all the time? They'd be long gone from the Mulligan by the time those squirts arrived.

And they were. In the fall they built the cabin right by the blue white-capped shore of Silver Lake, two men in the woods and a three-footed cat for a helper; they built it good and solid so it'd stand forever against the bitter winter wind that swept down from Lake Superior beyond the mountains; and then, for good measure, they put up a little barn and a woodshed; and by the time the first snow roared down out of the north, they were sitting inside by the squat iron stove, drinking beaver-castored whisky and arguing about where they'd put their traps. And Peggy purred all the time.

That camp, and the new one built later beside it, have been the home of four lonely men, the dam-keepers of Silver Lake. Ollie Nordtome, Neil Steffans, Dan Spencer—they in their turn slept where Peter slept, knew the quiet of Silver Lake.

When one died or drank too much or simply went away, another took his place, his right to the job unquestioned. It does not pay much, in money. It is a hard, lonely way of life. Solitude can be a disease in the north country. Yet solitude is part of the country's charm. There is the solitude of winter, when nothing moves in the woods but the wind through the tall timber. There is the dark solitude of a lake on a moonless night, when the only sound is the cry of a loon, long and high and weird, like the laughter of a woman gone mad. There is the solitude of the deep woods, and the solitude of the wild Big Lake, Superior, and the special solitude of the deep black holes that men have thrust thousands of feet down into the copper and iron ranges.

This book is about Upper Michigan, a section of the wilderness country, but mostly it is about some of its people. Some of the people who pioneered it with bateaux and snowshoes and dog teams and some of the people who live in it now. These people, and their land. It is a vast land, this wilderness country. It stretches from the east coast of Canada to the plains of the Athabaska. When the Jesuits came with cross and Book, they found the wilderness flowing without end along the coasts of the Great Lakes, westward from Quebec and up the Falls of Sainte Marie that we call now the Soo and on farther along the northern and southern coasts of the cruel Big Lake, Superior; this was the Upper Peninsula of Michigan, and it was also the country of northern Wisconsin and northern Minnesota, not the sections where the land is rolling and fertile and planted now to wheat, but the parts where the iron hills rise, where the pine blanketed mile upon mile of flat sand plains, where the tamarack timber skirts the desolate swamp; and the wilderness covered the great forests of Ontario and all the thousands of lakes and the mighty river systems that rise in the oldest mountain range of all, the Laurentian, and drain northward into Hendrik Hudson's Bay.

And later, after the Jesuits had come and gone, the fur kings sent their *couriers de bois* coursing through the myriad water highways of the forests, building empire for the Northwest Fur Company and the Hudson's Bay Company and for a German immigrant named John Jacob Astor. These men came and they departed, having seen the bloody intertribal warfare of the Indians give way to the confused War of 1812, when fog-shrouded British in rowboats captured the American fleet block-ading Mackinac Island. The fur men saw, too, the British move sullenly up into Canada along the shaky boundary line Ben Franklin drew and marked with non-existent islands.

For years after the fur barons left, no one took their place—no one but the surveyors and explorers who ran the line and dickered with the Indians. No one paid much attention to them; for twenty-odd years all this vast region was simply a part of Northwest Territory: unexplored wilderness known to the Eastern politicians only by legend and hearsay, country that some day might be divided up into states, but was probably worthless anyway. And then sud-denly the surveyors, wilderness men without peer who have been almost forgotten in their own country, found iron and copper and mentioned it in their field notes. And that set the pattern: from then on this was boom-and-bust country, mineral land, timber-land. Yet it always has remained wilderness country.

The heart of this Lake Superior country is the Upper Peninsula of Michigan. Take a map and stick one leg of a draftsman's dividers into the tip of the Keweenaw Peninsula—the copper country that is the topmost point of Upper Michigan—and circum-scribe a circle with a 300-mile radius and you will cover most of the wilderness country. You will cover all of Lake Superior and the wild Quetico National Park in Canada; you will come not far south of James Bay, the lower end of Hudson Bay; you will cover

the Soo and the now industrialized Lower Peninsula of Michigan
and all of northern Wisconsin. You will hit the great iron ports
—Duluth, Superior, Two Harbors, Ashland, Marquette, Escanaba.
You will have the copper country of Keweenaw, the only place
in the world where native copper is found pure in the earth in
commercial quantities. You will have the great iron ranges—the
Mesaba and Vermilion and Cuyuna of Minnesota, the Marquette
and Gogebic and Menominee of the Upper Peninsula. You will
have the vast sand plains and swamplands where the hell-roaring
red-eyed lumberjack army cut the great white pine on their way
from Maine to Oregon; the towns they made famous are still
legends of lusty bawdry: Seney and the lesser centers, and the
miners' sin spot, Hurley. You will have the Sault Ste. Marie Canal,
busiest in the world. You will have the fog-shrouded islands of
Lake Superior, Michipicoten and Isle Royale; and you will have
the vast still roadless wilderness that stretches darkly up toward
the pole from the north coast of Superior.

Big country, wilderness country; its heartland is the Upper
Peninsula of Michigan. It is hard country. Though much of it is
level, pocked only here and there by rugged hills, it all is wild
country, mining and lumbering country. Its boosters call it
Hiawathaland, and it is true that Longfellow drew on the legends
of the red men of the Upper Peninsula, but more Indians probably live here now than lived here two hundred years ago: the
country was too tough even for the Indians. It is called cutover
country and that too is true, but it is only a part of the story, the
lumbering part. They call it copper country, iron country; those
too are inadequate. Call it north country and let it go at that.

The gateway to the Upper Peninsula is Sault Ste. Marie. Here
the long low ships move up through the canal from the great steel
mills of Pittsburgh and the Chicago district and the Ohio lake
ports, into treacherous Lake Superior, bound for the iron-ore
fields. When the ice is out on the lower lakes, it still pounds at the
bows of the freighters on Superior; and after that come the fogs,
hanging low over the gray-blue water for weeks, shrouding islands
that seem to move in the mists, shrouding the ghosts of La Salle's
lost *Griffon* and all the other Flying Dutchmen of the lakes, veil-
ing the sundogs that the dying sun throws suddenly onto the

cloud banks to baffle mariners. A cold, heartless lake, Superior.

No softer is the land. Westward from the Soo stretches the vast Tahquamenon swamp; now the pine has been cut and the lonely tamarack, spare and gaunt, stands sentinel over the slumbering land. Beyond the swamp for endless miles of table-flat desolation are the sand plains where once the lumberjack labored and drank and fought. Here in the Chippewa country are the rivers he drove: the Two-Hearted, the Manistique, the Driggs, the Fox. You can jump across some of them and in the summer there's hardly any water in them at all, but hell, the river-hogs could drive a heavy dew.

Beyond the vast level Chippewa country the iron hills rise abruptly from Lake Superior behind Marquette; here iron ore was first discovered exactly one hundred years ago between what now are the twin iron towns of Ishpeming and Negaunee. And the Marquette Range lies westward, out past Humboldt and Champion and Michigamme and down the Michigamme River to Republic. Iron and steel made the twentieth century; this is where it came from in the beginning, and this is where it comes from today. The steel barons founded fortunes here, but they never quite succeeded in taming the wilderness, though they came into it in private railroad cars after the real men had done the spade-work. Long before the vast Mesaba Range was opened in Minnesota, the mining men of the Upper Peninsula ranges were learning, the hard way, how to avoid getting killed in the mine and still grub iron ore from the stubborn earth. And later, when the companies wanted a good diamond-drill man up the Burma Road or in Spitsbergen or Johannesburg or back in the Amazon River country, they sent for the men from the Michigan ranges.

North and south of the Marquette Range are more pine plains and their river highways—the Dead and the Yellow Dog and the Peshekee to the north, the Paint and the Michigamme to the south, and the great Menominee, which flows all the way down to Green Bay on Lake Michigan. And south too lies the Menominee iron range, second to be opened. Range towns here, some of them mines and mining locations that became towns: Vulcan, Norway, Iron Mountain, Quinnesec, Loretto, Crystal Falls, Iron River, Amasa. And below them the river called Brule after the French adventurer who cheated the Indians in Champlain's time and was murdered by them.

Westward farther to the end of the peninsula lies the third great iron range to be discovered near the end of the nineteenth century, the Gogebic Range, and its capital, Ironwood, and, across the Montreal River in Wisconsin, Ironwood's bawdy poor relation, Hurley.

Swing north across flatland to the Ontonagon country and the low-squatting Porcupine Mountains, where they prospected silver and mined copper. And now up north to the top, to the great copper trap range of the Keweenaw Peninsula: to Paines-dale and South Range and to Houghton and Hancock, the twin copper capitals that climb up the sheer rock cliffs from Portage Lake. And farther up the tip to Calumet and Allouez and Ahmeek and Eagle River and Eagle Harbor, and finally to Copper Harbor, the town at the tip which was once almost the capital of the Upper Peninsula.

"DAN DAN, DAMN FINE MAN"

IT IS an old country, this Upper Peninsula. Men were claim-jumping in the iron fields before gold was found at Sutter's Mill in California; when the forty-niners deserted the Upper Peninsula, they had to be replaced in the booming copper mines, and by the time Lincoln called for seventy-five thousand volunteers, the copper kings were sending labor lookers to Europe to bring in a fresh supply of men.

The early days in northern Michigan were perilous. There never was enough flour to last the winter, enough potatoes, enough salt, enough whisky, enough of anything. Men never really learned just how hard this country was. But somehow they managed, though many died; somehow they hung on.

And even when the pioneers came in the early forties, the Upper Peninsula was old. It is the oldest country in America. Ages ago, the first land that thrust up out of the primordial seas to form the North American continent was the Laurentian Mountain Range, with its low weather-scarred head in the Canadian highlands and its foot on Keweenaw in Michigan's Upper Peninsula. It remains today, a scarred welt across the level face of the northern Midwest. The Great Lakes slowly formed and settled in their troughs and the earth heaved fearfully and then slowly relapsed into sullen quiet, leaving deposits of iron and copper and gold and lead and silver in the pitted rocks. Long afterward men came, the first of them perhaps from Mexico, perhaps from Siberia; and after them the red men we call Indians; and then the whites, led by the Jesuits and the *voyageurs* and then the surveyors and the prospectors and the miners from all over the world and then the Wall Street capitalists and the Chicago lumber barons and the copper kings from Boston and even Henry Ford from River Rouge.

They fought over this ancient land and its riches. The unmarked wilderness muffled the songs of the *voyageurs* and the roaring of the miners and lumberjacks cursing the hard life they loved. They scrambled over the rocks and hills and swamps and rushing rivers; they fought cold of forty degrees below zero and they fought mosquitoes, and around the men and their country grew legends. Like the story of the boy who took a big copper kettle out to a sugar-maple tree and, attacked by mosquitoes, hid under the kettle, only to have two persistent mosquitoes drill through the heavy metal; he hammered their drilling beaks with a stone and bent the beaks and clinched them and then, unable to free themselves, they flew away into the swamp, carrying the kettle between them, the boy sitting on the handle, swinging. Or the legends of Paul Bunyan and his great blue ox, or the stories about how pigs discovered the fabulous Calumet conglomerate copper lode and about how the north wind blew over a giant pine and laid bare the great Marquette iron range.

These men coursed everywhere, and their mark is on the country even as its mark, a hard one, is on them and their children's children. Go into the woods today and when you think you are in wilderness never seen before by man, you will fall into a prospector's abandoned test pit or you will stumble over the brush-grown ties of an old logging railroad. Struggle all day to breast the swamps and rocky hills and you may end up in a thicket concealing a rusty four-hundred-pound stove that some forgotten trapper carried into camp piece by piece fifty or seventy years before you. Sail the Big Lake and get tossed about in your steamer cabin and be convinced that you are hardy; but do not forget that Douglass Houghton, exploring the coasts of the Keweenaw, was drowned because no boat bigger than a canoe was available.

Truly, it is a country of forlorn hopes, of ghost towns that never will come back but whose old residents, remembering the great days, cling to hope; a country of railroads that never quite got built, of ore docks that burned and were not reconstructed, of veins of gold that petered out, of yawning holes in the ground into which men dumped millions before they would admit the ore just wasn't rich enough. But it is not a dead country; its color is not gone; it does not live entirely in the past. It is still tough country, still fifty years behind the times, still fifty years closer to things—not ideas—than the cities. (But the men who manipulate the country like a feudal domain dwell in the cities.)

Here are the Cornishmen and the Swedes and the Finns and the Irish, who used to battle in the streets over the green of a necktie; here are the ghosts of boom towns; here are the wilderness lakes, the deer yards thick with deer in wintertime; here are the craggy copper cliffs, the old round iron hills with stubborn sullen faces; here are the wooded hills and the swamps and rivers and here are the people who battled them all: solid people, clannish people, people with long memories and doubtful futures, mining men and lumbering men and their women who worked for them "seventeen hours a day, seven days a week." This book is about these people of Michigan's Upper Peninsula.

When Peter Moore had built his cabin on the shores of Silver Lake, he was all set. Now let the loggers come; they'd leave damn fast. Or, if the mood suited him, would stay to have a drink of beaver-castored whisky. This was his land now; he could walk over it and kick it with his hobnailed boots. Tommy Wilson might drift away, ultimately; but here Peter Moore would live till he died. In the woods near by he found an old pine stump, ancient and gnarled and enormous; he grubbed it out of the earth and chopped it up for kindling. Pitchwood, it burned like kerosene. He split an old dry cedar from the jam-up by the dam; more kindling. Some second-growth maple he cut and corded for stove wood, a huge pile of it. All this he stacked in the little woodshed back of camp, piling it up to the roof before the snow fell. He cut hay in the clearing before the cabin was finished; when it dried, he baled it in the barn and now he wouldn't have to load his wagon half full of feed for the horses every time he wanted to bring in a load of chuck. He drove nails in the walls outside for snowshoes and inside for his rifles and his shotgun. Just a few hundred feet from the cabin door he found a big bubbling spring that never froze, the water so cold in summer it made his teeth ache. Good water—that was half the battle. And now he would walk around the cabin and the snow-covered clearing, peering at the neatly corded wood, studying the trees and planning improvements for the summer, surveying his domain. A tight little cabin, a piece of timbered land, enough wood cut to last the winter out, plenty of grub, guns, traps, a little drinking whisky—what more could a man want?

No man ever loved the woods more than Peter Moore. No man knew the woods better. Though he was past fifty, he still could have out-trapped the French who coursed the streams in the early days. He always kept thirty to forty traps out at a time and he would run the trap line every other day all winter. That meant a lot of work. He would climb out of his bunk long before dawn, with the temperature far below zero and the air so cold your breath froze as it left your mouth. He would stir up the fire in the heating stove and build a fire in the big cook stove; then, while the coffee was brewing, he would make up his pack: a little tea, a fire-blackened tin can for boiling water, eggs from the barrel of salt, a little deer meat (they only called it venison in the city). By the time he'd finished his coffee, dawn was breaking over the range of hills behind the camp. He would take his gun down from the nails in the log wall and step out of the warm cabin into the dawn cold and buckle on his snowshoes and start out along the frozen lake shore, swinging across the crusted snow with an easy shuffling gait that consumed the long white spaces as though they were nothing. Maybe the first trap was down below the dam at the lake outlet. There might be a mink in that little trap, hidden at the edge of the icy water.

Then on around the bay and up the lake shore, over the broken rocks and through the timber, darkly green against the white snow. By now the sun was red as blood in the sky; it was a fine clear day and the old man, his beard waving gently in the wind, felt good. He ran his trap line all morning, and by dinner time he was pretty close to the abandoned silver-lead mine on the west end of the lake. (You can still see the rock pile, monument to the men who hammered and clawed at the earth, picking at the tiny stringers of silver in the rock that somehow never widened into a real bonanza vein. But they took out mineral, all right; took it out by wagon and on their backs thirty miles through the woods to Marquette. Silver ore won't float like logs on a driving river.)

A little hot tea to wash down the deer meat, a couple of pipes, and then the old man would go on, till, near the early dusk when he got back to camp, he was hunchbacked with his pack of fur. The next day he would spend in camp, stretching the hides. And the day after that, back out on the trail again.

Every now and then he'd get a coyote, and there was a bounty on that. And a timber wolf was a real prize; so was a bobcat, most dangerous animal in the woods. Bears were not uncommon. One day, coming in off the trail, Peter found a bear caught by one hind paw in a trap he'd anchored to the old swill piles at the abandoned logging camp on the Mulligan. A big black she-bear. She saw him coming and reared up on her hind legs and swayed back and forth, roaring, towering maybe eight feet in the air, and she lunged and swung to get free of the jagged trap jaws. Peter unlimbered his 45-70 and waited till she was still a moment; then he shot her through the chest as she stood there, and she toppled with a crash to the snow. Skinning her out and butchering her and dragging the carcass to camp took hours. But it meant meat for weeks, and good money for the skin.

In the spring it was beaver all the time, and Peter Moore knew where they built their houses and how they could be trapped. Finally, along in May, the long winter ended, and Peter made his first trip into town in June, walking the twenty-one miles with his enormous pack of hides. He'd go first to Joe Schiller's Commercial House on Division Street and there he would transact his business in mysterious fashion. Peter never sold his furs in Ishpeming; he always sent them away somewhere. Everybody knew he got a top price and many a time the other trappers, coming on him in his cups, would try to find out where he sent his hides; but, drunk or sober, he never told. He used his high squeaky voice sparingly, especially where his personal affairs were concerned.

He might stay in town a few days or he might stay a week or two, depending on the weather and on how thirsty he was. He never was a man to make a stake, then come to town and blow it in one grand debauch. But he liked his liquor, and he always visited George Voelker's saloon and George Thoney's saloon—he always

called it "visiting my friends"—and sometimes he would go into
the place run by two Finns, Henry Manley and Alec Anderson,
whose real names were Henry Mantilla and Konstu Marjaneimi.
The Finns started coming to the Upper Peninsula in the eighties
and nineties and came and came until today they probably are
the biggest single racial group, but they had a hard time of it in
the early days. Racial prejudice is not dead yet, but in the nineties
it was bitter and real. The early settlers had been French and
Scotch and English; then the Irish and the Swedes had come, and
though the Irish fought the Swedes every year on St. Patrick's
Day and Orangeman's Day and nearly every other day, they
agreed on one thing: that Finns were no bloody good. When the
lumbering companies first put Finns out in the woods, the other
lumberjacks refused to work with them. Since sawyers always
worked in pairs and the Finns were unable to get partners, they
had to work as swampers, grubbing roads out of the muck, despi-
cable work. They had to sleep in designated corners of the huge
foul-smelling bunkhouses; they had to eat at the far end of the
table; and all winter nobody spoke to them except to curse them.
Many changed their names, but they could not change their high
cheekbones, their flat foreheads, their blond hair that somehow
has a different quality from the blondness of the Scandinavian.
But they were a tenacious people and they hung on grimly, keeping clannishly to themselves and working in silence. Grudgingly
the others accepted them and, though they still cluster together
and have retained perhaps more of their native traditions than any
other group, they now are a solid part of the community. And
this is as it should be; for this north country is peculiarly their
own; it is like their homeland, rocky and rough, with long winters,
covered from November to May with snow, pocked with blue-
water lakes and mantled with trees that are ever green.

Peter Moore was more tolerant of the Finns than many men
of his day. As tolerant as he was of any man. He was, his friends
remember, "set in his ways." He was independent, as were all his
successors at Silver Lake and as are most men who make the woods
their own. He was silent and he kept to himself. During his town
drinking he had few companions; mostly he stood by himself at
the bar. And when the time came to go back, he went alone, up

the logging road along the Dead River basin and across the Little Dead and the Mulligan and the Connors, where the sand plains were naked and flat as far as you could see; and then up into the hardwood, the big woods. Here, after he climbed the single enormous hill that rises from the rushing stream, he was among virgin birches and maples three feet through at the butt; here the sunlight rarely penetrated to the earth, and the forest floor was cool and clean. And then he topped the last rise and could see Silver Lake, shimmering blue and dazzling white through the trees; and there was Peggy to meet him, clawing at the door as he approached, mewing beside his legs as he entered, waiting for him to unshoulder his pack and pick her up and feed her.

He made his first trip out in May or June, his second in July, his last in September, just before the deer season opened (but was it ever closed season up in the big woods?). And then he was in for the winter. He needed three trips to bring in his chuck—a hundred-pound sack of beans, two hundred-pound sacks of flour, fifteen or twenty pounds of coffee, a gallon of molasses, five pounds of tea, five or ten bushels of potatoes (later he raised his own), but never, of course, any meat. And always a five-gallon jug of whisky. But only that one jug; it lasted him through the winter (unless, of course, a party of hunters happened to come in with a bottle), for, alone in the woods, Peter Moore was a temperate man. Only a little nip now and then each day; never any roaring lonely jags.

But he probably had enough to drink about. Nobody knew much about his past—not the details, that is. It must have been something less than fortunate; would love of the woods alone send him up to Silver Lake to spend his life? It is said that he had been married while he was back east, before he came out to the Upper Peninsula. And that he had a daughter. And that his wife died. It was after her death that he started following the pine and ended up at Silver Lake.

He had kept the dam there some fifteen years and was around seventy when three-footed Peggy died. Peter buried her out there at Silver Lake and did not mark the grave; *he* knew where it was; why tell the world?

But after that Peter was lonely. The woods were not enough

now. And he was growing old. He started thinking about his daughter somewhere back east. He had lost track of her. He put an ad in the personal column of an Eastern newspaper. And got an answer: a woman claimed she was his daughter and said she would be glad to have him visit her.

Peter must have pondered long alone in his cabin in the woods before he made up his mind to journey east. He was an old man; he had been around Ishpeming for thirty years or so and here at Silver Lake for twenty years. But now he packed a few things into an old suitcase and took a train east.

In a few weeks he was back, heading into the woods, saying nothing. "Saw wood and say nothing." But later it became known that he had seen the lady and they had talked. And now Peter sat up there in the cabin, thinking. This was his country. He had logged it and trapped it and hunted it; he had cleared this land and built this camp; this was his.

But it wasn't the same. Three-footed Peggy was gone. The pine was gone, and most of the short stuff. Even the beaver were thinning out. This was 1920, and when you went into town, the streets were full of Fords, puffing and snorting everywhere. The old board sidewalks, scarred with lumberjacks' calks, were gone. Peter had lost his battle with time. Might as well give up. He packed his few things and took a last look at the camp and hit the trail for town. He didn't stop in Ishpeming; he got aboard the eastbound train, an old bearded man sitting up very straight alone in a day-coach seat.

He never came back; he died out east, supposedly in his daughter's home. And they still say, around Ishpeming, that, though he only made some $35 a month as dam-keeper, he left some $17,000 when he died. He was a good trapper, "a good man in the woods," they say up north. It is their highest compliment.

Ollie Nordtome, a carpenter by trade, took over where Peter Moore left off. He wasn't satisfied with Peter's camp, so he built a new one, larger and lighter than Peter's, of enormous logs. Before it was finished, Ollie left and Neil Steffans took over. He completed the new camp, and when he got through, it was an amazing thing. This was no rude shack in the woods; it had a concrete porch floor and ornate glass doors. Taking cement on a sleigh over the drifted snow those twenty-one miles into the woods from Ishpeming was a tremendous job; the one hill alone was enough to break the back of a stout team.

Neil, big and raw-boned, was famed chiefly for his glass still. He kept it in the woods during the days of Prohibition—the dry era never did take hold in the north country—and his moon was praised with loud hosannas by one and all. Neil liked it pretty well himself.

Winter, famine, solitude—they are things to fight in the north country. Another is liquor. With it, the men in the woods have trouble. Having a drink may be more than a social occasion; it may be a defeat; the temperance ladies' slogans sometimes become meaningful here. Again, liquor can be as real a hardship as packing for a drinking man—getting it, keeping it, hiding it from the boys, bringing it into camp: these are difficult problems, to be solved only by devious methods. Some men spend more time at this than at trapping. For unless you are a real trapper like Peter Moore, there is little to do alone in the winter woods but drink. Neil Steffans was a pretty good trapper, but that glass still, shining and beautiful and efficient—it brewed strong liquor and plenty of it. Storing it was a major project. Neil, fittingly, stored it in the woods.

One time the game warden, Ed Sandberg, asked old Cal Olson if he wanted to go up to Silver Lake and visit Neil for a day. Cal said he might as well; didn't have nothing else to do anyway. Cal had quit his job as a bartender to go to China with a diamond-drill outfit to prospect for mineral; now, back in the States, it being dry here, he wasn't tending bar any more, wasn't doing much of anything right then; just mooching around and taking things easy. Cal had been born in Ishpeming in '73 just after his parents arrived from Sweden; he had lived all his life in Ishpeming and it had been quite a life, as we shall see.

So Cal and Ed Sandberg had dinner with Neil Steffans up at Silver Lake, and after dinner Sandberg left, promising to come back for Cal the next morning. But he didn't come back, not for a week, and Cal remembers that week as a long nightmare, spent in watching Neil drink all evening, in walking each morning three miles to the edge of the hardwood and sitting on a stump and looking down the trail, waiting for Ed Sandberg to come for him. The high spot came the night Neil's system broke down, his system of hiding his liquor.

About ten o'clock he finished the last bottle inside the camp and announced his intention of going into the woods after more. Cal tried to dissuade him, but Neil would have none of it: he was going to get another drink, by God, if he had to walk all the way to town for it. He flung open the door and plunged out into the darkness without a lantern. Cal, his friend, was afraid to let him go out into the night alone. He might step into a windfall, break his leg. And carrying a two-hundred-pound six-footer the twenty-one miles back to town would be no joke. Cal took a lantern and followed him out into the woods.

Neil had liquor hidden everywhere, but tonight he couldn't find it. He pawed around in hollow stumps, he plunged into the swamp and rooted under deadfalls and crawled on his hands and knees into tangled timber, hunting a jug. And all the time Cal timidly kept trying to talk him into going back to the cabin. And all the time Neil kept swearing at Cal and at the liquor. Just those two men, wandering around in the big woods, Neil on his hands and knees and Cal holding the lantern and pleading. Well, Neil finally found his jug in a hollow stump, and though he headed for Lake Superior instead of camp, Cal finally got him back to the cabin, where he promptly collapsed.

Neil's successor as keeper of the dam was Dan Spencer, a great lunking Scotch-Irishman from eastern Canada who wears a fierce white walrus mustache and has pink cheeks and a vocabulary profane as a mule-skinner's. He is a legend at Ishpeming, though he still is drinking his pint or so a day; it is said that when he and his twin brother celebrated their seventy-fifth birthday together in Ishpeming and Negaunee, they drank Negaunee dry. And that is something.

Dan was a miner when he first came to the iron range, and then he tended bar for Simons for many years. He was a state trapper, too, paid to trap coyote and other vermin, but he wouldn't trap very hard; he would wind up on a stump with a jug and maybe sometimes lose his traps.

The legend of Dan is complex and it runs to a pattern. Dan

encourages the legend, tells and retells it, usually in rhyme. About the time somebody brought the Indian princess to the Silver Lake cabin on her honeymoon. About the drawings of voluptuous nudes, spattered with bacon grease, on the wall near the cook stove. About the time—

Well, as he says, "Dan, Dan, damn fine man." He rhymes almost everything, often in soliloquy, explaining: "I talk to myself for two good reasons: number one, I like to hear a sensible man talk; number two, I like to talk to a sensible man. Yep, yep; guess so." He stands by the hour at the window of the cabin, one thumb hooked in his suspenders, the other hand stroking his mustache and his unshaven jowls, muttering to himself endlessly: "Yep, yep; guess so," and leaning forward, little squinty eyes always peering down the trail to see who's coming to visit him and bring "a gallon o' 'shine, to have a damn good time."

One time the constabulary came to visit him. Or, rather, tried to. Dan tells it. He heard the constabulary was coming up to raid his liquor cache. (Like many men in the Upper Peninsula, Dan, being Canadian, refers to the police as the constabulary.) So he quickly rounded up his bottles of whisky and home brew—why he made home brew is a mystery, for Danny needs whisky—and he hauled it down to the lake, chopped a hole in the ice, and dropped the liquor into the shallow water near the dam. Then he sat down in all innocence to wait for the constabulary. Sundown came and they didn't arrive; Dan worried about them, for the snow was deep and the night was dark; he lighted a lamp and set it in the window to guide them in. For hours he stood by the window in the lamplight, staring with watery eyes out into the darkness and waiting. Finally, though his throat was parched, he went to bed, leaving the lamp for the constabulary.

They didn't arrive next day, though he waited all day; that second evening he lighted the lamp again and waited. But by now he couldn't stand still at the window; he kept pacing the cabin floor, thinking about a drink and cussing out the tardy constabs. Maybe he ought to have that drink anyway. Maybe it wasn't true they were coming. (As it turned out later, they actually had got about half-way there before they turned back; the going was too tough for them.) But no, he'd wait another night.

He didn't sleep much that night and he was wakened before dawn by his great thirst. And not a drop of liquor in camp for a face-maker.

To hell with 'em; he was going to have that drink. He hurried down to the dam, re-chopped the hole in the ice, and, using a rabbit snare, began fishing with trembling fingers for a bottle of whisky. But it was bitter cold, his fingers grew numb; the water was deeper than he had thought. Where in hell was that damn whisky? Had the current carried it— He cried aloud in agony and he fished harder than ever. "I fished for nine hours and twenty-seven minutes," he says. Finally the snare caught on something, tightened. With infinite pains, as gently as though he were drawing the skin from a mink, he raised the prize. Careful now, not to bang it against the ice; should have chopped that damn hole bigger. He shifted his weight to the other knee to steady himself. The bottle broke water—a bottle, not of good red liquor, but of mealy home brew. He seized the bottle and he roared: "Danny don't want beer; Danny wants whisky," and he hurled the hated bottle back into the lake, ran back to the cabin, buckled on his snow-shoes, and tramped the whole twenty-one miles back to town. There his thirst awed strong men, and the story of the jag he got on that time still is legend.

But those were the great days. They are done. In the summer of 1943 the Cleveland-Cliffs Iron Company, paternal giant of the Marquette Range, took over the camp at Silver Lake, the dam, and the land that Peter Moore got the power company to buy. Old Dan, last of the legendary men, came into town for the last time, mumbling in his stubbly beard, his old sweat-soaked pack bulging with his belongings.

The graybeards in the Ishpeming bars shook their heads sadly. Old Dan was through. The CCI was sending a new man up to Silver Lake. A family man, some said. A skilled craftsman, long in the faithful service of the company. Times change. The old days are gone. And you know what? They're talking about putting a road right up through the hardwood, right up all the way to Silver Lake. Maybe they'll put in picnic benches, roadside tables. Damn good thing old Peter Moore's dead.

‹§ 3 §›

FOR GOD AND KING

A-HUNTING ONE DAY went Manabozho, the Great Spirit whose father was the West Wind and whose mother was a great-grand-daughter of the Moon. With him went a wolf, his relative. The wolf fell through the ice of a frozen lake and was promptly devoured by serpents. Transforming himself into a tree stump, Manabozho ambushed and killed the king of the serpents. At the command of the vengeful serpents, who were all manitous, the waters of the lake flooded the earth. Manabozho climbed a tree; it grew as rapidly as the flood rose and saved him. Nowhere was there any land—nothing but water. Manabozho enlisted the aid of a loon in the task of remaking the world. The loon drowned diving for some mud. Manabozho induced a muskrat to try; presently he too floated to the surface, apparently dead. But Manabozho discovered in his paws a particle of the precious mud, "and of this, together with the body of the loon, created the world anew."

Thus the Indians believed it was in the beginning, writes Parkman. (It also is written that Manabozho mated with a she-muskrat and propagated the human race.) Geologists might have a more scientific explanation of the earth's origin. But, as they stumbled across the rocky glaciated face of Upper Michigan they might have wondered if it were not true indeed that only the crazy loon of a crazy Indian's legend could have made a land like this.

Who inhabited it first is disputed. After the great glaciers flowed down from the Arctic and ice-locked the Upper Peninsula and all the United States down to the Ohio River, after the igneous rocks were thrust out of the sea to make a mountain range and were eroded away time and again until finally they settled in the Laurentian Range, after the granites and the gneisses and the schists were formed, and after the lava flows cooled and the copper and iron appeared and the receding glaciers formed the Great Lakes—after all that, millions of years ago, what men came first to inhabit this bitter up-ended land?

Certainly not the Chippewas, the red-skinned people whose southern brothers Columbus mistakenly named Indians. For when the white men came to the Upper Peninsula of Michigan, they found that the Indians had no traditions concerning copper. Yet somebody mined copper in Upper Michigan thousands of years ago. Modern miners have unearthed wagonloads of copper hammers and axes on ghostly Isle Royale far out in Lake Superior, and in the copper country of the Keweenaw Peninsula and the Ontonagon district, where occur the world's only commercial quantities of pure native copper. Who were these aboriginal miners? One authority has conjectured they were the Egyptians, coming for this copper from the other side of the world as early as 7000 B.C. Others believe the Aztecs walked and paddled all the way up here from Mexico to get the treasures that bedazzled Cortes. Others argue for the Mayans, others for the Phœnicians and Basques; one man has written a book to prove that this Upper Peninsula was the lost Vinland of the Norse adventurers whom Leif the Lucky led to the shores of the Western world a thousand years after the birth of Christ. (The Scandinavians who later mined the ore and fought the Irish on the iron ranges would like to believe this.)

Whoever these early miners were, they had disappeared and the Chippewas had replaced them by the time the first white men came. The fierce Iroquois had driven a part of the great Algonquin nation westward from the lower lakes region. They took refuge in the deep forests of the Upper Peninsula, splitting into various tribes—the Menominee, the Keweenaw, the Pequaming, and, largest, the Chippewa. Still the Iroquois pursued them, chasing the Hurons also into the Upper Peninsula, where they would give their name to a bay now dominated by Henry Ford and to a useless railroad grade that would cost visionaries their life sav-

ings. Harried and desperate, the Chippewas turned on their at-
tackers where a yacht club now stands on the shores of Portage
Lake at the foot of Keweenaw Point; here they licked the Iroquois,
who withdrew. Emboldened, the Chippewas turned bully, prey-
ing on the lesser tribes and driving the Keweenaws and Pequam-
ings still farther westward along the shore of Gitchie Gumme, the
Big Lake that the French named Lac Tracy ou Supérieur, driving
the gentle Menominees southward to final refuge in the rice flats
where the Menominee River empties into Green Bay, in Wisconsin, at the present southern boundary of the Upper Peninsula.

Obviously the Indian did more than fight. Wringing a bare
existence from the stubborn wilderness was in itself a full-time
job. He lived in filth and poverty, and famine stalked him, for the
virgin forests were not good grazing ground and the deer went
south in the winter, leaving the Indian stranded; it was a poverty-
stricken country, not the storied region of fabulous hunting
grounds. He practiced cannibalism, and warfare was more than
bravado. Beset by perils, he took refuge in magic; and so sorcery
and evil spirits and dread hobgoblins plagued him also. He was
brave, undeniably; he had to be courageous to survive in this
country.

Yet the Indians' lives were not lived in misery alone. For sport,
they gambled incessantly. They were "desperate gamblers, staking
their all—ornaments, clothing, canoes, pipes, weapons, and wives."
The braves were licentious. "Female life among the Hurons had
no bright side. It was a youth of license, an age of drudgery."

Murder was not so serious a crime as witchcraft. Thievery was
condoned, for the Indians were notorious thieves. All were story-
tellers. The legends were recounted only in the winter, when the
spirits slept and could not hear what was being said of them. Many
of the tales concerned the Big Lake, Superior, which they revered
and feared. It was a mysterious and terrible lake, too wide for
human sight to span, too huge for the mind to encompass, fraught
with shifting fog and fearsome storms and silent, crushing ice.
The dread god Missibizi dwelt on one of its islands, Michipicoten,
paddling it about at will through the vapors of the great gray lake.
(Missibizi is also spelled variously Mesabi, Mesaba, and Mesabe,
and means, freely, Giant; the name was given hundreds of years

later to the vastest iron range of them all, the truly giant-like Mesaba of Minnesota.)

By the time the Jesuits arrived in the early seventeenth century, the Upper Peninsula was largely controlled by the Chippewas; to their country came, two centuries later, a historian and explorer, Henry Rowe Schoolcraft, who recorded the legend of their great leader, Hiawatha. His writings were studied by Henry Wadsworth Longfellow.

While the Indian was trembling before his own gods and beating his women and struggling for existence, across the seas which he never saw the world was afire. The armies of kings were locked in battle for empire; the kings were scheming mightily and their courtiers were making maps and a boy in Genoa was dreaming. The westward surge came fast. In 1534 Jacques Cartier first beheld the sweet-water mouth of the St. Lawrence. And, curiously, in that same year Ignatius Loyola, wounded and disillusioned, forswore warfare for a vision and founded the Society of Jesus. Nearly two centuries later his disciples still would be battling the captains who followed his contemporary Cartier to the New World. For those are the two threads, at first parallel, gradually divergent, ultimately in hopeless conflict, that run through the whole early history of Upper Michigan—the patient labor of the Jesuit, the plundering of the iron-fisted French conqueror.

The name Jesuit has become a symbol of the cold analytical mind. It might also symbolize resolute purpose. The Jesuits traveled the globe and fought the church and their King and especially they battled the stubborn savage wilderness country of the New World. Always they were zealots, lit with the ineluctable fire of an idea. Your Jesuit is no ordinary black-robed cross-bearing man of God. Realistic, tough-minded, wise, hardy, he made the Lake Superior region peculiarly his own. He coursed the water highways of the wilderness for years alone, and he broke trail for the conquerors like La Salle and Joliet, laboring in the savages' vineyard, preaching the true faith, scribbling his notes by the light of an Indian campfire with the smell of bear grease and cooking fish strong in his nostrils. He, man of learning, product of the French civilization, was among a brutish flock. Truly there was work to be done.

But they were not all saints, these Frenchmen who came to this New World; the sinners came too. Back east, Sir Walter Raleigh had made the first discovery of iron ore in the United States when Champlain sent his protégé, Étienne Brulé, one of the most unscrupulous adventurers of all, from Quebec into the wilderness where the truly great iron deposits lay undisturbed.

Though young, Brulé was worldly, tough, fearless, cynical, brutal. At the outset, he was one of Champlain's bright young men, as was Jean Nicolet; but before Brulé's violent life was ended, "Champlain says that Brulé was licentious and otherwise depraved." Quick-witted, by a ruse he escaped Indian torture at the stake and brought back to Quebec tales of copper deposits in the western wilderness which fired Champlain's imagination. (Seventy-odd years earlier, similar tales had lured Cartier into a costly expedition which produced nothing but "a shipload of iron pyrites or fool's gold, and of quartz crystals that he believed to be diamonds.") By Champlain's order, Brulé traveled westward through the wilderness alone, living among the Indians, growing more savage than they, until virtually all traces of France slipped from him. No man knows precisely what he did during this period, but the Jesuits hinted that he robbed the Indians and was robbed by them, that he was everlastingly becoming involved with the squaws and being run out of town. The Indians murdered him. The Sieur de Champlain, having heard of Brulé's deeds, did not claim the adventurer's body. Father Le Jeune relates: "We would have had much difficulty in resolving to make on this occasion a private Grave, and in transporting to consecrated Ground a dead man that had lived so scandalous a life in that Country, and had given to the Savages so bad an impression of the morals of the French." Years after Brulé's death a plague overtook the Indians, who swore they saw, on a frosty night, the Frenchman's sister flying over the countryside, spreading pestilence and desolation with her fiery-tongued breath. Today Brulé's memory is preserved chiefly in the name of a trout stream where President Coolidge once went fishing. It is generally forgotten that Brulé was the first white man to gaze on the brooding gray coasts of Lake Superior, two years before the *Mayflower* anchored at Cape Cod.

Nicolet followed him to the Soo and went on to Isle Royale in 1634. At the Soo he found an Indian settlement, permanently situated there because the rapids remained ice-free for fishing through the winter. Nicolet stepped from a birch-bark canoe to the shores of Green Bay clad in a mandarin's silk robe to bedazzle the Chinese he thought to find there.

But it was the Jesuits and not the adventurers who performed the prodigious labors. Their terrible course was charted for them succinctly by their leaders, comfortable in Paris: "You should love like brothers the Indians with whom you are to spend the rest of your life. Never make them wait for you in embarking. Take a flint and steel to light their pipes and kindle their fires at night, for these little services win their hearts. Try to eat their sagamite as they cook it, bad and dirty as it is. Fasten up the skirts of your cassock, that you may not carry water or sand into the canoe. Wear no shoes or stockings in the canoes, but you may put them on in crossing the portages. Do not make yourself troublesome, even to a single Indian. Do not ask too many questions. Bear their faults in silence and be always cheerful. Buy fish for them from the tribes you will pass; and for this purpose take with you some awls, beads, knives and fish hooks. Be not ceremonious with the Indians; take at once what they offer you, for ceremony offends them. Be very careful, when in the canoe, that the brim of your hat does not annoy them. Perhaps it would be better to wear your night-cap. There is no such thing as impropriety among Indians. Remember that it is Christ and his cross that you are seeking; and if you aim at anything else, you will get nothing but affliction for body and mind."

Quebec was the jumping-off place. Here, on the gray rock heights above the St. Lawrence, France had founded an empire; here in 1634, a hundred years after Loyola was visited by his vision, Father Le Jeune, Superior of the Residence of Quebec, held spiritual dominion over uncounted souls in a vast and desolate region. Even the simplest beginnings presented problems. Language, for instance—Le Jeune knew Latin as he knew French, but of Algonquin he was ignorant. The French interpreters who had preceded him knew the language, but they were in the pay of the fur traders; too often they regarded the Jesuits as interlopers who would befriend, not exploit, the Indians. (Thus began the long hidden struggle between priest and captain in New France, a struggle that ended in defeat for the black-robes and, ultimately, in disaster for France.) In the end the cultured Le Jeune was forced to turn for instruction to a young Indian ne'er-do-well who hung around Quebec, mooching tobacco from the commandant of the fort.

For months the patient father practiced diligently on snow-shoes. In October he departed with an Indian band to see for himself this region which he must bring to Christ. On his back he carried an enormous pack, like any Indian, and it seemed to thrust him down into every treacherous snow-hidden windfall. But the days of the trail were at least clean and crisp. The nights in camp were hideous. In a hut thirteen feet square he crouched and tried to read his breviary while all around him squatted nineteen nearly naked savages, men, women, and children. Dogs were every-where, rooting in the meager food. The smoke blinded him, and he wrote: "Unhappy infidels, who spend their lives in smoke, and their eternity in flames!" The wind whipped through the cracks in the bark hut; sometimes he thought he must surely freeze; other times the roaring pitchpine fire got out of control and cooked his flesh. As though this were not enough, he was bedeviled by a sorcerer who delighted in taunting him and trying to frighten him; he succeeded in neither but he did succeed in keeping the good father awake most of the nights by ceaseless thumping on a skin-covered drum. They nearly starved that winter in their miserable hut. And coming home, Le Jeune, sick and weak, nearly was drowned in the gray ice-jammed St. Lawrence.

But soon he was planning new missions westward and writing to France for pictures of hell and souls in perdition: "A few were sent us on paper; but they are too confused. The devils and the men are so mixed up, that one can make out nothing without par-ticular attention. If three, four or five devils were painted tor-menting a soul with different punishments,—one applying fire, another serpents, another tearing him with pincers, and another holding him fast with a chain—this would have a good effect, especially if everything were made distinct, and misery, rage, and desperation appeared plainly in his face."

Now, in the 1640's, Englishmen and Dutchmen were astir along
the Eastern seaboard and the great men were coming to New
France—the black-robes Ménard and Allouez and Dablon and
Marquette and Jogues and Joliet and Hennepin; and the swash-
buckling captains, La Salle and Cadillac and Du Lhut, des Groseilliers and Radisson. Some of these men would labor for the glory
of God, some for the glory of France, some simply for greed or
pure adventure.

The captains and adventurers were laying the foundations for
the fur trade, Upper Michigan's first boom. But the Iroquois
watched jealously while the *coureurs de bois* brought great car-
goes of pelts in their bateaux down the lakes, and finally they
struck, murdering two Jesuits and blockading the canoe route for
nearly twenty years.

But the Jesuits labored on. No lonelier spiritual outpost was
manned anywhere by the priests than that at Sault Ste. Marie.
Father Raymbault and Father Jogues went there in 1642 and,
finding a Chippewa village of two thousand at the rapids,
preached to the savages on the rocky shore. Raymbault became
ill and Jogues took him back to Quebec, where he died. (Nicolet
was drowned in the St. Lawrence about the same time.) Soon
after, Jogues and two companions were captured by an Iroquois
war party. The savages chewed off their finger-ends and beat
them into insensibility with clubs, then forced them to run the
gantlet down double lines of braves armed with clubs and knives.
When they fell senseless, the Indians revived them with burning
brands. One of them showed such stoic courage that he was
adopted into the tribe. But Jogues and the other were carried from
camp to camp and tortured as they traveled. And Jogues devoted
the hours between tortures to missionary work, carving the name
of Jesus on trees and baptizing a captive Huron with raindrops he
caught in a cornhusk.

After long captivity he was traded to the Dutch, who took him
to New Amsterdam. Thence he returned to France for new
orders, pausing to allow the Queen to kiss his mangled hand. But
his orders were not new: he was to go among the savages and
preach the gospel. He went, knowing he would not return alive,
and he was right, for on his first trip into the wilderness he left a

box of clothing which the Indians found and regarded as a sort of Pandora's box, believing it contained smallpox or some other pestilence; when Jogues returned for it, they ambushed him, captured him, tortured and in the end murdered him.

He was not the only one to die. René Ménard was one. On October 15, 1660 he reached the head of Keweenaw Bay and established Upper Michigan's first permanent mission at L'Anse (The Bay), beneath the eminence that was to become known as Dynamite Hill in the roaring days of mines and lumber. Here Father Ménard's teachings were rejected by the taunting Indians. He took a single Indian companion and started westward for Chequemagon Bay, where Ashland, Wisconsin, now stands. On the portage across the base of the long narrow Keweenaw Peninsula where the copper lay as the Mound Builders had left it, either he was betrayed by his Indian guide or he simply wandered off into the woods; his body never was found, only his crucifix.

The year he arrived at L'Anse two travelers reached Sault Ste. Marie and embarked on a career that was to bulk large in the coming French-English struggle for supremacy. They were Pierre Esprit Radisson and his brother-in-law Médart Chouart des Groseilliers, young *voyageurs* courageous enough to defy the Iroquois and reopen the French fur trade with the western tribes. Having disappeared into the wilderness for so long that many thought them lost, they came swinging down the St. Lawrence in 1661 at the head of 360 canoes loaded to the gunwales with pelts. The fur route was open once more. But they were greeted not with rejoicing, but with a demand from the French Governor, Argensen, for a full third of their profit in taxes. It may have been one of those great blunders that change the course of history. Radisson and Groseilliers gave the Governor his third but, embittered and vengeful, they went over to the English. It was they who opened the eyes of the English, preoccupied with colonial troubles on the seaboard, to the riches of this vast unknown western country. It was they who broke the trails that led to the Crees and Sioux and Assiniboines and it was they who supplied the dream that became the Hudson's Bay Company, famed throughout the north country for two hundred years as simply The Company. Seventeen years after it was chartered, fabulous Louis XIV

of France advised his Governor in New France to try to capture
Radisson or, failing that, to buy him over. The Governor accomplished neither purpose, and The Company prospered beyond its backers' wildest dreams. Fur had become big business.

Britain now was reaching for northwest empire. The head-on
collision with France was not far off. But still the Jesuits had
much work to do before they were swallowed up in imperial warfare; their finest hours lay ahead. The martyred Jogues was gone,
but he had worthy successors.

There was Father Claude Jean Allouez, who followed the trail
on which Ménard had perished. He succeeded in reaching
Chequemagon Bay, where in 1665 he founded the famed La
Pointe mission. Returning to Quebec, he brought with him samples of native copper from the Keweenaw country (he probably
was the first white man who actually saw copper in the Upper
Peninsula). In 1667, the same year that William Penn was converted to Quakerism, Allouez and Father Louis Nicolas arrived
at the Soo to establish the mission that Allouez had dreamed of.

And there was Jacques Marquette, who arrived a year later at
the Soo. Subsequently he replaced Allouez at La Pointe but,
threatened by hostile Indians, shepherded his flock back toward
the Soo and set them up in another mission at Michilimackinac,
beside the straits at what became St. Ignace. (Marquette knew
this country; one of the great works attributed to him and Allouez is the making of a map of Lake Superior, which, published
in 1672, is amazingly accurate.) And there was Claude Dablon,
who became Superior of all Canadian missions and who sent
Marquette to the Lake Superior country. He and Allouez made
a perfect team, ranging this wild region with the curiosity of
explorers as well as the fervor of black-robes.

The same year that Marquette fled back to St. Ignace, the
French cavaliers became aware, belatedly, of the British peril.
And so, on June 14, 1671, the captains and the priests joined in
a great ceremony at the Soo where, by grandiose proclamation,
they claimed for France all lands "adjacent" to the Soo, "bounded
on the one side by the oceans of the north and west, and on the
other by the South Sea." Brave words; but less than a hundred
years later France had lost Quebec itself.

Encouraged by this rapprochement with the cavaliers in the face of the common British peril, the Jesuits set out on new expeditions with heightened zeal. Even stern Marquette became an explorer; reluctantly he left his beloved mission at St. Ignace and, with the adventurer Joliet, whom Frontenac had sent, embarked on the southward journey which took him to the Mississippi River and an enduring place in history. And to death: he died in May 1675 on the banks of a Michigan stream that later was called the Père Marquette.

Three years later Robert Cavalier de La Salle and his one-handed, iron-clawed aide, Henry de Tonty, and the huge bearded friar Father Hennepin, continued the union of sword and cross which had served Cortes so well: in the *Griffon* they sailed down to Green Bay, where they disembarked, loaded the *Griffon* with furs, and sent her back toward Niagara. She never was seen again, except, of course, on moonless nights when Great Lakes seamen swear they see her scudding through the fog, skimming the surface of the great gray waves, her sails full-bellied though there is no wind, her tiller firm though she has no crew.

La Salle, despite misfortune and importunate creditors, reached the Gulf (and later was killed in Texas by his own men); Hennepin was captured by the Sioux and taken northwest into the dark wilderness beyond Lake Superior. Here he was rescued by a band of bearded Frenchmen whose leader was Daniel de Grosollon, Sieur Du Lhut. One of the more flamboyant of the high spirits who ranged the north country, Du Lhut built a private army and a private fur empire and gave his name, misspelled in modern times, to the lusty cliffside iron port that now broods over the head of Lake Superior.

The travelers were coming to the north country now that the Jesuits and adventurers had broken trail, now that the fur traders had established order to safeguard their business. These travelers started many of the legends that plagued the Upper Peninsula pioneers for years. Radisson had written of sea serpents; another writer declared that copper, gold, diamonds, even steel and "certain blue transparent stones more valuable than turquoises" were to be had in the Upper Peninsula by anyone with the energy to pick them up. Baron L'Hontan and two Englishmen, Alexander

Henry and Jonathan Carver, contributed to the legends of fabulous mineral wealth which, like will-o'-the-wisps, lured prospectors ever onward into the wilds. L'Hontan in 1688 told of pure
copper mines in the Upper Peninsula, though he called the region
"the fag end of creation."

L'Hontan, a man of acid opinions, wrote scornfully of the
Jesuits' futile work. In truth, the missionary period was about
ended by 1700, when the Duke of Marlborough distinguished
himself on the battlefields of Europe. The English won Gibraltar
the same year that Joliet died. They were moving fast into the
northwest country, spurred by the Hudson's Bay Company. And
their enemies, the French, were divided. The old rift between
captains and churchmen reopened. The sanctimonious French fur
traders and the British alike sold liquor to the Indians in order to
get them drunk and cheat them out of their furs. The Jesuits
fought the practice. They won a temporary victory; Louis XIV
decreed that any persistent blasphemer should have his tongue cut
out. And he also ordered the *voyageurs* to settle down and take
wives and stop running around the country seizing furs and passing out liquor. Frontenac ignored him, and the traders had free
rein. To consolidate the fur centers against British encroachments,
the post at Michilimackinac was abandoned; this was the blow
that meant final defeat for the Jesuits, for the Indians followed
the traders to Detroit, and of what use were missionaries without
savage parishioners? The black-robes burned their mission and
retired to Quebec. They had tried to shield their charges, but the
world was moving too fast for them. This country now was a
pawn of empires. This wilderness which they had worked to
tame now never would be tamed; it would be crushed. For now
the rape by the empire-builders had begun, the first wholesale
rape of an Upper Peninsula natural resource: fur. In their time
timber and copper would be stripped with prodigal waste from
northern Michigan; now it was fur that the white men wanted.

But the French secular rulers neglected the country and the
Indians as the Jesuits never had neglected them. Narrow, shortsighted, greedy, the royal regime made stupid mistakes. Gradually
Indian loyalties swung to the British, and by 1731 the Soo was
abandoned and the Hudson's Bay Company was moving south-

ward and westward rapidly, its way blocked by only a handful of French traders. The King made a last effort to use individual enterprise to save his empire for him when, in 1750, he granted an enormous tract of land at the Soo to a private citizen, the Chevalier de Repentigny; title to this feudal domain, the largest ever carved out of Michigan, was not decided by the United States Supreme Court until after the American Civil War. But 1750 was too late to stem the tide of British encroachment with any makeshift medievalism; four years later a young lieutenant-colonel in the Virginia militia, George Washington, fired a shot on a French force near Fort Duquesne and thus began the war that ended all the colonial contests for empire.

It was a big war; indeed, it was, in a real sense, a world war, though Americans call it simply the French and Indian War. It began in 1739, and it gathered momentum until, by the sixties, nearly all of Europe was aligned on the side of either France or England. But although warfare was conducted everywhere from the Mediterranean to the Philippines, it was in North America that the decisive battles were fought. There England was out-maneuvered and out-lucked for two years until William Pitt came to power; concentrating his armies in the New World, he cut down the old-line brass-hat fuddy-duddies and named as commander-in-chief young James Wolfe, the lanky, red-haired son of a British country squire, who died one night on the Plains of Abraham above the dark St. Lawrence, but died knowing he had won Canada for his King.

Once sovereignty had passed to the British, the traders came rapidly. Alexander Henry arrived at the Soo with the British conquerors and wrote rapturously of this north country, his enthusiasm blunted not even by the days he spent hiding in a cave on Mackinac Island to escape the Indian massacre at Michilimackinac during the conspiracy of the great chief Pontiac that failed so narrowly to overthrow the British rule. Henry continued to write of the riches of the Upper Peninsula, not only of its furs but of its deposits of native copper to the westward. Indeed, it was he who led the first white man's mining expedition into northern Michigan.

He had traveled first alone westward from the Soo in 1765–6,

coasting the southern shore of Lake Superior to the mouth of the
Ontonagon River, where Indians showed him specimens of native
copper weighing twenty pounds and told him tales of silver and
of a single chunk of copper weighing five tons. (This may have
been the mass of native copper later famed as Jim Paul's boulder.)
By 1770 his and Carver's writings had so excited Londoners that
a mining company was formed with the backing of such notables
as George III, the Duke of Gloucester, and Secretary Townshend.
(They were the first of many moneyed Englishmen to invest in
Upper Michigan's minerals.) The miners reached the Soo and,
having hired Henry as guide and built the first covered-deck boat
on Lake Superior, a sloop of forty tons, they set sail in the spring
of 1771 for the western end of Lake Superior.

After a profitless search for gold on the Island of Yellow Sands,
the party landed near the mouth of the Ontonagon River. Here,
below the beetling brow of the Porcupines, some twenty-odd
miles up-river from Superior, they found an ancient Indian pit
and, amid the debris left by forgotten miners, evidences of a copper vein. Henry, having performed his duties, left them and returned to the Soo, presumably to await the royalty checks. The
following spring he sent a boatload of provisions to his brave
company; when the boat returned, it bore the embittered miners.
They had commenced operations all right; they had proposed to
drive an adit—that is, to dig a horizontal tunnel—into the hillside.
But the clay kept falling in on them, they encountered obstruc-
tions, their tools were inadequate, the workers were discontented
and easily discouraged, and they grumbled constantly after the
first glow of discovery had passed and the real work of mining
had begun. When they had driven their adit some forty feet, they
quit. The country was too tough for them. Northern Michigan's
stubborn earth had licked the first white men who tried to wrest
from it its riches. Henry, recovering from his first chagrin, concluded that "The Copper ores of Lake Superior can never be
profitably sought but for local consumption." Moreover, what
they really had wanted was silver and gold, not copper.

Intermittent warfare consumed more time than fur trading and
mining during this middle period, and for fifty years the Upper
Peninsula lay fallow. Although the British held the area militarily,

they were plagued by Indian trouble; they were threatened even by the Spanish, who for one day occupied Niles, Michigan, across Lake Michigan from the site of Chicago; and when it wasn't the Indians or the Spaniards, it was the damned Yankees. They and their thirteen colonies pulled away from the mother country and, theoretically, won all the territory that included northern Michigan: Ben Franklin, treaty-making at Paris in 1783, insisted that the Upper Peninsula and northern Minnesota and even Isle Royale, far out in Lake Superior, be included within the United States. Whether he was guided by the celebrated Franklin foresight or the error of a map-maker who spotted non-existent islands is disputed. The British agreed to abandon northern Michigan, but they didn't do it; they kept right on trying to re-establish the fur trade. Congress passed the Ordinance of 1787, organizing the Northwest Territory. The British lay low and probably would have withdrawn peaceably, but by now Harrison had overwhelmed Tecumseh and the Prophet at Tippecanoe and thereby created a campaign slogan for 1840, and the Americans were feeling their oats; they believed, inaccurately, that the British had fomented the Prophet's uprising, they wanted war, they wanted all of Canada. Mad Anthony Wayne planted the first American flag on Michigan soil and took Mackinac (which most people still fail to pronounce properly: Mackinaw); the Territory of Michigan was created in 1805 and the Yankees seemed determined.

But now the world-wide Napoleonic Wars engulfed the young United States, and the British up north took up their guns. The history of this War of 1812 in Upper Michigan is a history of American indecision and mistakes. They lost Mackinac and Detroit; they couldn't retake Mackinac, though they had it blockaded. But finally, after the Treaty of Ghent, they got the British out of the Upper Peninsula of Michigan. And John Jacob Astor moved in. He built an empire and founded one of the great American financial dynasties on the wreckage of Upper Peninsula's fur resources. And on the wreckage of uncounted Indian livers. Astor, with his American Fur Company, was not the first to debauch the Indians, but he was one of the most successful. He ruled his vast domain like a feudal fief, employing a small private army to keep order.

Gustavus Myers writes: "By means of Government favoritism and the unconcealed exercise of both fraud and force, he obtained a complete monopoly." Myers points out that Lewis Cass, Governor of Michigan Territory, in 1817 received from Astor $35,000 "for services not stated." Within three years the Government posts were abandoned, leaving Astor without competition. Cass, one of Michigan's most famed men, became President Jackson's Secretary of War and Minister to France; he went into the 1844 Democratic convention the leading candidate, but lost to the first compromise dark horse in United States history, James K. Polk— "Who is James K. Polk?" Clay would hoot in vain. Finally nominated in 1848, Cass was engulfed in the imperialist tidal wave that swept into the White House Old Rough and Ready, profane General Zachary Taylor; beaten in convention by another veteran of the Mexican War, General Franklin Pierce, Cass became a vociferous "54-40 or Fight" Senator and a Secretary of State devoted to strong nationalism.

Having pyramided his fortune, Astor pulled out of the Upper Peninsula, leaving it stripped of fur resources. Thus he became the first of a long line of Easterners who came to Upper Michigan, plundered it, and left it to shift for itself. When Astor departed, the few white men who had come to northern Michigan to grow up with the country must have shaken their heads and mumbled: "We're done for. There's nothing here now for a young fellow. This country's through." A great many times in the next hundred-odd years men would mutter the same thing. But always there would be a few who would repeat stubbornly: "The country's bound to come back."

It didn't seem so, though, in the early 1830's. True, Lower Michigan was being settled fast; the Erie Canal was open and settlers were streaming westward from New York State. But they didn't come on up north very much. Why should they? The land in the Lower Peninsula was better farming country, the winters were not so terrible, there were a regular mail service, better roads, more of all things that meant civilization and an easier life. The Upper Peninsula was little but uncharted wilderness. The Jesuits and other early Frenchmen had poked along the coastlines of the Big Lake, and Lieutenant H. W. Bayfield had explored its western end for the British. Even the *voyageurs* stuck strictly to the streams. What secrets lay locked in the woods beyond the waters?

There had been rumors, of course, many rumors, of minerals; nearly all the early travelers had brought back tales, mostly inaccurate, of copper and gold and silver and lead, and some had even mentioned iron. Henry Rowe Schoolcraft, with Governor Cass, had made tentative explorations across the Upper Peninsula commencing as early as 1820, listening to the stories of *voyageurs*, making treaties with the Indians, who ceded their lands piece by piece to the United States. Still, by the early thirties no one actually knew much about northern Michigan. It was a big piece of land. Now that the British were finally driven out, what was the United States going to do about it?

Few people cared. No one wanted the land anyway, not even the bonus army that besieged the Government after the War of 1812. With the veterans in mind, the Government had sent its surveyors into Michigan. Edward Tiffin, of the Surveyor General's Office at Chillicothe, had reported to Washington in 1815:

Sir:—

The surveyors in Michigan Territory have been obliged to suspend operations. . . . They continued at work, suffering incredible hardships, until both men and beasts were literally worn down with extreme suffering and fatigue. . . . There would not be more than one acre out of a hundred, if there would be one out of a thousand, that would . . . admit of cultivation . . . nor is it worth the expense of surveying it. Perhaps [I should] . . . pay off what has been done and abandon the country. . . .

The country . . . is (with some few exceptions) low wet land with a very thick growth of underbrush. . . . Many of the lakes have extensive marshes adjoining their margins, sometimes thickly covered with a species of pine called "Tamirak." . . . The balance is a poor, barren, sandy loam land, on which scarcely any vegetation grows, except very small, scrubby oaks . . . swamp beyond description; . . . taking the country altogether so far as has been explored . . . it is bad."

And a month later Tiffin wrote: "Subsequent accounts . . . make the country out worse (if possible) than I had represented it to be."

Tiffin's recommendations apparently carried some weight; Congress found land for the veterans elsewhere. The amazing thing is that Mr. Tiffin's suffering surveyors were working in the Lower Peninsula, mild hospitable country, gently rolling plains checkered today with neat sleepy farms. What would they have thought if they had been sent to the geological nightmare called the Upper Peninsula? (Even today men of the Upper Peninsula are humorously contemptuous of the softies from "down below.")

The good people of Lower Michigan, now in 1835 framing a constitution at Detroit for admission to the Union, wanted the Upper Peninsula no more than Mr. Tiffin did. What they wanted was a part of Ohio, the strip of land along Lake Erie that now includes Toledo. The original boundary line, which young Robert E. Lee had run, cut straight across country at the bottom of Lake Michigan. Ohio had pre-empted the Toledo strip. Now feeling ran high; there were mass meetings and harsh words; this was frontier country. At the border armed men gibed at one another. One mule was shot dead. That ended hostilities in the bloodless Toledo War. For a compromise had been proposed: the Federal Government offered to give Michigan the Upper Peninsula, then a part of Wisconsin Territory, if Michigan would relinquish its claim to the Toledo strip. Indignantly the men of Michigan rejected this offer. Scornfully a contemporary writer called the Upper Peninsula "A wild and comparative Scandinavian tract—20,000 square miles of howling wilderness on the shores of Lake Superior." More excitement at the border; the armed men of Michigan sang:

> *But now the song they sing to us*
> *Is—trade away that land,*
> *For that poor, frozen country,*
> *Beyond Lake Michigan.*

But in December 1836, a rump session of the convention accepted the compromise, and a month later Michigan, including the Upper

Peninsula, was admitted to the Union. Thus it came about that today more than 150,000 people live in Michigan west of Chicago. And this worthless piece of land, this Upper Peninsula, which, it can be argued, should belong to Wisconsin by all the logic of geography, this land so rich in timber and minerals, has paid into the state coffers in taxes two hundred times the amount that the Toledo strip has paid to Ohio. Yet because of this accident of compromise politics the Upper Peninsula always has been so far from the seat of government at Lansing that it is a stock saying today among men in the northern woods: "The big shots at Lansing *still* think this is Indian country." And indeed Upper Michigan's history might have been guided more happily if it had not been separated wholly by water from the other peninsula. Even today it is the lodestone of Chicago or Milwaukee, not Detroit, that draws many people from the Upper Peninsula of Michigan.

Well, in 1837 they had a state. The destiny of the Lower Peninsula was set—it would be farming country, and, much later, a great industrial area centered on Detroit. But what of the Upper Peninsula? True, it was part of a state of the Union. But there were only two counties in it, and only 664 people lived in Mackinac County, most of them at St. Ignace, and only 366 in vast Chippewa County, most of them at the Soo. There might be minerals, there might be timber, here. What were the governors of Michigan going to do about it?

First they had to find out what there was in this wilderness country. So they put surveyors to work, northland surveyors, cut to a different pattern from Mr. Tiffin's Lower Peninsula sufferers. And it is the surveyors, ranging the unbroken inland wilds despite summer mosquitoes and autumn storms and winter snows, marking with their cries of "Chain!" a line straight as a die through swamps and up sheer rock cliffs and across rushing torrents and through tangled underbrush that lesser men would skirt—it is the surveyors who are truly the great men of this era. They opened the country. Nobody ever did a better or a tougher job.

❧ 4 ❧

"CHAIN!"

❧

WILLIAM AUSTIN BURT was a shaggy-haired, tight-mouthed man with staring evangelical eyes; he looked more like a Methodist circuit rider than a surveyor and woodsman. But he was one of the best woodsmen who ever surveyed the Upper Peninsula; a latter-day geologist wrote: "It is to Burt's energy and to his discovery of ore that later developments of the iron district are due."

He was a man of cold precise mind. Inventive, scientific, he regarded the day he discovered the fabulous Marquette iron-ore field simply as a day of triumph for his solar compass. He had courage and fortitude; he was strong and determined; no hardship could deter him from running the line through the wilderness. Yet he viewed himself as anything but heroic; he wrote thousands of words about the survey and none about himself; he was simply a man with a job to do, and he did it.

No writers ever were more chary of words than the surveyors. Their sparsely-written field notes, composed by the light of campfires after a twelve-hour day running the line, are among the world's great works of understatement.

A sample page from a field book, almost unintelligible to the layman:

Subdivisions of Fractional Township 41N R13W of the first Meridian of the State of Michigan. Commenced August 28th, 1845, and finished September 4th, 1845. by John Burt, Deputy Surveyor.

South Between Sections 1 and 2 Vr 3° 30' E Z Pine 14
S 33 1/2 E 1.05.

44

27.52 W Birch 3
34.40 Stream 50 CSW
40.00 Set qr Section Post
W Pine 12 N52 W 17.
do 12 N44 E25.
51.14 W Pine 14
71.80 Z Pine 8
79.19 Intersect Bay and Set Post
W Pine 7 N2 E 1.20.
do 9 N 29W
Land in ridges parallel with Bay Shore 3rd rate
Tamarack Cedar Fir W and Z Pine

What did all these cabalistic entries mean? Of what value were they? Well, they opened this particular township, these particular acres, of the Upper Peninsula to settlement and development. On them were based claims to land that might be worth hundreds of thousands of dollars.

Wilderness land is useless. You've got to know what is on the earth's surface and beneath it. The surveyors found out. They did more than run lineal surveys; as though that were not enough, they collected geological specimens, mapped swamps and rivers and lakes and hills, and reported on the kind and amount of timber and on the quality of the soil on the land they covered.

As the Indian claims to Michigan lands were extinguished, the Government pressed its survey north and westward. A system was established by law in Jefferson's time which, amazingly practical and thorough, has stood up through the years. Principal meridians were run north and south at various points on true meridians of longitude; the first principal meridian runs north from the mouth of the Great Miami River; the one going north through central Indiana is the second; the one north from the mouth of the Ohio through Illinois is the third; and so on. Intersecting these principal meridians are base lines, running east and west across the nation and intersecting the meridians at right angles.

The primary survey divided the country into tracts six miles square (23,040 acres) called townships. Townships were numbered east and west of the principal meridian lines and north and south of the base lines. Any tier of townships north and south, piled on top of one another like blocks, was called a range. Thus a description of a township might read: Township 47 north, Range 26 west; or simply T47N, R26W.

Each township was subdivided into thirty-six sections, each one a square mile (640 acres) in area. The corner of each section was marked with a corner post.

After the primary survey was completed, the sections were further subdivided into halves and quarters and "forties" (forty-acre tracts).

In Upper Michigan this meant dividing an area stretching some 325 miles westward from the Soo and some 200 miles north from the mouth of the Menominee—and it meant an enormous amount of labor for the surveyors. We shall see them in action. Perhaps the greatest of them was William Austin Burt.

Born at Petersham, Massachusetts, June 13, 1792, he had only six weeks of schooling. After having served in the War of 1812, he married when he was barely twenty-one. He was not a man who found himself when he was young; he struggled through nine years as an unsuccessful merchant in upper New York State. His family increased—ultimately he fathered five sons—and his business failed to prosper. He was getting nowhere. The West was opening up. Settlers in the plains states wrote back home describing the wonders of this new country across the Appalachians. Restless, Burt journeyed as far west as St. Louis, in 1817 little but an outpost of Astor's fur company; he walked back, all the way to Detroit, on foot. Here he saw the Great Lakes and heard stories of the northwest, of the Upper Peninsula. This was new country, big country; it made York State seem dull. He went back there because his family was there, but he remained only as long as he must. He moved to Michigan in 1822, when he was thirty years old, and, settling in Macomb County in the Lower Peninsula two years later, engaged in construction work.

His affairs prospered. He knew how to grow up with the country; York State was old, settled; Michigan was new, turbulent, exciting. Burt grasped one opportunity after another. He was a member of the Territorial Council for two years, in 1826 and

1827. In 1829 he patented a "typographer," later renamed "type-writer." And he found time, despite the long days spent in building mills, to pursue in the evenings those studies which were to fit him for his real life work.

Of a scientific bent, in his search for knowledge he had been thwarted in his youth. At that time scientific studies, and especially that of geology, were neglected all over the United States, and out here in this frontier country science was a total stranger. Burt procured textbooks somehow and taught himself mechanics, engineering, surveying, and the rudiments of geology. More, perhaps, than any of the other Upper Peninsula pioneers, he fits the pattern of the early American great man, laboring hard all day, studying at night by a guttering lamp until his eyes gave out.

Burt's studies were rewarded. In 1831 he was chosen county surveyor of Macomb County, an office he held for three years, and about 1832 the Territorial Governor named him district surveyor. Rapidly his educational accomplishments in this region of unlettered men were forcing him to abandon his construction business. He became postmaster of Mount Vernon. He found time to invent a printing press. His erudition must have impressed, not antagonized at least some of his fellow settlers, for they elevated him to the Macomb circuit court bench in 1833. It was in the autumn of that same year that he was appointed United States deputy surveyor. Immediately he dropped everything else. At forty-one he had begun his life work.

It was a lonely work, which took him into the wilderness and kept him from his family for months on end. But it was his work; this was the job he had to do; he could no more have gone on building mills than he could have remained an unsuccessful Yankee merchant.

He led survey parties north of Fort Gratiot, Michigan, along the shore of Lake Huron, and into Wisconsin and Iowa. Encountering mineral bodies which deflected the needle of his magnetic compass and made it useless, Burt, unruffled and resourceful, invented the solar compass, an instrument which finds direction by means of astronomical observation rather than by magnetic polar attraction. He patented the instrument in 1835 and constantly improved it; he considered it his crowning achievement.

(Actually, it was indeed a valuable instrument in its time, but to-day is little used.)

In 1840 Burt pushed his surveys into the Upper Peninsula, and it was there that he did the work for which he became famous.

William Austin Burt, in his quiet way, knew everything there was to know about surveying and woodcraft and kindred subjects. He wrote a lot of it down in a little pocket-sized manual, published in 1855, called *A Key to the Solar Compass, and Surveyor's Companion*. A glance at its contents suggests the breadth of knowledge required of these men: use of the nautical almanac, mathematical tables of fixed stars, methods of determining latitude and time of day and of making telescopic measurements in meandering rivers and of constructing rafts, a discussion of the system of survey of the U. S. lands, and suggestions for an outfit for a surveying company of six men for four months. Burt, self-educated, was scientist enough to instruct young surveyors on "corrections for the Moon's parallax and refraction." But he also could remind them they must take needle and thread and boot-nails into the woods with them. He was no textbook surveyor.

In late April the snow was almost gone from the woods. It was time to get started. William Austin Burt set about putting into motion his plans for this season's survey. All the long winter he had been cooped up at home in the town, writing reports on last season's work, perfecting his solar compass, planning this year's work. All winter he had gazed at the vast white spaces on the western portion of the map of the Upper Peninsula, the section into which he had not penetrated and where all but the shoreline of Lake Superior was white space, unknown territory. These white spaces fascinated him; he was impatient to have at them.

He had gone over his plans time and again. He had selected his assistants, the most delicate task of all, for he would have to live with these men four months and must depend on them: an assistant surveyor, two chainmen, two axmen, the cook and packers.

The mud in the streets was drying as Burt walked down to the store—"Gen'l Mdse"—and noted the blue of the sky, the new warmth of the sunshine. (But in the woods the snow was still three feet deep in ravines.) At the store, redolent of spices in square glass jars and of vegetables in wooden bins, he made his purchases. Eight barrels of flour and two and a half barrels of clear pork, first, and three bushels each of beans and dried apples. (The storekeeper and his assistants gave their full attention to Judge Burt.) Seventy pounds of ground coffee and a hundred and twenty pounds of "good dry sugar." Twenty-five pounds of rice, ten pounds of "saleratus"—baking soda, today—for baking; and, for seasoning, a pound of ground pepper and a small bag of table salt. Four pounds of soap. And that was all. Somehow, from this they would prepare three good meals a day for four months; they would supplement their rations with game and fish, with berries from the woods (everybody liked blueberry pie in late July) and other delicacies.

The packers would pick up the chuck; now Burt assembled his camp furniture. First a large tent for the surveying company, preferably a military tent, and a smaller one for the packmen, for a question of caste was involved here. Six mackinaw blankets for warmth and three "common blankets" to spread atop the balsam-bough beds. Two dozen boxes of matches ("best kind," Burt cautions, for fire means everything in the woods) and a good chopping ax—only one, but a good one. What if you should lose it? You simply didn't; and since you had to keep the weight of the outfit down, you couldn't carry a spare. Four pails that would telescope, constructed of heavy tin with covers and handles riveted so they wouldn't separate over the campfire; the largest held twelve quarts. Fourteen tin basins six inches in diameter and one and a half inches deep; so many were needed because they served as plates, cups, soup and meat dishes. Seven spoons, but only a single set of knives and forks: the men's own jack-knives were sufficient tools for eating. For the cook, one good butcher knife, three light frying pans and two mixing cloths a yard square, made of heavy cotton drilling; two tin pepper boxes, two half-round cans for storing grease and saleratus. Finally, six "soldiers' drinking cups, also needles, awls, thread, twine, small cord, etc." And four papers of three-ounce tacks for nailing boots; boots took a terrible beating in the rocks and woods and rivers.

Burt left nothing to subordinates. He supervised the expedition, from the time it was planned in town until the last field note was written in the fall. He might hire a good packer, but he saw to it that the packer took along proper equipment—"one or two good horses, or mules, as circumstances require; one pack saddle; a ball and spancil for each. Twenty stout bags, that hold one and a half bushels each. Four linen bags, for pork. Six small bags, for beans, dried apples, knives and forks, etc. Three India Rubber bags for sugar and coffee (should be lined). Two strong drilling cloths, two or two and one half yards square, to do up the camp equipage into packs; also, strap and cords, to secure the packs to the horse and saddle."

Now Burt collected his instruments. First, of course, was his solar compass. And, far down the list, two pocket compasses, as a concession to cloudy days or places where the foliage was so thick he couldn't get a shot at the sun. A standard chain, the crux of surveying; running the lines consisted in measuring along a straight-sighted line with this chain, which was 100 links long, each link being exactly 7.92 inches in length; thus the length of the chain was sixty-six feet; measurements were entered in the field book in chains and links, not feet and inches. (A measuring chain half as long also was required by law.) A telescope sixteen or eighteen inches in length, for sighting the line. Eleven tally pins for marking each half-chain distance along the line; these were pointed steel stakes a foot long, heavy enough at the tips to drop perpendicularly and with a loop or eye at the upper end to which was fastened a bit of red cloth in order to make the pin easier to locate in high weeds. Since section corners often were marked on trees standing at the corners, two small marking axes for blazing the trees and a set of marking tools for inscribing the required data must be provided. A tape measure also was required, and a case of good drawing instruments was indispensable. A hatchet was useful around camp, and of course the party must carry two whetstones and two three-cornered files for sharpening axes and two small round files for sharpening marking tools. And in addition the surveyor needed in his pack "field books, mapping and writing paper, ink, pens, pencils, India rubber, mouth glue and a small valise (or box) to carry them in."

At last everything was ready. The party assembled and, watched by a crowd of gaping children on the town's main street, departed. The men never said they were leaving civilization and going into the wilderness for four long months; they simply said they were going into the woods.

They might go on foot directly into the woods from the Soo. Or, if they already had pushed their survey farther westward, they would avoid the rough, time-consuming overland trip and load their entire outfit on small boats and run down the coast to the place where they had left off last year. Here they would plunge into the woods and send the boats back to civilization. Now they were on their own. They would see few other human beings all summer.

Burt's first task was to locate the last section corner he had marked. It might be a tree blazed and marked with the range and township numbers. Or, if he had found no tree growing at the exact corner, it might be a cedar stake buried in the ground. To find this stake, he would hunt for the bearing trees standing near the corner which he had blazed and marked and noted in his field book. "W Pine 7 N 2 E 1.20," his notes might read, meaning that there was a blazed white pine 7 inches in diameter standing exactly 2 links north and 1.20 links east of the corner stake. Here it was—the stake, put down a year ago at the northwest corner (the upper left-hand corner, so to speak) of the township, where the north-south range line and the east-west township line intersected; here the stake would remain for years, located by the bearing trees.

From it Burt could continue running the lines where he had left off the year before. Setting up his 'scope, he turned ninety degrees north and sighted the range line north into the woods. His assistant pushed his way north a couple of hundred feet and set up a rod, a vertical pole striped red and white, lining it up with the 'scope. While another man held it, the assistant went on another couple of hundred feet and set up another rod. (They could handle only a few hundred feet at a time, for in this rough country vision was restricted by hills and trees and underbrush.) And now, with the line marked out by Burt, the axmen started cutting the brush along it. Following them came the two chainmen, starting by plunging a tally pin into the ground directly in front of the instrument. One stood there, holding the chain loosely in five-foot loops, while the other carried the other end of the chain forward through the clearing hacked by the sweating axmen. At every half-chain length he set a tally pin in the earth, tagged with red cloth. When he encountered trees too big to waste time falling, he had to run a deflection around it, guided by Burt. As he approached the end of the chain, the rear chainman cried "Chain!" and the forward man went ahead cautiously, setting another tally pin at the end of the chain.

Now the axmen came back and, under Burt's direction, blazed the larger trees that stood on the line. These Burt noted in his field book as bearing trees.

The process was repeated until five chains had been run and all eleven tally pins set. When this had been done, the forward chainman cried: "Tally," and each chainman registered the distance by slipping a loop on a tally belt he wore, much as a billiard-player marks a point on the rack. The rear chainman then came up, pulling out the tally pins as he came, and, having counted the pins in the presence of the forward chainman, took the forward end of the chain and started out on a new tally. Thus the chainmen alternately changed places, "so that one is forward in all the odd, and the other in all the even, tallies; which contributes to the accuracy of the measurement."

Accuracy was an obsession with Burt. But not all the surveyors were as painstaking as he; some of the surveys actually were full of errors. In parts of Minnesota and northern Wisconsin the township and range lines run in curiously wavering patterns, quite unlike the firmly traced checkerboard squares that Burt laid out in the Upper Peninsula. Some surveyors used amazingly bad judgment; one marked a section corner with a sawmill; in a few years, of course, it was abandoned and before long it disappeared entirely, leaving nothing to mark the corner. Other surveyors did their work too hurriedly, making many errors. (One surveyor's field notes say that he surveyed and subdivided an entire township, thirty-six square miles, in ten days, an impossibility if any degree of accuracy was to be attained.)

But, in truth, the wonder was not that these men made errors, but that they made so few. Their obstacles were almost insurmountable. In his calm way, William Austin Burt gave advice about how to overcome a few. He told how to take the level, or horizontal, measurement in hilly territory. This was not prairie country; this was the country of the iron hills, whose bluffs sometimes rose five hundred feet of sheer granite above a swamp. Later surveyors scrambling up these cliffs clutching the chain in one hand and Burt's placid book of instructions in the other might have cursed him for a schoolroom visionary had they not known that every sentence he wrote was based on experience. He had been there.

Rivers and lakes were formidable obstacles. They dotted and threaded the country everywhere, their shorelines rough and broken. To measure and map them, Burt worked out a method in which the telescope was mounted on a skiff or light raft. Not only the shorelines but the surface area of "rivers, lakes, and miry-marshes" must be surveyed; many "cannot be measured with the chain," so Burt devised a trigonometric system for the task. In discussing it, he wrote casually: "It may be remarked here, that in surveying large districts of new country, many obstacles of this kind are to be expected, and are met with sometimes under many difficulties, such as the direction and swampy or thickety character of their shores, also, the annoyance felt by the presence of increasing swarms of blood-thirsty flies and moschetoes, which largely infest such shores in summer; hence the importance of the best management, and correct and expeditious methods of passing such obstacles."

It is his only reference to hardship. Here are no complaints of "incredible difficulty and labor" such as the celebrated Douglass Houghton (and Mr. Tiffin's sufferers in the Lower Peninsula) addressed to the Surveyor General; here are simply notes on difficulties which "are to be expected" and obstruct the accurate prosecution of the survey. Burt did not protest against them. He patiently overcame them.

Did the party come to a river too deep to ford? Burt put his men to work building a raft. In his handbook he detailed a method of construction which sounds simple enough. But you had to know what you were doing or you would be building your raft out of tamarack logs and it would sink; or you would be using green or waterlogged lumber, heavy and unmanageable; or you would get the raft out of proportion and it would not steer properly. And if you did not balance your outfit carefully, somebody was going to get wet—no joke on a crisp September day.

When the country was too broken even for horses or mules, the men did their own packing, using the "portage strap," a leather strap ten or twelve feet long with a wide middle section designed to rest snugly on the forehead (the ends were bound around the made-up pack). With this, or a five-strap rig, the men commonly carried between 75 and 120 pounds each.

The men all dressed alike—a wool hat, heavy trousers, a light coat with numerous waterproof pockets, "a light India rubber cape in which to wrap documents and compass during wet weather." (Protecting his field notes and field maps was a twenty-four hour a day obsession with any surveyor; he kept them always on his person, carrying them on his back by day, at night putting them carefully under the rolled-up clothing he used for a pillow.) "Flannel for under clothes, is preferable to cotton, for all seasons and all kinds of weather." Burt gave particularly careful attention to boots, outlining precisely their shape and construction. He also suggested that "A large silk handkerchief, of any colour but red, to tie over the ears and neck, is a good protection from flies and musquitoes."

The survey party moved in a line straight as a Roman road over the hills and swamps. Indians or prospectors might skirt tangles of fallen timber, but the surveyors clambered over them or cut their way through them. And these tangles might not be simply isolated patches twenty feet square; the surveyors sometimes encountered a tangled area that stretched for miles through the woods, "a big blowdown," evidence of a sudden cyclone that had funneled between the iron hills, cut a swath through the timber, and struck down every standing tree. It might take a week to run one boundary of a township through such a place. Nor could the surveyors avoid marshes.

They ran each line twice, as a double-check on accuracy. And after all day at that work, camp must be pitched and food prepared. Every so often the cook must bake bread, mixing his dough on the square of cloth he spread on the ground atop a blanket and baking in frying pans before the fire. After supper

Burt must sit by the dying embers, even after the other men had turned in, writing in his field notes, making them jibe, going over them time and again hunting infinitesimal errors, filling in his rough field map against the next winter when he would make his final map. Those maps included everything from swamps to geological formations.

Burt studied carefully the geology of the country he passed through and he wrote that surveyors should be able "to make a proper collection of geological specimens; and also, to observe the character, stratification, dip, etc., of any rocks in place, or other mineral deposits. Such services afford pleasure and profit to the surveyors, while they contribute to the public interest, and to science."

Burt divided the Upper Peninsula rocks into five principal groups: the primary rocks, the traps, the conglomerates, the sandstones, and the slates. (The granites were described in more detail by Bela S. Hubbard, who worked with Burt and Douglass Houghton.) Subsequently Burt went into more detail about the greenstones and hornblende-slates, the quartzes and feldspars. He mentioned fourteen exposures of iron ore along the lines and concluded that the Upper Peninsula region was richer in iron ore than any other section of the United States. All the geologists who studied the country later were tremendously indebted to the work of Burt and the other early surveyors. But though Burt was the first man in the whole fabulous Lake Superior district to discover iron, he never became an iron king.

By the time he found iron ore, he was working under the general supervision of Douglass Houghton, a bright young favorite of Government officials whose rise was so meteoric that he almost qualifies as a boy wonder. He is far more widely remembered and revered in the Upper Peninsula than Burt or, indeed, than any of the other surveyors and geologists. He came to Michigan from New York when he was barely twenty; already, having had the advantages of a formal education, he had been an assistant professor at his alma mater, the Rensselaer Polytechnic Institute at Troy, New York, and had been admitted to the practice of medicine. The public lectures on geology and chemistry which he had been hired to deliver at Detroit were said to have been well received, but he continued them only a few months, leaving to accompany, as botanist and physician, one of Schoolcraft's exploring parties to the headwaters of the Mississippi. On this expedition Houghton saw the famed copper boulder along the banks of the Ontonagon River which had so excited Alexander Henry and all the other early travelers. Houghton chiseled off some specimens which he took back to Detroit.

There he practiced medicine from 1832 to 1836, performing particularly valuable services during the cholera epidemic of 1834. He also occupied his time during this period by reading many books and learning to play the flute.

Michigan was wrangling over the Toledo strip and fighting shy of the Upper Peninsula, and William Austin Burt, at forty-one, was starting out on his first survey when young Douglass Houghton began his own life work. Young, earnest, intense, good-looking, he gained the ear of prominent citizens and politicians. Among his friends was Steven T. Mason, who was to be Michigan's first Governor. No sooner had statehood been attained than the new Governor wangled an appropriation for a state geologist out of the new legislature. Promptly he appointed Douglass Houghton, twenty-seven years old, to the office.

Houghton entered into the prosecution of the geological survey with a whirlwind boyish enthusiasm. His reports have been described as cautious, as they were in warning that copper could not be found in the Upper Peninsula "pure and without labor"; but at least one of his opinions was rash: he doubted if the ores of zinc, lead, iron, and manganese occurred "in sufficient abundance to prove of much importance." He qualified this by possibly excepting zinc and iron from the statement, in which he turned out to be half right. The point is that when Houghton made this statement in 1840, he could not have known what he was talking about: he had not personally examined the iron fields, as, indeed, no man had; not for four years would plodding, exact Burt discover the Marquette iron range. Houghton in 1840 had simply made his first geological expedition to the copper country. (Like the early travelers who were so impressed with the Ontonagon mass of native copper, he interested himself more in the Upper Peninsula's copper than in its other minerals.)

In 1840 Houghton led his party to the Lake Superior mineral district. By that time he had accumulated able assistants, Bela Hubbard, who also worked with Burt, and Columbus C. Douglass. In his party, which reached Mackinac by steamer from Detroit May 23, 1840, were, in addition to those two assistants, Frederick Hubbard, in charge of instrument observation; H. Thielson, a civil engineer; and Charles W. Penny, "a young Detroit merchant" whose presence is not otherwise accounted for. At Mackinac two boat crews were made up, consisting of six Canadians, *coureurs de bois*, men of mixed French and Indian blood. They could row twelve or fourteen hours, Hubbard reported, unpack the boats, pitch tents, pile up the baggage, and prepare the evening meal, all without displaying signs of fatigue.

At this time Burt was surveying the eastern and central portions of the Upper Peninsula. Impetuous Douglass Houghton, anxious to get to the mineral fields, overleaped Burt (and the iron region too), heading westward straight for the copper country, that long narrow slanting band of rock which stretches northeastward from the Ontonagon River to the tip of Keweenaw Peninsula. Here slight young Douglass Houghton would make his reputation.

In all this Upper Peninsula, Bela Hubbard estimated, lived not more than a thousand persons. There was a fur company factory at L'Anse, at the head of Keweenaw Bay, and another at the famous La Pointe mission. There was a Baptist mission at L'Anse and a fur post and garrison at the Soo. Occasionally transient fishing camps appeared briefly. And that was all. This still was Indian territory.

Houghton and Hubbard and their men set sail westward along the southern shore of Lake Superior. They were sailing the course of the Jesuits and the cavaliers. West from the Soo, Hubbard noted, they passed first an immense tract of broad sandstone steppes, distinguished by the fabled Pictured Rocks, towering stone cliffs eroded into fantastic shapes by centuries of wave action. Farther west, along the hump, all the way from what later became the city of Marquette to Keweenaw Bay, Hubbard was impressed with the ranges of granite knobs rising in the Huron Mountains and, around them, the series of quartzites, slates, and metamorphosed sandstones. He did not know that at the southern foot of these hills lay the great Marquette iron range.

They went on to Point Keweenaw's rockbound coast, a lofty range rising from four to nine hundred feet above the lake. Within these hills were locked veins of native copper. Here, at Copper Harbor, the party halted on July 3, 1840 and started blasting for ore. Houghton, without identifying the locale specifically, wrote: "In opening a vein, with a single blast I threw out nearly two tons of ore, and with this were many masses of native copper, from the most minute specks to about forty pounds in weight. . . . Ores of silver occasionally occur with the copper. . . ."

The party's meals were almost lavish here. Hubbard wrote that dinner included pigeons, fried and stewed, corn and bean soup, shortcake and hardtack, pork, and a can of oysters. They could afford the burden of these delicacies because, unlike Burt, they were not packing their outfit for months in the woods; they were coasting the shores with six *voyageurs*.

When they landed at Ontonagon, a group of "Buffalo Indians" came out of the woods and the explorers were startled to observe, dangling on the breast of the chief's son, a medal bearing a likeness of John Quincy Adams (who had been out of the White House eleven years). These Indians sought to deter the geologists from going up the Ontonagon River to observe the huge copper boulder that had been reported, but the white men appeased them with a bag of flour and a keg of pork.

At the end of the season's explorations Houghton returned to Detroit, taking with him four or five tons of "copper ores," much of which must have been native copper, not true ores of copper, for Upper Michigan's copper is mostly native. Analysis showed Houghton's specimens to be of higher grade than the ores of Cornwall, then the center of world copper production. He sets all this forth in his 1841 report to the legislature, which has been called the first definite information on northern Michigan's copper resources.

In it Houghton, writing astutely in the self-effacing third person, "regrets that the hardships to which he has been exposed in conducting the field work . . . have so far impaired his health as to render it impossible to enter into so minute details as had been anticipated." Yet, withal, canned oysters. Constantly Houghton reiterated his high resolve in connection with "these important subjects . . . to draw no conclusions but such as are strictly based on observations." Houghton, young, educated, dramatic, had a sense of history-making which Burt, the tireless surveyor, totally lacked. Houghton was acutely conscious of the romanticizing of earlier explorers; to Burt accuracy was a matter to be assumed.

Yet they worked together. If Houghton intended to impress the legislators, he failed; his appropriation was not renewed after his report of 1841. The original act of 1837 had paid him sums increasing from $3,000 the first year to $12,000 the fourth year. Now it had expired. But Houghton continued his labors to a point where, in 1843, he reported that the field work for the geological survey was completed; and despite his repeated warnings that copper could not be picked up by handfuls on the beaches, the boom was on: prospectors shinnied up and down the craggy copper cliffs by the scores.

All this while Houghton, no longer on the state's payroll, had been maturing a grandiose scheme for conducting a simultaneous mineralogical, topographical, magnetic, geological, and linear survey of the entire United States. In 1844 this plan came to fruition, and thus the bright young man came into direct contact with William Austin Burt.

Friend of politicians, young Houghton went to Washington while Congress was in session in 1844. James K. Polk had retired as Speaker of the House, but a few months later he would be lifted from relative obscurity to the Presidency. Houghton proposed his plan to the Secretary of the Treasury. The Secretary listened sympathetically; public lands were a problem all right; had been, ever since the King drew his no-entry line along the Appalachian chain before the Revolution; it'd be a good idea to know just what was on those western lands before they were disposed of. And no question but what it would be cheaper to have the linear surveyors turn in geological reports too. But the Secretary doubted if deputy surveyors were sufficiently versed in the sciences to perform such a task successfully. Houghton offered to take the contract himself. As a starter, he proposed to complete the survey

of the Upper Peninsula at a half-cent per acre in excess of the sum
to be paid for the linear survey. The Secretary agreed. Houghton
would receive $5 per mile for every mile of line run and marked,
with a maximum of 4,000 miles.

All these negotiations took time. Then Houghton hurried back
to Michigan and collected assistants. William Austin Burt, already
a United States deputy surveyor for some eleven years, was one
of them. Fifty-two years old, a practical inventor, a retired judge,
an experienced woodsman, veteran of thousands of miles of surveying, he may have looked slightly askance at the buoyant young
man who proposed to lead the survey, the young man who never
went into the woods without wearing a white collar. But if Burt
smiled at Houghton, he smiled to himself. Houghton was running the show; Burt went on surveying.

Houghton's real interest soon became evident. Time was running out; the previous year, in 1842, all land west of the Chocolay
River near Marquette had been ceded by the Indians to the United
States, and now, with the always rather hypothetical Indian
menace removed, prospectors and settlers were flocking to the
copper country. Captain Walter Cunningham had arrived at Copper Harbor, the boom town of the Keweenaw mineral district, on
the first boat in the spring of 1843 and, on behalf of the War
Department, had opened the office of the mineral land agency for
the Lake Superior district. Already claims were being filed with
gay abandon on land not yet surveyed. And that was the point:
this copper country that was Houghton's pet must be surveyed,
and surveyed in a hurry. But this couldn't be done until the survey
was pushed westward. Methodical William Austin Burt had been
plodding along in the eastern end of the Upper Peninsula; he now
had reached the middle portion; Houghton must prod him, must
speed up the rollback of the white spaces that stretched across the
bulge between Iron Bay (later Marquette) and the copper country. Already, in July 1844, much of the short surveying season
had been wasted, Houghton, always sore beset, wrote to the Surveyor General at Cincinnati. He would do his best and would get
an early start next year.

Houghton's party assembled at Mackinac the first week in
August, the party which he was to abandon a month before it

made the history he loved so well. Burt had left Detroit August 1, 1844, with his assistants, William Ives, James King, Jacob Houghton (Douglass's younger brother), Harvey and Richard S. Mellen; at Mackinac they met the boss, Houghton, and Norman McLeod and two Indians named John Taylor and Bonny. The entire party went by boat to the mouth of the Escanaba River, their disembarkation point.

Here they found "a number of men in the employ of Mr. Smith engaged in daming the river, preparatory to the construction of a saw mill," Richard Mellen wrote, failing to explain how this Mr. Smith happened to be out here a hundred miles from nowhere twenty-odd years ahead of the times. The surveyors wanted to build a flat-bottomed boat in which to haul their provisions up the Escanaba; unable to obtain lumber at Mr. Smith's mill site, they were forced to carry their chuck along the riverbank until they reached another mill, unnamed, where Burt bought lumber and had a flatboat built.

It is interesting to note that, according to Mellen's eyewitness account, it was Burt who bought this lumber and supervised the boat-building. The inference is that Houghton already had left the party, having seen it start up the river. And Mellen states flatly in another place that Houghton and McLeod returned to Mackinac "about August 15"; he well may have been gone by the time the party reached this up-river mill.

But Houghton himself, in his subsequent report to the Surveyor General, clouded the exact time of his return and sought to give the impression that he was with the party longer than he actually was. He wrote that "we" built a flatboat "and after incredible difficulty and labor" towed it up the Escanaba River to the south boundary of T43. Here "we" went to work, extending the survey west to the west boundary of Range 26 and up to the north boundary of Township 47. One line, that between Ranges 24 and 25, was projected all the way to Lake Superior.

After detailing other labors which "we" performed, Houghton reports: "The surveys in all the Townships 45, 46, and 47 [which include the rich Marquette iron district] have been exceedingly difficult in consequence of the hilly, almost mountainous character of this country. The northwesterly portion of these surveys reached the Iron District, which has been described in my state reports, and here for many days the needle was absolutely useless, the variation sometimes amounting to 90 degrees, and at other times being nearly reversed. This Iron District is highly interesting . . . and there can be no doubt but it will eventually become of great practical importance." Thus Houghton, although he had run off to Detroit and, later, to the copper country in characteristically peripatetic fashion and was not present when iron was discovered, reverses his earlier impetuous judgment on the value of Upper Michigan's iron ore.

Mellen recalls that the surveyors loaded their new-built flatboat with provisions and towed it by hand up-river, wading a total of twelve miles, the "bottom of stream covered with cragged rocks of limestone, and, after having clambored over them in the water for several miles, we felt no slight degree of relief when we arrived at the place where we were to commence surveying." Mellen adds that dragging the boat "was by no means an easy or agreeable task." Burt's field notes are silent on the subject.

The party began work on the southern boundary of Township 43 north and ran the lines up to the south boundary of Township 48 north, a distance of some thirty miles. "We camped at the corner of townships 47 and 48, north of range 24 and 25 west, about the 18th of September. [This is on the shore of Lake Superior, about two miles southeast of the present Marquette city limits.] From this place we ran west twelve miles to the corner of townships 47 and 48 north, ranges 26 and 27 west, near Teal Lake. Thence we ran south on the east boundary of range 27 west, township 47 north, and on this line about the 21st of September we found iron ore."

It was no wonder that they found iron ore; it was everywhere; this is the Marquette range; these are the two richest Michigan iron townships, land descriptions that still have a ring of greatness about them: T47N R26W and T47N R27W. Hear Mellen's story of the discovery:

"I well remember the day. It rained all that [September] day and part of the next night, when it commenced snowing, and it snowed the remainder of the night and part of the day following. Our [magnetic] compass needle was of no use to us while we were in the iron region. (We used the solar compass.) We were nearly out of provisions and were anxious to pursue that course which would soonest bring us to the place where they were left."

But they found iron. One of the party, Jacob Houghton, tells the story:

"So soon as we reached the hill to the south of the lake, the compass-man (Mr. Ives), began to notice the fluctuation in the variation of the magnetic needle. We were, of course, using the solar compass, of which Mr. Burt was the inventor, and I shall never forget the excitement of the old gentleman when viewing the changes of the variation—the needle [of the magnetic, not the solar, compass] not actually traversing alike in any two places. He kept changing his position to take observations, all the time saying, 'How would they survey this country without my compass?' . . . At length the compass-man called for us all to 'come and see a variation that will beat them all.' As we looked at the instrument, to our astonishment the north end of the needle was traversing a few degrees to the south of west. Mr. Burt called out, 'Boys, look around and see what you can find.' We all left the line, some going to the east, some going to the west, and all of us returned with specimens of iron ore, mostly gathered from outcrops. This was along the first mile from Teal Lake. We carried out all the specimens we could, conveniently."

Near this spot a prospecting party later located an iron outcrop and opened the first iron mine in all the Lake Superior district; a monument marks the place today, erected by a mining company between the twin iron cities of Ishpeming and Negaunee.

Burt never got rich from what any prospector would have called the richest strike in a lifetime. Houghton reported his discovery, other men made millions out of it, in a few years a mad scramble was on for land in this fabulously rich district. Burt went on surveying.

On that particular day, having collected ore samples, he continued to run the line. His party was short of food and anxious to hurry back to the provision cache; iron or no iron, starvation in the unseasonable snow was not pleasant to contemplate. Mellen continues: "Some of our party proposed that we try to 'angle' the township; but to this Mr. Burt objected, saying that it would be quite impracticable, since the needle was too fluctuating. So, by his suggestions, we continued on south, ranging through by stakes nearly two miles which took us a day or more [in this rough country]. We had then got so far south that we thought the compass needle might be of some use to us and we tried it again, but it failed to guide us aright. The weather became clear so we could use the solar compass. When we had reached the southeast corner, six miles from Teal Lake, and were turning east, the packers who were ahead discovered three hedge-hogs on a birch tree. They cut down the tree and secured the porcupines." (For many years porkies have been protected from hunters in Upper Michigan because, while not esteemed as a delicacy, they are the easiest edible animal a man lost in the woods can catch and kill.) "We ran the line but a short distance east, when our appetites, which were keen before, were rendered, by the prospect of a porcupine steak, quite irresistible, and we fired a big pine stump, warmed ourselves, dried our clothes, cooked one of our hedge-hogs and devoured him. This was in the first part of the day, and in the afternoon we built another fire and cooked the second. The third we made into a soup for our supper. The next day we reached our provisions, having subsisted for six days on the food we had intended for two days."

A year later Douglass Houghton was drowned in Lake Superior while on a geological expedition. Thus he became the young martyr, better remembered than Burt and Hubbard and Foster and Whitney and the other early surveyors and geologists. When he died, he was only thirty-six; he had been in the employ of the United States only a little more than a year; he was still engaged in his race with time to complete his surveys before the copper rush got ahead of him. Appropriately, he was drowned off the rugged Keweenaw coast. With four *voyageurs*, he left Eagle Harbor, October 13, 1845, in an open boat to keep an appointment eleven miles up the shore with another surveying party, led by Sam W. Hill. This accomplished, Houghton re-embarked, hoping to reach Eagle River the same night. Although the evening was fine, one of the *voyageurs* thought a storm was coming. Houghton disagreed. They had rowed for three miles in choppy seas when a northeaster sprang up and the *voyageurs*, experienced boatmen, wanted to put ashore at Sand Beach, but Houghton refused; it was only a little farther now, the men should row faster. Already they were rowing for all they were worth, but the boat was shipping water and, as it began to snow in the quick darkness, the seas became monstrous. One of the *voyageurs* advised Houghton to don his life preserver. As he reached for it, a heavy sea crashed into the boat and filled it. Then it was Houghton who proposed going ashore. But it was too late, the *voyageurs* told him; they had passed Sand Beach; here the coast was a ragged mass of rocks. Stubbornly, as the survivors later recalled, young Dr. Houghton "immediately put the boat about, saying 'We must go ashore; we can do nothing here.' Within two hundred yards of the shore, [we] shipped another sea which was followed by a larger billow, and the boat capsized with all hands under her."

One of the *voyageurs* hauled Houghton from under the water by the collar of his coat and told him to hold on to the keel of the boat. "Dr. Houghton then remarked, 'Peter, never mind me, try to go ashore if you can; I will go ashore well enough.' Instantly a heavy sea struck the boat, throwing it perpendicularly into the air. It fell over backwards, and Dr. Houghton disappeared forever."

Though nearly drowned or beaten to death on the rocks by the pounding seas, two of the *voyageurs* got ashore and, after a futile search for their companions, walked to Eagle River. On the way it was dark, there was no trail, nothing but rocks and thickets; one of them fell down several times from exhaustion and cold. They reached town near midnight. A searching party was formed. But that night three feet of snow fell, the search was impeded, and it failed; not until the following spring was Houghton's body recovered and taken back east by his brother for burial.

Many of Houghton's notes were lost with him, but from other notes he left, Burt and Hubbard prepared a report which the administrator of Houghton's estate described as "not as complete and accurate as it would be if prepared by Dr. Houghton himself."

Burt did not die in such spectacular fashion. He grew old in the field, surveying till he was nearly sixty. Even then he did not retire; he served in the state legislature and took part in the preliminary survey for the canal at the Soo. Until his death, when he was sixty-six, he maintained his interest in the development of the Upper Peninsula's mineral resources. And when he died, he was working to perfect an equatorial sextant which he had patented.

The surveyors had broken trail through the wilderness. On their heels came the Government geologists. This Upper Peninsula was a geologist's paradise. General Cunningham, stationed at Copper Harbor, made a trip to the iron region and reported in 1845 that "important discoveries of lead ore" had been made "in the vicinity of Death River." These lead deposits, which turned out later to be rather trivial, also interested other investigators, such as Samuel Peck and A. B. Gray. Most of the claims which Gray showed on his painstaking map were filed by prospectors who, like Gray himself, were interested not so much in the iron that was everywhere in the two great iron townships of Michigan but, rather, in the lead and copper and gold reported farther north, near the Dead River. Only Joseph Stacy bothered to report that there was "an inexhaustible amount of compact and micaceous specular iron ore in that district."

In 1846 the Lake Superior mineral lands were taken from the War Department—the war veterans long since had been settled on more hospitable earth—and put under supervision of the General Land Office, then a division of the Treasury Department. Dr. C. T. Jackson was named to make a geological survey of the area. He picked as one of his assistants Dr. John Locke, who is remembered chiefly for one deathless sentence describing the iron district: "So far as I have observed, it is a gold region 'all but the gold,' a silver region without silver, and a copper region with veins and bunches of ore so thin and scattered as to be unprofitable for working." But Locke did note iron ore and he called the region, in reference to its general geological make-up, "the Cornwall of America," a rather apt description.

In 1848 Dr. A. Randall, an Assistant U. S. Geologist, reported iron ore in northern Wisconsin, just south of the Michigan-Wisconsin line in the extreme western end of the Upper Peninsula on what was to be called, thirty years later, the Gogebic Range.

But thus far the explorers had only been nibbling at the edges. Now Jackson sent to the Upper Peninsula a pair of geologists unsurpassed in Michigan's history. J. W. Foster, a round-cheeked man with Pickwickian sideburns, traced the iron range westward from the two iron townships to Lake Michigamme, one of the largest and most beautiful of Michigan's lakes. Here on the north shore he found hornblendic and argillaceous slates forming a range of hills that encompassed the lake on its north shore; within the hornblende were beds of quartz. This, he thought, meant iron ore; and the men who not many years later built the hell-roaring doomed town of Michigamme confirmed his opinion. By canoe Foster went down the Michigamme River through gorges of towering gray rocks, stopping frequently to hack with patient curiosity at the mountains with a pick. Seven or eight miles downstream from the lake he found an almost perpendicular cliff composed of specular oxide of iron so pure that its mineral associates were difficult to determine. This pure ore formed the brow of the cliff, and here was to be sunk the shaft of the Republic Mine, called in the eighties the greatest of them all, but now, in 1943, abandoned, its town, like Michigamme, a ghost of greatness.

Foster's running mate, J. D. Whitney, another of Jackson's associates, found almost chemically pure peroxide of iron in quantity beyond calculation on this rich Marquette Range; the ore, he reported, was "in solid ridges and knobs, evidently of igneous origin, the highest being about 1100 feet above the level of the lake, and some of them being half a mile long." Small wonder that the early mining men who swarmed in after the geologists referred excitedly to "iron mountains."

These matters excited Dr. Jackson. In 1848 he received a specimen of rich hematite from the Marquette Range; about the same time a French-Canadian sent him some magnetic iron ore which an Indian had found farther south, along the Menominee River, which Foster was exploring. Hastily Jackson assembled his report, a fat, curiously conglomerate collection of myths and statistics and geological facts; then, with a sort of "What are we waiting for?" dispatch, he closed his desk in Washington, resigned his office, and caught the first boat to the Upper Peninsula mineral lands to see if he couldn't cut himself in on these riches. He was not the only fugitive from Washington; by now the copper fever was running high. No sooner had the Chippewas ceded their land to the Government than the Secretary of the Navy, David Henshaw, resigned and promoted a company that grabbed forty entire square miles of rich copper veins on Keweenaw's rock-ribbed back. Henshaw was the first Boston Brahmin to exploit the copper country; he was to have many successors. And they were to come fast. For by now the Upper Peninsula's first boom was not only well started, it was subsiding. Already men were abandoning the copper country to join the forty-niners, and the companies were harassed not only with the bad guesses of geologists but with a labor shortage. Yet these, in truth, were the least of the hardships suffered by the men and women who pioneered old Keweenaw. The period of exploration in the Upper Peninsula was ended; now came the period of first boom. It had started in the copper country in 1843.

THREE : KING COPPER

◄§ 5 §►

TWO MONTHS' POOR SLEDDING

𝒱

IN 1843 AMERICANS knew little of the Lake Superior region. Not
all of it had been surveyed; Houghton had reported copper, but
Burt had not found iron ore. The boundary between the United
States and Canada had been settled finally only the year before.
Only that spring had the Indians relinquished their claim to the
Upper Peninsula. True, settlers were moving westward rapidly
to put plow to the plains states; it was the eve of the land rush,
the pre-emption laws were prime political issues, the people of
the new West were in the saddle, and they had sent their champions, Andrew Jackson and Old Tippecanoe, to the White House.
The people of the West were throwing out their chests; they
were ready to fight Indians or any nation of the world, and before
long they would fight the Mexicans and win Texas and California
and half of Mexico itself. It was a time for expansion, a time of
restlessness; the new nation was stirring uneasily; men were moving, moving constantly, moving westward in one of history's great
tides of emigration. Already some of them had gone to California,
where they would find gold. But somehow these men had neglected the Lake Superior region, by and large; certainly they
had neglected the inhospitable northern peninsula of Michigan;
they hadn't known enough about it; only this spring had the
settlers started coming, and most of them were not really settlers
at all, properly. They were men who knew something about

mining, men who had read Houghton's reports, men with a mission.

They came mainly by boat to Copper Harbor, the mining camp on the rocky tip of the long Keweenaw Peninsula. Copper Harbor is but a summer resort today; in the 1840's it was the capital of the booming copper country and, but for the Soo, the first city of Upper Michigan. Here were established the second largest hotel and the second largest newspaper of the entire state, surpassed only in Detroit. Here the oval landlocked harbor always was white with sails. Here the crisp days rang with the clatter of hammers and axes, the shouts of stevedores and teamsters, the shriek of whistles at the mines, the rumbling roar of incessant blasting in the hills.

A mile behind the village the mountains rose, stern, silent, rugged, untouched as they had been when the Jesuits first beheld them. The wilderness was at Copper Harbor's back and, in the winter, at its throat. At night there was silence, the noisy silence of the north country, where wolves howl and bobcats scream like children in pain; silence and blackness in the brooding mountains.

Many men—Cousin Jacks they were called—came here direct from the tin and copper mines of Cornwall. Everything was mining here; the talk in the saloons was mining talk, the rough-handed men you passed on the straggling streets were miners, the whiskered men with packs on their backs and suspicious glints in their eyes were prospectors, the new mules unloaded from the boats, and the men too, were being brought in to work in the mines. The broken ribs of the old schooner *John Jacob Astor* stood like a stark lonely sentinel on the beach, with the big gray lake beyond, hazy at sundown.

The town was growing, growing fast. The first boat through the ice fields in the spring of 1843 had brought General Cunningham to open the Government land office, and it had brought also twenty miners. They came in a steady stream after that, overrunning the town and the near-by hills, and building to a climactic year in 1846. Boarding houses sprang up overnight; their beds were never made, for the men were sleeping in three shifts. Years later a woman who had owned one of these houses came back to Copper Harbor clad in silks and satins; she had bought copper stock of the great Calumet & Hecla Company when it was worth next to nothing and she had ridden it up to close to a thousand dollars a share.

At the head of the little bay stood the Brockway House, built by Daniel D. Brockway, who came to Copper Harbor from Father Frederic Baraga's mission down at L'Anse. He was one of the few who brought his wife and family to this remote region; he became one of its remembered men, making and losing fortunes. Opposite his hotel was the tiny rock knob called Porter's Island, and on it perched the Government House, office of the all-powerful Federal land agent.

The town was crowded with saloons, jammed with miners far from home, who "abandoned themselves to drinking and gambling; vice and wickedness prevailed." One early apologist noted that "The early forties in the Copper District were days of heavy drinking, of mingled feasting and fasting, of hard labor and carousing . . . but the troops were never called on to suppress rioting, subdue violence, or maintain order. The pioneers were a wild and hardy lot, but honest and neighborly." No vigilante committees were needed; the district "was perhaps the only great mining district of the world so suddenly populated . . . which did not finally require the services of Judge Lynch." Nevertheless, "litigation was commonly settled by a stand-up-and-knock-down fight between the plaintiff and defendant."

Back from the shore of Superior was Lake Fanny Hooe, nestling blue and clear at the base of the mountains. Here the prospectors were scratching at the cliffs diligently; here the Clark Mine was opened and the manganese mine. It was logical that Copper Harbor should be the first center of activity in the copper country. Since there were no roads, immigrants must come to this region by water; of necessity, they went around the Keweenaw Peninsula, and at its tip they found not only a safe anchorage in stormy weather but also copper outcrops: a greenish band of ore on the very end of land, known to the *voyageurs* as "green rock." This point was included in the first lease issued to a prospector; he sold his claims to Easterners who, in 1844, put down the first shaft in the copper country.

Copper Harbor is the topmost end of Michigan's copper-bearing "trap range," which runs, like a copper filling in a giant's tooth, 140 miles southwest to Ontonagon, at the base of the Porcupine Mountains. Along the whole narrow length of the Keweenaw, the rocks are tipped northward. On the edges, near the lake, are bands of sandstone; down between them æons ago flowed the lavas; this is the trap range. Copper-bearing rocks here are of two types: amygdaloid and conglomerate. The amygdaloids are the tops of the lava flows, rocks which were made porous by gas bubbles rising through the earth as it cooled. Later copper-impregnated water washed over these rocks and slowly, infinitely slowly, the copper settled into the bubbles, or amygdules. The conglomerate formations are, in essence, beach pebbles cemented with red sandstone or hematite and mingled with copper; "puddingstone," the Cousin Jacks called it, and thought it worthless. Indeed, no company except the Calumet & Hecla ever worked the conglomerate profitably (but C. & H. became the greatest mine of them all). Nowhere else in the world is copper found, in commercial quantities, in its pure or native state. (There are some ores of copper on Keweenaw, but they are of less importance than the virgin copper deposits.) Copper is everywhere in this region; the problem is to find it in paying quantities. In that quest fortunes were thrown away. The various companies have spent, in a hundred years of prospecting, more than a hundred million dollars, and there is truth in the saying: "It takes a gold mine to make a copper mine." But other fortunes were made. Calumet & Hecla alone has paid more than two hundred millions of dollars in dividends on a capital of two and a half millions. Nine billion pounds of copper have been taken out of the range and sold for a billion and a half dollars, much of it at a premium, for of such high quality is Keweenaw copper that for years it commanded a premium on the market and set the standards of purity for copper the world over.

Southwest from Copper Harbor for twenty-odd miles the Keweenaw Peninsula is a serrated broken range of hills a thousand feet high. The wonder is not that the early prospectors found so few paying veins here; the wonder is that they were hardy enough to prospect these hills at all. Farther to the southwest the peninsula flattens out into a high plateau which ends abruptly in a bluff overlooking Portage Lake. Somewhere near here Father Ménard lost his way on the portage and died. The lake, long and narrow, lies athwart the base of the Keweenaw; today a ship canal to Lake Superior has been cut at either end of the lake, making the Keweenaw Peninsula actually an island. On the steep north shore of the lake stands Hancock; across the water its twin town of Houghton climbs up another bluff to the South Range. This range, an extension of the Keweenaw, continues southwestward along the shore of Lake Superior to the mouth of the Ontonagon River, at the foot of the Porcupines.

Here in the early days was the other copper settlement: Ontonagon. Thus, although the middle portion of the range, the Portage Lake and Calumet district, proved to be the richest of all, it remained wilderness for several years while the early prospectors worked inward from the extreme ends, from Copper Harbor and Ontonagon.

Copper Harbor was settled early through the logic of geography; Ontonagon was settled early because a backwoodsman named Jim Paul heard (he could not read) the old tales of the enormous mass of copper on the banks of the Ontonagon River. Jim Paul, restless wanderer through the West of the thirties and forties, came to the mouth of the Ontonagon in 1843 with a half-breed named Nick Minclergue. "He came for copper and he got none," writes his biographer, James K. Jamison, in one of the best of all the books about the Upper Peninsula. "He suffered unbelievable hardships. . . . He came to get rich quickly and depart, but he stayed and died in comparative poverty. He came like a young adventurer, a gaunt, indomitable, fiery and experienced Indian fighter fresh from the Black Hawk war, and he doddered out his days poking up the fires and doing the chores of a village tavern."

Paul founded the town of Ontonagon on the east bank of the river's mouth. There was an Indian village on the west bank. He built his log cabin and started out in search of the "historic pebble," the huge copper mass up-river which Jonathan Carver, Alexander Henry, Lewis Cass, Sam Hill, and Douglass Houghton, each in his turn, had marveled at. By the time they had finished hacking off chunks to carry home, it still weighed nearly two tons. Paul's halfbreed partner palavered with the Indians and they went up-river and found the great shining mass of pure copper three miles above navigable water. What happened then is obscure; a long controversy arose over ownership of the mass, for the Indians appear to have sold it to anyone who came along. Before the wrangle was finished, Jim Paul had defied the United States Army, and a Detroit hardware merchant had triumphantly loaded the boulder onto a boat and shipped it about as a twenty-five-cent exhibit, much as certain later entrepreneurs were wont to encase whales in ice and cart them around the country until health officers interfered. In the end, after weighty debate in the halls of Congress, Jim Paul's pebble came to rest in the Smithsonian Institution, where it is today.

It was the first of many great masses of pure copper found in the Upper Michigan district. Perhaps the largest was that taken from the Minesota Mine, near Ontonagon; twenty husky men worked fifteen months to cut it up and raise it to the surface, and it weighed more than five hundred tons. Jim Paul went on looking for mass copper, and so did most of the other early prospectors. But the truth was that copper wasn't gold; you couldn't make a fortune off one chunk of copper, however big.

Nor was Jim Paul's transaction with the Indians a peculiar case. The threat of Indian trouble was real to the early settlers. The sudden unexpected rush of prospectors to the copper country in 1844 was driving the Indians from their land sooner than either the Government or the Indians had foreseen when the treaty was signed. The Office of Indian Affairs didn't want to retard the opening of the mines but "would advise no step that could be tortured into harshness towards these poor people." Furthermore, there was another consideration, less high-minded: "Nor would it be politic to deal with them harshly until the question about Isle Royale is adjusted." The Indians, indeed, appeared resentful. As a consequence, and with the added thought of fortifying a point not far from potentially hostile British Canada, the Government built Fort Wilkins on the outskirts of Copper Harbor. Actually no massacre ever occurred and in fact the Indians of that day were a sorry lot. They were in the throes of being evangelized, civilized, settled in towns and on farms. The

change-over was difficult. An Indian agent at the Soo wrote in
1846: "There appears to be a decreasing disposition on the part
of [Indian] parents to send their children to school. Many of them
who have left school apparently derive little advantage from what
they have learned, and frequently fall into dissipation and indo-
lence. . . ." There was a lot of trouble of all kinds. Each year the
Indians left the Soo and went to a summer resort at Whitefish
Point; the preacher was forced to follow them. They complained
constantly that their "annuities" did not arrive till they had been
vacationing at Whitefish Point for six weeks. Sometimes they
drank up their annuities anyway. The Indian carpenter and blacksmith at L'Anse settlement resigned. The Indians there pooled
their "treaty money" and bought a yoke of oxen; they raised
potatoes—so many potatoes that they became a glut on the market
and spoiled, while seventy miles up the bay the prospectors at
Copper Harbor were without potatoes.

The prospectors were walled in by the winter, a snowbound
little settlement on the fringe of the wilderness. Lake transportation ended usually in November; from then until April or May
only the slender thread of a trail bound them to the civilized
world, so far away as to seem non-existent. Mail came in by dog-
sled. Often the carrier would lighten the overloaded sled by leaving sacks of mail along the trail; he hung it in trees, intending to
pick it up on a later run; but on the later runs he was overloaded
too; often the mail that got left was never delivered. Small wonder:
it was a run of nearly three hundred miles to Copper Harbor from
Green Bay, the post office and nearest town of any size. The sled
which the dogs pulled was much like an ordinary toboggan; on it
were loaded the sacks of mail and the blankets and food of the
carrier. He snowshoed behind the sled, covering perhaps twenty
miles a day in good weather if no accidents occurred. But accidents did occur, constantly. Sometimes the mail got wet. Once
an Indian carrier fell through the ice while crossing Green Bay
and was hauled out of the water at the end of a rope with the mail
on his back. The letters were thawed out and read as avidly as
the annual reports of the mining company agents. The arrival of
each mail was enough to stop all work in town for a day. Newspapers weeks old were as fresh as the day they were printed. A

lighthouse keeper was told in the spring that Franklin Pierce had been elected President the previous November. The mail-carrier was a hero; after the mail was unloaded, he would sit for hours by the stove in the village store, telling the prospectors of his journey.

Once the mail sled reached Ontonagon not only two months late but also nearly emptied of mail: three bags had been thrown off at Escanaba to make room for a barrel of pork. The towns-people did not complain. For food shortage was a chronic peril in the copper country. Famine was as real to the first prospectors as it had been to the Indians before the French came; perhaps more real, for the Indians didn't care about copper; they had sense enough to stay near Whitefish Rapids, where the water was open all winter for fishing. But the white men stayed near the copper. Some of the pioneers might escape actual privation; few escaped boredom in the long winters. They snowshoed the twenty miles from Copper Harbor to Eagle River to attend a dance at the big Senter Hotel. They passed the heavy-hanging time by visiting friends for a few days, though they had to carry their own provisions and blankets on their backs and to make up pallets on the floor because few homes had extra beds.

The company agent was the leader of the settlement. He was the on-the-ground representative of the moneyed Eastern men who owned the mines; often he was an Easterner himself, sometimes less a mining man than a relative of the majority stockholder, sent out from Boston when he finished school. He was strictly a white-collar man. The miners themselves were a rough lot—rough in speech, rough in dress. They wore mackinaw coats, flannel shirts, heavy boots. One, a sport who enlivened all the winter dances, wore white duck trousers, a red sash for a belt, a blue flannel shirt heavily embroidered on bosom and collar with multi-colored silks, high leather boots, and a stovepipe hat.

Dances often broke up in brawls; men who had been twenty miles out in the woods for weeks or months simply had too much hell-raising stored up inside them to be content with dancing. By the end of the evening they had put away enough forty-rod—so-called, it is said, because its aroma would kill a greenhorn at forty rods—to fight the devil himself. Fighting diminished toward spring, for the saloonkeepers usually ran short of whisky and diluted what remained with water; sometimes the miners were paying for a shot of almost pure water by the time the first boat came through in the spring.

Its arrival was the signal for a complete shutdown of all work, for a general celebration. A lookout had been stationed previously on a high point of land; when the vessel approached and he gave the signal, whistles were blown, the mines and stores closed down, every man, woman, and child rushed down to the dock. The crowd stormed aboard as the boat landed; winter-starved, they rooted in the cargo like children on Christmas morning, and until they had carried off the things they had been deprived of during the winter, the crew was unable to unload. A week after a pastor at Ontonagon found his church utterly deserted, he remarked wryly: "Divine service will be held at this house next Sabbath morning at the usual hour, provided no steam boat arrives at that time."

The winters of 1847–8 and 1850–1 were two of the worst. Late in the fall of '47 word came that the last boat had burned, the one that was to bring the winter's supplies to Copper Harbor. Everybody knew that starvation would be no joke this year. A vessel was chartered hastily and loaded at Detroit, but when it had not arrived by early November, things looked hopeless. Samuel W. Hill visited the mining camps and inventoried provisions. Hill was a rip-roaring surveyor and mining man; he had surveyed with Douglass Houghton, and his propensity for profanity was legendary. His neighbors, retelling his tall tales in polite society, substituted "Sam Hill" for the more lurid phrases, and Hill's fame spread far beyond the Copper Country; he became, indeed, a part of the American language as mule-skinners roared: "What the Sam Hill!" all the way from Bent's Fort to Manassas Junction. But in the copper country Sam Hill was also a man of respected judgment. As he went now in this terrible winter from store to store, from house to house, he realized the truth: there wouldn't be enough food to get through to spring. There was only one thing to do: all the single men would have to get out of the country. There might be enough food for the family men and their wives and children, but that was all. Where would the single men go? To Green Bay; it was the only place; Green Bay, three hundred miles distant over snowshoe trails with short rations. Hill went to hundreds of lonely dwellings, some substantial homes in the settlements, some only rude boarding houses or squatters' shacks, some the loneliest homes of all: snow-mound hovels deep in the woods occupied by men hired, in accordance with Government land regulations, to maintain residence on a mining claim in order to keep title to the land. In these places Hill squatted and scratched in the dirt floor with a stick while he talked, explaining patiently that the single men would have to leave, that if they remained they would starve and would drive women and children to starvation. The men understood. But there were a thousand questions. What of title to the claims? The Government said that a man had to be kept on the property constantly in order to point out its boundaries to anyone who might inquire. Wouldn't somebody jump the claim? And what about food for the long trek to Green Bay? "My snowshoes are wore out; they'll never stand a trip like that." Or "I'd have to borrow a good gun; man can't go into the woods with a gun like this." Or "My misery's been comin' back; don't know whether I could make it or not." Or "I been here three years now; I just plain don't like cities." Or "My dog—he's too old to make the trip. What'll happen to him?"

Hill argued, cajoled, promised to look after a thousand details. And the men sighed and said they guessed there wasn't nothing else to do. They made up their packs.

But when Hill got back to Eagle Harbor on November 11 he heard almost unbelievable news. The propeller *Independence*, which was finishing its second season as the first steam-driven vessel on Lake Superior, had reached Copper Harbor with supplies. Laid up for the winter at the Soo, the *Independence* had been put back into commission again when the chartered boat arrived from Detroit, the supplies had been rushed across the portage at the Soo and loaded onto the *Independence*, and she had fought her way up the lake at five miles an hour under forced draft, through the quick-forming ice floes to Copper Harbor, arriving there just before the winter closed down tight. No boat ever was greeted with more rejoicing. But even with this windfall, food still was scarce during this winter. Famed Captain Charles Gratiot of the Phoenix Mine explained to the stockholders that profits were meager because the miners had to spend most of their time hunting game for food.

Sam Hill made the rounds again on snowshoes in March 1851 when provisions ran low. But the spring breakup came early, permitting a boat to arrive ahead of schedule; once more the copper country had squeaked through.

Once a trek actually was made from the copper country to Green Bay in midwinter, with tragic results. The summer of 1854 had brought a fresh rush of miners to the region. But in January 1855 the Eastern capitalists who owned the mines ordered expenses cut. The decision made in well-heated Boston board rooms threw men out of work a thousand miles away at the hardest time of year. Boarding houses could not afford to carry the miners till spring. Facing starvation, some four hundred men left to walk to Green Bay. Many were not woodsmen, they were miners, come here from more hospitable climates to work in the mines, not to roam the woods. The winter had been unusually hard, even for this region where the climate has been described as consisting of "ten months of winter and two months of poor sledding." There had been a great deal of snow, and some of the men, ignorant of the hardships ahead, set out for Green Bay with insufficient provisions. Some didn't even have snowshoes. They started as a group, but inevitably stragglers fell behind. To wait for them was dangerous; the woodsmen pressed on. No Moses appeared to lead the party. In the end, the survivors who reached Green Bay told tales of terrible hardship. Five were known to have died along the trail. Many others never were heard from. Nearly all suffered frozen hands or feet or faces.

Jane Masters, one of the first pioneers at Copper Harbor, lived through all this hubbub and confusion and privation, yet remained untouched by it. Her father was a privateer in the service of the King, her mother was an English gentlewoman, and she was reared, in cloistered fashion, in Cornwall. She worshipped her father. He died when she was a girl. As soon as it was seemly, Jane's mother became engaged to remarry. Young Jane was horrified; she never quite forgave her mother her second marriage. Jane, seventeen and already, by the standards of those days, nearly an old maid, forthwith married a local boy named Job Masters; her mother took her second husband a few days later, and the two couples packed up and left England for good, honeymooning together to the wilderness of the New World.

Why to Upper Michigan? Perhaps Jane's father had brought home tales of the new West. It may be that the two couples planned their hegira only so far as New York and that they heard of Michigan there. A little-known region in 1843, it was a strange destination for two honeymooning English couples. They reached New York after a rough six weeks' passage in a sailing vessel. Going by train to Buffalo, the honeymooners visited Niagara as their children and their children's children would do. Below the Falls they embarked on a lake boat for Detroit, which they considered a disgusting little settlement rowdy with burgeoning commerce. They paused but briefly there, re-embarked, and headed up Lake Huron to the North Channel. There, at a settlement called Bruce Mines on the Canadian shore, they disembarked.

Bruce Mines never was much of a place. Located in a copper, silver, and gold region east of the Soo in Ontario, this village, huddled on the wilderness coast of Lake Huron, was a booming mining camp in Jane Masters's time. It was settled by Scottish miners from the lead mines around Glasgow and by Cornishmen from the tin and copper mines of Cornwall, and many of the men and women who pioneered Upper Michigan's copper country stopped first at Bruce Mines. One of the early Scots had located a quartz vein eight miles from Bruce Mines, which he sold to a Toronto syndicate for $8,000; these gentlemen got $20,000 for it a few weeks later from some Chicago speculators, who in turn sold it to some Londoners for $1,500,000. (As things turned out, the claim was worth about the original $8,000 which the prospector got for it.)

Not long after Jane's party reached Bruce Mines, the plague arrived. There they were, marooned in the little hamlet in the wilderness, with no boat due for weeks; and everywhere men and women were dying nightly in their beds. Jane's groom, young

Job, was a carpenter, and he was kept so busy making coffins for the plague victims that a man who was killed in a fall out of an apple tree went unburied two weeks for lack of a coffin.

Jane and her party left on the first boat that braved the terrors of the plague. But they were not turning back. They sailed on, up to the Soo, where their baggage had to be unloaded, carried in wagons around the St. Mary's River rapids, and loaded again on a sailing vessel in Lake Superior, for the Soo canal was only a dream.

Being a carpenter and a bridegroom, Job Masters had both the ability and the incentive to build a better home than most of the other first-year pioneers at Copper Harbor. But the mines were taking most of the timbers and boards that the little sawmill could cut, so the Masterses' first house was built of logs and had a dirt floor. Job built it, not on the flat land immediately behind the harbor which was settled first, but back a little on the hillside, so there was a view of the sea, and the clamor of the port would be less intrusive in their lives. Job got a job at a mine, timbering the openings of the adits that the miners bored into the sides of the rock bluffs, erecting field offices and other surface structures.

All her life Jane loved beautiful things. Into the rough-hewn cabin she put the belongings she had brought with her all the way from England: the massive oak bookcase, the books in fine bindings, the pewter, and the brilliant-colored shawl which her father had brought her from the Orient, and the enormous Bible, the flyleaf of which would be filled to overflowing with the names and birth dates of her eighteen children. The fireplace was the most important feature of the house. On either end of the mantel Jane placed a heavy ornate candlestick, and over the fireplace she hung a picture of Queen Victoria and the British royal family, draped with a British flag.

Now she was ready to receive. But there were no guests she could properly entertain, only miners and Indians. And a few women. But Jane spoke to none of the women she passed on the board sidewalks. Just because she was a pioneer was no reason to lower herself. There still were decent people, and there still were impossible people, here in the wilderness as much as back in England. She violated the first law of the frontier: neighborliness. She considered her fellow pioneers revolting, partly because they were unwashed, but also because they were downright dull, stupid, unread, rude; she was impatient of their ignorance. And so Jane admitted to her log-cabin salon only three persons: the local physician, the company agent, and the itinerant minister who rode the circuit in the wilderness.

Jane Masters didn't mind the bitter winters, with the bad food. She could combat without complaint the deer flies and mosquitoes and the tiny irritating insects which, so small as to be almost invisible, today are called nosiums in Upper Michigan, from "big-bite-um, no-see-um." She could endure all the ordinary hardships of the wilderness; but the Indian peril—that was something else. The company agent told Jane that if she ever heard the bell at the fort ringing, it would mean an Indian uprising. She was to take the children (there were children by then) and some food and run into the stockade.

Another worry was the Indian chief who came to her house every day. It wasn't that he looked dangerous; he was an old man. But he must have—well, friends. He came every afternoon, and when Jane opened the door, he entered silently, walked to the mantel, filled his pipe from Job's jar of English smoking tobacco, and sat the rest of the afternoon, smoking in silence, ignoring Jane and the babies. When he had finished, he departed without thanks or threats. And returned the next day at the appointed hour. Jane was afraid to deny him entrance; no telling what he and his friends might do. Some of the pioneer women set out pans of milk on the stoop in an effort to appease the Indians, much as their forebears in the old country propitiated the little people. Though Job grumbled, Jane considered a little tobacco a cheap price if it warded off a massacre.

But when one day she heard the clamorous ringing of the bell at Fort Wilkins, she thought her offerings had failed. Alone, she snatched up her children and what food she could lay hands on, and fled precipitously to the sanctuary of the fort. All over town she could see other women running, crying out to one another. And were those Indian war-whoops mingled with the cries of the full-skirted running ladies? When finally she reached the stockade, she found a crowd of women surrounding a single embarrassed soldier. A cow, he was trying to explain, had got its foot tangled in the bell-rope; there was no alarm—only a wayward cow. Everyone went home, feeling a little cheated. It was the town's only massacre. But Jane never forgot the awful night she and the children piled into the old spool bed when they heard a sound as of Indians creeping outside the house. The ropes which the spools were strung on broke and she and the children all crashed to the floor, but they were too frightened to move; they lay there all night.

She bore Job eighteen children there in the wilderness, and she reared all but one. She herself was an only child. Once, while she lay still abed with her fourteenth, her bewildered mother said: "Jane, Jane, what ever can you be thinking of?" It was the only time she ever mentioned her daughter's fecundity.

Raising a family that size in the wilderness is an almost incredible feat. Somehow she and Job managed. He never had much of a job; he was a carpenter all his life, setting timber at the mine or else making coffins. Coffins seem to have occupied much of his time. He had a workshop back of the house, and he stored the better boxes in the living-room, where the eighteen children played in them. (Victoria made the best corpse; she could lie still longest.) Jane was always thankful that Job didn't work in the mines. Mining was common labor, but a carpenter was, to her, a craftsman of sorts. Besides, mining was dangerous, and when the ambulance clattered through town and housewives wondered fearfully who had been killed in the mine, Jane knew that after work Job would come trudging down Garden City Hill. Job was another who never caught hold as the band wagon went by. There were hard times, plenty of them. And with eighteen kids—well, eighteen is a lot of kids. Lack of money kept Jane from going back to England for a visit. Once she even had to box one of her son's ears because he put expensive syrup in his tea. Through all those years of child-bearing and privation and loneliness she never changed, she remained the *grande dame*. In later life she actually seemed to acquire a physical resemblance to Queen Victoria. Once, at a friend's house, her son played the organ and did it well; on the way home Jane bought an organ for him, though she knew they couldn't afford it.

Her home was her pride, her home and her children. The family did not live long in the log cabin. Soon Job built a proper sort of house, of milled lumber, with a wood, not a dirt, floor, which the hired girl had to scrub daily with sand and water. Soon this house proved inadequate; the family was increasing fast. There were fourteen children and fourteen kittens (Job and Jane always were surrounded with life, so much life that it would have oppressed most people). They moved into a big house that they rented from a Jew who had gone through the copper country with a pack on his back, selling notions to the housewives at the mining locations; now he was wealthy and owned a big store in Houghton; later he would go to Chicago and become a merchant prince. His name was Leopold, and one day, in the 1920's, his grandson Nathan, with another rich man's son, Richard Loeb, would shock the nation by murdering a small boy just to see if they could get away with it.

Jane Masters saw the copper country develop from nothing. Dog teams disappeared. Steamers became trustworthy (time was when you could expect the boilers to blow up any minute). She saw men come broke and die rich, saw them come young and hopeful and die broke. Gradually the Indian menace faded. With roads and better boats, starvation ceased to be a threat. But when a boat was wrecked on the rocks and a cargo of pigs, trying to swim for shore, cut their own throats with their cloven hoofs and were washed onto the rocks dead, Jane was not above sending the older children out to scavenge with the common people. Loneliness departed a little too when the roads were built. Copper Harbor bought its own fire horses; in the early days, when a house caught fire, they had to unhitch the horses in the mines, bring them up to surface, and hitch them to the fire wagon, and usually by the time the laddies arrived in their red helmets, the fire was out.

Jane lived through all the tumultuous days, and yet somehow the fever seemed to escape her. She lived apart. Men drank and roared and battled in the streets; they scrambled over cliffs and clawed at one another in their wild search for ore. None of it ever touched her, really; she was remote, somehow still a lady on the hedge-trimmed lawn in Cornwall.

Her mother died, having outlived her second husband, and was buried near Eagle Harbor. Jane lived on, a matriarch. Her children scattered; one became a contractor, one an architect, one a mechanic, one an engineer. A daughter who married a man who mistreated her must have had a lot of Jane in her, for she walked away from a farm in the Dakotas in midwinter, taking their nine children with her; she divorced her husband and put all nine children through college. Another daughter went to New York with a family whose children she had cared for at Copper Harbor; not until forty-five years later, when the girl had married well, did Jane consent to receive her. A son sailed away from Copper Harbor and never returned. As Jane grew older, it saddened her to have her children move away. They must come back at Easter. But when they did—and they always did, each year, without fail—she did not unbend. She received them as a queen might have done. Once she told a daughter-in-law: "I should think you'd think enough of your husband to appear in silk at least on Easter," for Jane invariably wore black taffeta and a little white lace collar and a cameo pin; the daughter-in-law had appeared in cotton. Jane always insisted that her grandchildren wear white kid gloves when they called on her, for little English girls did. She never knew how much some of these grandchildren feared her and dreaded the half-hour their parents made them spend with her.

She was as impatient of a person's size as she was of his mind and his clothes. She was proud of her small size; it was refined. One of her daughters was tall, and this disturbed her. Once, to this daughter and a tall Danish girl who was a prospective daughter-in-law, Jane said: "It's too bad you're both so tall." The Dane replied: "You never see short women in fashion magazines." For once Jane had no reply.

Job died when he was seventy-two; Jane grieved, but remained outwardly calm. Small, wiry, she might have lived forever if she had not broken her hip when she was in her nineties. Even after that she lingered several years, propped up in bed and ordering the servant about her home imperiously, arranging her children's affairs, playing till the end the part of a grand matriarch. When she realized that she must lie in bed the rest of her life, she had the picture of Queen Victoria and the royal family and the British flag removed from the mantel and brought into her bedroom, where she could look on them from her bed. When she died, at ninety-seven, her eyes were fixed calmly on the portrait of her Queen.

Even in death her impatience, her imperiousness, her snorting contempt for so much in living remained. Though Job had bought one of the first Fords in Keweenaw County, Jane always had refused to ride in it, and she often had said she never would ride in a horseless buggy, not even to her own funeral. Her wishes were respected. In 1923 her body was borne from Calumet to her grave at Eagle Harbor in a wagon.

COUSIN JACK AND
COUSIN JENNY

ALTHOUGH A FEW Cornishmen like Jane and Job Masters reached Copper Harbor in 1843 and 1844, the great influx did not come until the opening of the mines around Portage Lake a few years later. During 1856 many Irish came also to the copper country. Trouble was chronic. Fifty miles southwest near Ontonagon, the Minesota Mine and two smaller ones near it were booming, and so were the three towns they supported. The Irish and the Cornish could work together side by side all day, but at night they fought. One Sunday morning, April 24, 1857, the Cornish and the Irish met at the Minesota Mine and a general brawl ensued. Beaten, the Irish retreated and hid in the second story of Dan Ryan's saloon at Rockland. It was set afire. The Irish leaped from the windows and doors. The Cousin Jacks met them. Somebody started shooting. In the thick of the fray was Johnson Terrell, a burly Cornishman with fists like the smashing heads of a stamp mill. As he bored into the mob of escaping Irishmen, he saw a fallen comrade. Stooping, he sought to aid him. Somebody swung an ax at Terrell's back, cleaving it; he died almost instantly.

Rioting became general. The Cornish drove the Irish out of Rockland. They went up to Portage Lake and told their story. Immediately work stopped and four hundred Irishmen gathered at the Quincy dock. They would march through the woods to Ontonagon like an avenging army; they would clean every bloody be-damned Cousin Jack out of Ontonagon County, out of the whole copper country. They set out, stopping now and then in the woods to swear a little more, to take a few more slugs of forty-rod. Word went ahead of them to Ontonagon; to escape the invaders, the outnumbered Cousin Jacks clambered aboard the steamer *Illinois* and she put out into the lake jammed with refugees. The army of angry Irishmen stormed on. But when they got three miles southwest of Portage Lake, they halted to have another drink; that one tasted all right, so they decided to have another, wondering: "How do they make it so good?" Somebody said that, look, they'd only come three miles in all this time; that meant they had about forty-seven miles yet to go. It'd take them two or three days to reach Ontonagon. Where would they eat, four hundred men? And where would they replenish their dwindling stock of forty-rod? And would they still feel like fighting after tramping through the woods for a couple of days? They straggled back to Portage Lake, took the rest of the day off to tell one another in saloons what they'd have done to the Cousin Jacks, took the following day off to recover from their hangovers, then went back to work.

Yet even today the Cornishmen and the Irish have no use for each other. Racial prejudice is rooted deeply throughout the Upper Peninsula. Every town has its tales of street fights between the Swedes and Finns, the English and Swedes, the Irish and everybody. Usually the stories are funny. Sometimes they are not. Sometimes sheer go-to-hell bravado becomes something vicious: plain race prejudice. Usually the men fought because they had come out of the woods or mines full of spit-and-vinegar, because they simply were spoiling for a fight; in combat they hunted comrades; the easiest basis for rapport in the early days before the races were assimilated was a common language, a common culture, vague memories of the old country and vague similarities in physiognomy. The easiest basis for comradeship was race. Brawling was happy-go-lucky, senseless, irresponsible. But gradually men learned English, widened their acquaintances, no longer needed fellow countrymen for companions. They could converse with anybody. Yet race stuck, as a common bond. Racial prejudice, blind and brutal, remained. It is today one of Upper Michigan's shames.

The Cornish were more Welsh, almost, than English; they had the Welshman's mysticism, his gentleness, his great strength. The prowess of Cornish-style wrestlers became legendary; these barefoot men in loose duck jackets battled mightily in sawdust arenas all summer long across the Upper Peninsula, attracting great crowds and provoking general Cornish-Irish riots. Their hammer-and-drill contests also were bitterly contested. On the Fourth of July three-man teams from the various mines would pound away at huge blocks of marble, and the team that could drill the deepest in the given time won a barrel of beer.

The Cornish brought with them unique dialect and mannerisms and mining savvy. A mine was a "bal," to take a smoke was to "touch a pipe," a tale was a "plod," to shut the door was to "close 'ome" the door. "A passel of people," meaning a lot of people, is said to be of Cornish origin, as is "tuckered out," meaning exhausted.

The pasty is the Cornishman's great gift to Upper Michigan; it is as popular there today as, say, scrapple in Philadelphia. A pasty —although it looks like a misspelling of "pastry," it is pronounced to rhyme with "nasty"—resembles a meat and vegetable pie. The Cousin Jenny got up before dawn to bake them for her miner husband; he stuffed them still hot into his shirt and they kept him warm on the long walk to the mine through the crisp morning air; then, while he toiled sweatily through the forenoon deep in the mine, the heat of his body kept the pasties warm till dinner time. Or so the story went. Bloody street battles have been fought in the mining camps over the proper way to make a pasty. Although the pasty was usually made in individual sizes, here is one recipe for a larger pasty, which is offered in all humility:

Into a "sieve full, not quite a quart," of flour work two pieces of ground-up suet, each the size of an egg, and a half cup of lard. With this mix enough *cool* water to form a smooth dough. Roll this flat and place it on the bottom of a pie plate. Pile on half the dough the following ingredients: five or six potatoes sliced thin or diced; about two pounds of diced or cubed beef, or beef and pork mixed ("and make sure your beef's good beef"); add onion and parsley, salt and pepper, to taste. Fold the other half of the dough over on top of the vegetables and meat, crinkle the edges, place in a moderately hot oven, and bake for fifty or sixty minutes. Optional touch: ten minutes before removing from the oven, add a ball of butter through a small hole cut in the top of the pasty. This recipe serves four people.

It has been written in Cornish dialect:

I dearly love a pasty;
A 'ot leaky one,
With mayt, turmit and taty,
H'onyon and parsley in 'un.

The crus' be made weth suet,
Shaped like a 'alf moon,
Crinkly h'edges, freshly baked,
'E es always gone too soon.

When spring came, the prospectors, long winterbound, hurried into the hills to begin the desperately short season of exploring. One marvels at their temerity and trembles at the thought of the riches that lay beneath the hills they trod, at the thought of the multi-million-dollar enterprises which grew out of claims that were staked, then gambled away or forgotten. There are few stories of down-at-the-heels prospectors who struck it rich and died wealthy, many of men who passed by or sold for nothing land worth millions. The fortunes were made—and lost—by the Easterners. Copper mining (and iron mining too) is unlike gold mining; you cannot grub out a fortune with a pick and your two hands; you need heavy machinery, capital to carry a payroll over several years of unproductive shaft-sinking during which time not a pound of ore is taken out.

But in the early days the prospectors knew little of this. Most of them were simply men hunting mineral. When they found it, they filed their claim with the War Department, which granted them at first nine square miles and later one square mile that they were to work on a sort of partnership basis with the Government. They paid royalties to the Government on mineral obtained. In the first two years of exploration about a thousand such grants were made. (The tremendous volume of business done in land offices throughout the nation in these days of westward expansion created a phrase still in the language: "to do a land-office business.") Before long, owing to chicanery and inaccuracy, claims to copper lands overlapped two and three deep. To straighten out the hopeless confusion, the Lake Superior Land District was established, and after that land was sold outright for $5 an acre. Later this was cut to $1.50.

Speculators moved in. Trading in claims and leases became big business. The value of acre after acre spiraled upward fantastically from $1.50 to thousands of dollars until the bubble was pricked and somebody, the last sucker, was ruined. Claims worthless in the beginning became bonanzas; claims a quarter of a mile away were simply promotion schemes, theoretical holes in the ground into which widows poured life savings. All the gaudy legend of any mining region is here.

Strip away the legend and you find simple men hunting for mineral, as there always have been rough-handed illiterate men searching for riches in the earth. Were they ignorant of geology, were their methods crude? Even the early mining companies backed by Easterners used crude methods. The wonder is not that most of the companies went broke, but that they managed to grub out any copper at all. A hole dug in the earth with pick and shovel, the face of a cliff pocked with hand drill and sledge, then blasted loose with gunpowder—a hole in the ground and then some buildings around it that became a town. It is the story of the towns in the iron region of Upper Michigan as well as in the copper country. Today a shaft is dug into the earth vertically or on an incline following the lode; from the shaft, drifts are driven horizontally into the ore. The shafts reach amazing depths; the Quincy shaft has been sunk nearly 10,000 feet, not far short of two miles, on the incline, or more than 6,200 feet vertically. (Only a few mines in Brazil, South Africa, and Canada are deeper.) Far down there in the heat men punch holes in the rock with pneumatic drills, charge the holes, blast, haul the ore to the shaft. Powerful hoists bring it to the surface. Machinery crushes it and conveys it to the stamp mills, where it is ground into a fine powder. The copper is separated from the worthless rock and sent to a mechanical melting plant, where it is cast into plates or bars and shipped to the rolling mills in the East, in Pittsburgh or Detroit or

Connecticut. And then, after all that, the copper is sold for twelve cents a pound—and the companies make money.

Today the whole process is highly mechanical in startling contrast to the early days. Most of the mining then consisted in driving an adit, or horizontal drift, into the bald face of a cliff. Powder holes were drilled, not by pneumatic drills that bite into the rock as though it were soap, but by three men, one of whom squatted and clutched in his bare hands a pointed steel bar that his two partners battered with synchronized sledge-hammer blows. The rock blasted loose was broken up with sledges. The miners hauled it out in wheelbarrows or "chariots" and beat off as much of the worthless rock as possible with hammers. They graded it. Into shipping barrels they packed pieces of ore containing thirty per cent or more of mineral (this was called "barrelwork" and comprised the bulk of early production); lower-grade ore they sent to the crude stamp mill, where it was beaten into a powder. At "strakes," or washing troughs, the miners stirred the residue from a preliminary washing with a shovel to separate the metal from the mud. The washing process had to be repeated many times, and the Cornish miners were particularly adept at it, using a peculiar spade with a bent narrow blade instead of the conventional rake or hoe.

The boss of the miners was called the captain, as he is today in the iron as well as the copper mines of Upper Michigan, and he was a figure of vast importance and prestige, never addressed as "Mr." but always as "Captain." He was an oracle. Usually he had been a shift boss; when he proved he could lick any man on the shift (and that he knew mineral from rock), he became captain. Most of the captains in the early days were Cousin Jacks, Cornishmen, and the saying ran that the old Cousin Jack captains had a nose for ore, which sounded good but produced some strange results. Professor James Fisher, who should know, cites one such result to students of mining engineering as "probably the finest example extant of 'how not to do it.'" He refers to the Wheal Kate Mine, south of Houghton, where, in 1851 and 1852, the captain's "eye" for running drifts and "nose" for ore induced the company to sink a vertical shaft forty feet into the rock, drift twenty feet south, then sink an inclined shaft fifty feet from the end of the drift. From the bottom of this shaft they drove a drift a hundred feet west; striking a seam of laumontite there, they drifted fifty feet south on the seam and then sunk another inclined shaft forty feet. And so on, up, down, around corners, trying to follow the capricious trail of the vein of ore; and all underground, burrowing in the dark like moles gone mad. In the end a diagram of the mine resembled a psychiatrist's maze designed to baffle white mice. Using windlasses and buckets to hoist the ore, they must have had to fill and dump the stuff four times, wheeling it twice a total distance of 170 feet before they reached surface. Such crude methods, using wheelbarrow and hand drills and black powder and buckets, persisted into the 1870's.

In those days no mining engineer was thought necessary. Indeed, mining by textbook was scorned. The captains and executives came up from the ranks. Today a miner might become a shift boss, but he rarely could rise higher; technology and scientific mining engineering have built a ceiling over his head. It was inevitable; as the lodes were worked through the years, the richest ore was exhausted until the Cousin Jack captain simply couldn't make money for his company in low-grade ore. The mining engineer stepped in. At one time the companies lost money if their ore ran less than sixty pounds of copper to the ton; now they are lucky if they get twenty pounds to the ton, and they still make money. Mining engineers, though they are held in contempt by the old-timers, have kept the iron and copper mines of Upper Michigan profitable through the days of lean ore.

The copper mines always have been remarkably dry and clean, in sharp contrast to the muddy soft-ore iron mines. But ventilation has always been a problem since the early days. In the winter the cold surface air penetrated to the shallow galleries; but in the summer the air became "incapable of supporting the flame of a candle." Fan-bellows were used at first; later these were supplanted by pumps. The miners' own breathing and the candles which they burned for illumination fouled the air, as did repeated blasting.

Gunpowder was used exclusively for many years. The first attempt to introduce high explosives into the copper district was resisted stoutly. If ever a man juggled a hot potato, John Mabbs did. Agent for the Isle Royale Mine about 1870, he was a forward-looking man, dissatisfied with the black powder in common use in the copper country. He had heard of nitroglycerine, a comparatively new explosive said to be thirteen times stronger than black powder, and, despite tales of terrible accidents in the Pennsylvania coal fields, he went to New York and bought 4,000 pounds of pure nitroglycerine oil packed in one hundred forty-pound tin cans. After considerable difficulty, he induced a railroad to accept it for shipment to a lake port. But the news traveled ahead and a mob assembled and stopped the train. The nitroglycerine was sent back a hundred miles, transferred to another railroad, and finally, by a circuitous route, reached Cleveland secretly. There Mabbs, fearing momentary arrest for violating city ordinances, negotiated feverishly for a steamboat to carry his explosives to the copper country. No master would accept it; the trade on the Lakes was booming; business—that kind of business—was not wanted. Mabbs turned to sailing vessels. But few of them went as far up the lakes as the copper country any more. And all the time Mabbs, feeling more like a criminal than an enterprising mining engineer, dodged Cleveland's finest. Finally he persuaded the master of a vessel to accept the shipment and, sighing with relief as the last tin can was handed gingerly down into the hold, Mabbs went to his cabin and the vessel weighed anchor. Mabbs's troubles had only begun.

He intended to store the explosive in a powder magazine above Hancock, one of the twin copper cities on Portage Lake. But authorities there heard of the plan in advance and, meeting Mabbs at the dock, ordered him to take his infernal oil elsewhere. He didn't know what to do. He could not hire men for friendship or money to help him handle the stuff. Only his brother had confidence in him. By night the two of them unloaded the hundred cans and deposited them, one by one, in an abandoned stope, or gallery, of the Isle Royale Mine, for which Mabbs was agent.

He got in only a few inconclusive blasts before orders came from the East to close the mine. By then he was getting stubborn about the thing. He had lugged this nitroglycerine halfway across the continent, risking death and arrest; he would not see it unused. After long argument he persuaded the agent of the Huron

Mine to permit him to experiment with it there. The Huron was a going concern; at last he had his opportunity. Enthusiastically he built a little magazine near the Huron and stored one can of the nitroglycerine there; then he prepared to blast. He had to work entirely by night, so as not to arouse the miners. But they discovered his plan anyway. Highly excited, they threw down their tools and quit work. A mob gathered, determined to ride Mabbs out of town on a rail and destroy his witch's brew. He went into hiding. That night the mob blew up his little magazine, thinking it had destroyed all the nitroglycerine. Word leaked out that Mabbs had more. The mob formed itself into a posse and commenced a thorough search of the countryside. Mabbs knew it was only a question of time before they would find and destroy his cache in the abandoned stope at the Isle Royale. Again working at night, Mabbs came out of hiding and, with his brother, moved the nitroglycerine into the woods. Next day the mob got close to it. The Mabbs boys moved it again. And again, and again, working without lights, stumbling around in the deep woods at night, cradling forty-pound cans of nitroglycerine in their arms.

Finally they saw it was no use; they couldn't keep this up forever, and the mob was determined. They loaded the stuff on a yawl and started for Marquette, capital of the iron range and more than a hundred miles away by water. Storms beset them; their little boat, with its cranky cargo, came within an ace of being tossed on the rocks. But they managed to make Marquette. And there, in the iron field, they were welcomed not by vigilante committees but by highly interested mining engineers. They demonstrated successfully the efficiency of their explosive and sold the remainder of their stock. Thereafter nitroglycerine was used in limited quantities on the Marquette iron range, although, as we shall see, the residents had reason on at least one occasion to regret that they had ever heard of John Mabbs's murderous potion. Not until new methods of making the stuff were developed was it admitted to the copper range.

"There is no danger of exhausting the ore," ran the report of the Lake Superior Copper Company, organized in 1844. "If the ore runs out at a considerable depth, say two hundred feet, it will be a matter of little importance to the present generation, though it might be to posterity." Prophetic words. Less than a hundred years later the towns that depended on the mines of this district were little more than ghost towns. And, indeed, the report was preposterously over-optimistic in regard to "the present generation": three years later the company had failed, even though such men as David Henshaw, C. C. Douglass, Dr. Jackson, and Charles H. Gratiot were associated with it, and its first operations produced ore of phenomenally high assay. The main shaft had been sunk on a pocket of copper and silver, which was soon exhausted, and the miners carried off nearly all the silver. For forty years various capitalists and engineers tried to work the location successfully, refusing to believe the first rich assay had been a fluke; their stubborn faith is characteristic of mining men all over Upper Michigan. All together, stockholders poured some two and a half million dollars into the hole and took out only one dividend: twenty thousand dollars paid in 1877.

But the original success of this company was one of the principal magnets that drew a rush of prospectors to the tip of Keweenaw in 1845 and 1846. Near this shaft on the Eagle River some twenty miles below Copper Harbor, the first real bonanza strike was made when, in August 1845, explorers discovered the famed Cliff Lode. They were working for the Pittsburgh & Boston Company, which now abandoned its other workings and concentrated on the Cliff. But shaft-sinking was expensive. Before long the Boston financiers, their enthusiasm already dampened by one assessment, refused to pay another; in the crisis one of the Pittsburgh stockholders, Dr. Charles Avery, relied on the judgment of his Cousin Jack mining captain and put his personal fortune into deepening the mine; in eighteen months it not only had repaid him but had declared the first dividend in the copper country. And Eagle River, with a huge new dock, a good road, a big stamp mill, warehouses, and streets lined solidly with boarding houses and saloons and miners' homes, was on its way to supplant Copper Harbor as the big boom town of Keweenaw.

While all this was going on at the upper end of the trap range, down at the southern end near Ontonagon a prospector named

Sam Knapp found a curious depression in the earth and, excavating, discovered a great litter of stone hammerheads and beneath them a shining vein of pure copper. He had stumbled on the great Minesota Mine. Before Sam Knapp and his Eastern backers were through, they had taken from the old pit ten wagonloads of artifacts, the largest single mass of copper ever found, and gold and silver and copper that paid the stockholders nearly two million dollars in dividends.

These were the golden years in the copper country, the years when the Cliff Lode was paying regular dividends, when the Minesota management yawned and reported to the stockholders that veins of gold and silver in their mine were becoming a nuisance because they excited the miners so greatly they could not work efficiently. Boomed by the Minesota, Ontonagon became a city of 6,000. Prospectors swarmed everywhere at the extremities of the trap range; they commenced to work inward toward the Portage Lake district. They left a trail of mines, great names in their day, now nothing but weed-grown rock piles hidden in the woods, marked for tourists by quaint roadside signs the WPA erected: Garden City Mine, Washington Mining Company, Iron City Mining Company, Delaware Mine, Madison Mine, Central Mine, Meadow Mining Company, Humboldt, Petherick, Gratiot.

All over Upper Michigan—indeed, all over the United States— these years in the middle and latter 1840's were years when great things were happening. A cocoon had burst. New steamers brought immigrants as never before from across the seas to the New World; new railroads, new canals, new prairie schooners carried them across the vast land mass of the North American continent. There was empire to be won. Back east the Abolitionists were beating their breasts, and in the Midwest bigotry was whiplashing the Mormons into their monumental trek, but in the West a man could breathe fresh air, could fight Indians or Californians or Mexicans or do as he damn pleased. Somehow Upper Michigan seemed more a part of the West than of the Midwest in those days. It had been an eddy in the earlier current of westward expansion; it was, as it is today, behind the times. (The Alamo had been avenged and Sam Houston was President of the Republic of Texas nearly a year before Michigan was admitted to the Union.) But now, in the roaring forties, the Upper Peninsula surged ahead with the West.

Curiously, the whole Lake Superior region has been neglected by historians; they have studied the Jesuits here and the War of 1812, and they have skipped on over to more recent times, but unaccountably they have overlooked this middle period of the forties, the fifties, the sixties. Yet, in all truth, what happened here in the Upper Peninsula during those years is as significant, in its way, to the whole United States as the more familiar events of settlement elsewhere in the nation. Jane Masters and her neighbors lived lives as meaningful as those of the men and women who rode the prairie schooners across the Great Plains; mineral strikes here were as important as the gold strike at Sutter's Mill—perhaps more important ultimately to the nation's economy. Modern civilization means steel, steel means iron ore, iron ore means the Lake Superior region. But look at a conventional map of the United States in the fifties and you will see that the Upper Peninsula of Michigan is all white space, marked in the legend "unsettled." Unsettled was it? Hell, man, those were the great days. The region was coming alive. By the time Polk asked Congress to declare war on Mexico, a sick, half-blind contractor from Ann Arbor had staked the first claim on the Marquette iron range where Burt had found ore. The Irish were beginning to come to the Upper Peninsula and, far out in Lake Superior, prehistoric copper mines were being reopened on mist-shrouded Isle Royale about the time that Johnny Frémont led the Bear Flag revolt in California; Kearny's weary men took Santa Fé after their incredible march overland from Kansas before the first iron was made from Lake Superior ore. By that time, early in 1847, Zach Taylor had won the Battle of Monterey and was marching on Buena Vista, where he would lick Santa Anna, thereby winning the admiration of Polk the statesman, but incurring with reason the jealous displeasure of Polk the Democratic politician. John Jacob Astor was by then the richest man in the United States. And the first sawmill already had been established on the great pine plains near Escanaba that would be the first Upper Michigan lands to be denuded by the rip-roaring lumberjacks. (Not far away bearded, brawny

King Jesse Strang was setting up his Mormon kingdom on Beaver Island, in Lake Michigan.)

By the time old Fuss and Feathers, Winfield Scott, bought off Santa Anna and ended victoriously America's imperialistic war, the prospectors at Copper Harbor and Ontonagon were talking about the Cliff Lode and the Minesota and, listening to Sam Hill, were beginning to realize what the burning of their supply boat would mean during this winter. But they got over that hump; they were on their way into the tumultuous golden years. They had stayed remote from the Mexican War; it was Upper Michigan's last isolation. In 1849 many of the prospectors left to seek gold in California, but enough remained that year to make Michigan the biggest copper-producer in the Union. And that same year they were talking once more—and now in concrete terms—of a canal at the Soo which, by providing cheap transportation for both iron and copper, would open Upper Michigan to exploitation still undreamed of. They were exploring everywhere for ore. Loggers were thinking about moving north into the Upper Peninsula from the cutover lands in the Lower Peninsula. Big-scale immigration and colonization were beginning; the land rush was on and so was the land-plundering by the railroad and canal promoters. They would build private empires in this wilderness. The prospectors, working in toward the middle, opened up the Portage Lake amygdaloid district; on the brow of the bluff above Hancock, overlooking Portage Lake, they sank the Quincy shaft, and it sank and sank until it became the deepest of them all. That same year, 1852, the first iron ore was shipped from Marquette and the Government made a grant-in-aid to facilitate building the canal at the Soo. And next year Ed Hulbert came to the copper country, where he found the fabulous Calumet conglomerate.

Luck always was against Ed Hulbert. A sad-eyed, long-faced man with a beard, he learned the geology of the copper region while running surveys. He became associated with hell-roaring Sam Hill in a survey for a Government military road which was to connect Fort Wilkins with Fort Atkinson, clear down in middle Wisconsin. Conceived not long before the Civil War, this was a land-grant project. Hill and his associates were to receive four sections of land for each mile of road they built. The sections were to be chosen from a strip three miles wide on either side of the road. The joker was that Hill and the boys selected their sections first and laid out the road to embrace them; following copper lodes willy-nilly as it did, the result was a thoroughfare slightly resembling the labyrinthine shafts and drifts dug by the old Cousin Jack mining captain. Hill and his boys had a nose for ore too. They promptly sublet the road contract, paying subcontractors one section per mile, and got busy mining the other three themselves.

One of the subcontractors was Dan Brockway; short of cash to meet his payroll, he sold some of his lands; part of them were in Iron County, near where the town of Crystal Falls would be built; years later two and a half million dollars' worth of iron ore was taken out of the lands Brockway sold for whatever he could get. Brockway never quit trying. He prospected and contracted and operated a hotel and a mercantile business and various mines, and when he was sixty-four years old he went to the Black Hills and nearly died staking a couple of claims; but somehow, though his name is perpetuated in the Brockway Mountain Drive that winds up to the tip of Keweenaw, he never got both feet planted firmly on the band wagon that carried others to fortunes in this booming country.

Yet his tribulations were nothing beside Ed Hulbert's. While he was surveying on Hill's road about midway between Portage Lake and Eagle River in a region supposedly barren of mineral, Hulbert found, in a curious pit in the woods, copper boulders different from any he had ever seen. (Legend says that they actually were uncovered by a herd of pigs which strayed from Billy Royal's wayside saloon and that Ed Hulbert, helping search for them, found them rooting in the pit and thus discovered the copper-bearing boulders.) Here Hulbert found the Calumet conglomerate. Contemptuously, the Cousin Jack captains called it puddingstone; there wasn't enough of it in the world, they said, to buy a shift boss's drinks. But the company that worked it made more money, for a time, than any other mine of any kind in the world.

Having formed the Calumet Mining Company in addition to the Hulbert Company, Ed Hulbert went to Boston and borrowed

$16,800 from Quincy Adams Shaw, who was a brother-in-law of Alexander Agassiz, a young man who made his name as a naturalist. By July 1866 rumors about the richness of the lode had sent Calumet stock from a dollar to seventy-five dollars a share. Ed Hulbert was riding high; already one of the greatest men in all the copper country, soon he would be a true copper king. The only trouble was that, actually, the Calumet Company wasn't making money, was, in fact, sucking $12.50 a share in assessments out of each of the Bostonians. They blamed Hulbert. Shaw foreclosed and Hulbert was out. To replace him Shaw sent Alexander Agassiz out from the East. In a couple of years the Hecla Mining Company paid its first dividend; a few months later Calumet did likewise; in 1871 the two companies, together with two others, were consolidated to form the Calumet & Hecla Mining Company. Under Agassiz's unwilling but gifted guidance—he wanted only to be a naturalist—C. & H. became the big bonanza, the most profitable on the range, the index to the fortunes of the whole copper country. When C. & H. was up, good times were here; when C. & H. was down, people went on the county.

What of Ed Hulbert? He always swore that Quincy Adams Shaw squeezed him out. Shaw pensioned him. Embittered, he went to Italy and let it be known that he knew the location of another vein of conglomerate far richer even than the Calumet Lode. Legend says he furnished notes to an old Cornish mining captain who, working in secret and at night, sought the location. If he ever found it, nothing was done about it, and Ed Hulbert died at Rome in 1910, taking his secret with him. Even today you can hear whispered tales in the copper country of the richest vein of conglomerate of them all, still sleeping beneath centuries' accumulation of leaves and earth and rock, waiting for the magic touch of another Ed Hulbert.

It should be noted, in extenuation of Hulbert's apparent incompetency, that no company but the Calumet & Hecla ever worked the stubborn conglomerate profitably. There can be little doubt about C. & H.'s success. It has paid more than $160,000,000 in dividends on a capital of $10,000,000; its stock hit a thousand dollars a share in 1907 (and was given away with sets of dishes during the depression of the 1930's); the company became the paternal giant of the copper country, building whole towns of company houses, installing electric light and sewerage systems, sprawling all over three counties, and, inevitably, mixing in local politics. The old debate arises: is the company a kindly grandpa or an evil octopus? It depends on where you sit. C. & H. built schools and paid enormous taxes; it also fought the 1913 strike on behalf of all the companies because, being most enlightened, it was in the best position to do so. This strike was Upper Michigan's bloodiest labor trouble; during it more than fifty miners' children perished in a panic following a mysterious fire alarm. C. & H. has raised wages and bettered living conditions for its men; but in the early days it issued company money and operated company stores. Sure, said the early companies, a man can quit and leave this country any time he wants to; but it so happened that, if he wanted to take his earnings with him, a miner had to exchange his company scrip at the company office in, say, the Portage Lake district, for a requisition on the company's Federal agent at Eagle River, thirty miles northeast. The miner had to walk there and get the company agent to give him an order on the Government agent, whose office, it happened, was at Ontonagon, eighty miles back southwest; only thus, by walking nearly a hundred and fifty miles, could a miner get real cash money for his company scrip. C. & H., octopus or benevolent giant, has without doubt over-shadowed all other companies on the range in richness of rock, amount of production and profits.

The Civil War made trouble for a while: men were drafted, labor grew scarce, wages went up, the price of copper went down temporarily. But the mine operators sent labor agents to Europe and they brought in whole shiploads of new immigrants from the Scandinavian countries. Unfortunately, draft dodgers met these men at the Portage Lake docks and offered them three hundred dollars apiece to go to war for them. Most of the newcomers took the offer; they had come over for the boat ride anyway, they'd rather fight than grub in the earth. But somehow the mines got labor and they got a price for their copper too; fortunes were made, and after the war, with the Soo canal open, great days dawned. Brawling went on, but who cared? Dividends were the thing—dividends and land grabs. (Roads were often built double, two roads serving the same terminals and roughly parallel to each other: a low road built in the valleys so you wouldn't have to climb the steep hills, a high road over the hilltops for use in the winter when snow blocked the low road. It was an old custom; in Loch Lomond land they wrote a song about it.) Other men got land by promoting canals and railroads; the Government gave away tracts worth millions. Contracts were loosely drawn; the Government was generous; it had plenty of land and wanted the canals and railroads built. Thousands of acres went to the builders of the canals connecting Portage Lake with Lake Superior; thousands went to Hill and the boys who formed the Keweenaw Land Association, still potent in Upper Michigan; thousands went to the builders of the Marquette, Houghton & Ontonagon Railroad, and its master mind dreamed of a railroad running all the way from Ontonagon to the Gulf of Mexico. Those were days for dreams. And many of the dreams came true. Sure it's a fact that, out of more than a thousand filed claims, only eighty-odd companies took out enough copper to report the amount to their stockholders. Sure only thirteen of the eighty paid back to the stockholders more than the capital paid in. Sure eighty millions of dollars have been poured into the ground in assessments. But look, man—more than three times that much has been paid in dividends.

Sure there have been hard times. Sure Ontonagon was burned to the ground the night the Diamond Match Company caught fire, and it's true that Diamond Match never rebuilt; the pine was gone anyway, Ontonagon was through. Sure the silver boom in the Porcupine Mountains turned out to be mostly a real-estate promotion scheme. Sure Phoenix is a ghost town—remember when they opened up the Cliff Lode near there?—and there are a dozen, a score maybe, like it: Mandan, named for "that man Dan," and other towns burnt out by fire, wiped out by pestilence, abandoned when the vein petered out or the Eastern rich boys simply decided to cut the melon and call it quits. But hell, man, this country's got a future. There'll always be copper here. Calumet & Hecla alone (may her name be blessed) is enough to keep this country going. The 1930's, when seventy-five per cent of the people of Keweenaw County went on relief, were a long way off in the eighties and nineties.

⋘ 7 ⋙

BRIGHT MOUNTAIN

℣

IRON IS THE GIANT of Upper Michigan. Somehow it symbolizes the timeless richness of this land—the hope of the future, the struggle and romance of the past. Truly, here memory and aspiration are bound up in a rock formation.

Iron ore is old; for æons it lay undiscovered, fallow in the wilderness. Men found it a hundred years ago and, since, have hacked at it and scrambled over it and fought about it bitterly. It remains. Men have cut down Upper Michigan's trees; they have dammed its streams and killed its game and emptied its copper veins. Iron ore remains, somehow eternal as the land itself is eternal.

Wresting iron from the earth is a dirty dangerous heart-breaking business. It is also as romantic as flight. Men who once "go underground" in the mines would no more work in the sunlight than a sailor would desert the sea for a bookkeeper's desk. Indeed, they are somehow akin to seamen. They have the same tight-lipped fatalism, the rough intelligence, the quiet power that the sea gives men. They speak a language of their own, and even their mining talk has a fascination—they sink a shaft into the rock, they drive a drift or a raise a thousand feet underground to get at the hematite ore; they "rob a pillar" and invite disaster; they speak of formation, of dyke and hanging wall and the breast of a drift. "Nice-looking rock," they say of a commonplace freight carload of ore, and thereby invest it somehow with dignity and greatness, thereby somehow express their own feel for the earth. In all their thoughts and talk is the wisdom of men who struggle against the earth which they inhabit and who, if they lose, do not complain. Always they live close to violent death, but never speak of it. They will chase an ore pocket to hell.

That the hold of iron upon men's lives is tenacious can be made plain by a glance at the towns of Upper Michigan. There are few true ghost towns in the iron region—that is, towns utterly deserted. True, towns once booming and now idle are common. But always a few loyal citizens refuse to move away. They came when the mine opened; around the shaft house they built their town, a "mining location"; the mine now is idle, the machinery in the shaft house is rusted, most of the saloons and hotels and bawdy houses and homes are filled with cobwebs and rats. But still the shaft house stands, a weatherbeaten symbol of past glory, of hope for the future; it becomes, gradually, a totem; long after it is nothing but an empty symbol above an exhausted ore body, its people remain huddled about it and worship it. The hand of iron lies heavy on the minds of men.

The twentieth century means steel, steel means iron, iron means the ore fields of the Lake Superior region. The first great ore range opened there was the Marquette Range of Upper Michigan. Its opening follows a familiar pattern—the frantic scramble of men beholding for the first time riches in the wilderness, the disillusionment after the first excitement of discovery has passed, the years of toil and disappointment, the gradual leveling off, and finally the rebirth and the slow growth of giant corporations.

Even geologists marveled at the "mountains of pure iron"; small wonder that the first mining men thought there were millions in it. There were, but not for them. When, naïvely confident, they wrestled chunks of ore about in the wilderness, they did not know that only engineers and financiers can make money out of a hole in the ground on the iron range. It is Jim Paul's pebble all over again.

The first man who opened the Marquette Range was not even a mining man; he was a canal-builder and a merchant. Philo Marshall Everett, who in later years resembled a parsimonious schoolmaster more than an explorer, arrived with his wife and child in the Lower Peninsula of Michigan in 1840, when he was about thirty-eight years old. He operated a wheat commission business at Jackson, Michigan, for five years, but he suffered greatly with ague, chills and fever, like many of Michigan's early settlers. Illness made him totally blind for a year, and for the rest of his life his sight was poor. Like William Austin Burt, Everett had had no particular success in business down below, and the tales of mineral riches which were filtering out of the wilderness were enough to excite any wistful invalid. The combination of prospective riches and a healthful life in the open was irresistible. Everett, sick and half-blind, embarked on an arduous journey which was to make him the first mine operator on any Lake Superior iron range.

At the Soo, casting about for guides and information on the country, Everett and his brother-in-law, Charles Johnson, met a halfbreed named Nolan; he had talked with the men who had been with Burt when he observed those mad fluctuations of the compass needle near the Dead River. Everett, like most men of this and earlier periods, was more interested in silver and lead, gold and copper than in iron. But Nolan was persuasive: Burt's party had picked up everywhere chunks of iron ore unbelievably rich; mountains of iron rose like natural pyramids from the plain. And, after all, the iron fields would not be far off Everett's route to the copper country.

Nolan led them to Teal Lake, south of which Burt had found iron ore. But though the halfbreed searched the swamps and bluffs diligently, he failed to locate the outcrop. Disgusted, Everett and his party left him and pushed on westward toward the copper country. By chance, the story goes, they met an Indian chief, Marji Gesick, whose pre-treaty hunting grounds had embraced the Dead River country and who now had gone to L'Anse to collect the annuity due him from the Government. He confirmed the stories of iron ore. Something in what he said must have been impressive, for Everett, sick, half-blind, disappointed, exhausted by the hard trip, turned around and went back to Teal Lake, this time led by Marji Gesick. Although the Indian refused to go all the way to the iron hills, since they were the dwelling place of the dread god of thunder and lightning, he did lead Everett's party to the vicinity and furnish explicit directions to the precise location of the ore. The iron outcrop was most easily seen beneath the uprooted stump of a giant pine tree at the foot of a hill. There Everett's party found it, about the middle of Section One, T47N, R27W, the line which Burt had run the year before; there they staked their claim. An earlier claim, half-forgotten, was withdrawn; Everett's company paid the Government $2.50 an acre for the land from which would be taken, before operations ceased in 1924, some five million tons of ore. Everett formed the Jackson Mining Company, so named because its thirteen backers lived in Everett's home town, Jackson, Michigan. For services rendered, Marji Gesick was given a scribbled document assigning him twelve undivided one-hundredths interest in the company. But the company did not fulfill the agreement; Gesick died in poverty, cherishing the crumpled scrap of paper dated "River du Mort, May 30, 1846," which he had hoped would make him rich; not until long after his death did the courts decide that his claim was legitimate. In all fairness, one writer points out, the original members of the Jackson Company made no more money out of their holdings than did the Indian.

But their hopes were high in the beginning. Everett wrote that their holdings included "a mountain of solid iron ore, 150 feet high. The ore looks as bright as a bar of iron just broken." Better still, it contained "something resembling gold," perhaps gold and copper. When spring came in 1846, the Jackson Company sent four men to explore the location further. And now the eager would-be iron kings began to appreciate the difficulties ahead. Certainly there was iron ore here, lots of it, enough, perhaps, to last the United States almost forever. But even after the ore was broken loose from the stubborn vault of the earth, it must be transported to some place where it could be made into usable form. For this was no copper country virgin lode. This was not iron but iron ore, containing perhaps fifty per cent pure iron; it must be smelted, refined. How could this be done in the wilderness?

How, indeed, could the men even exist in this wild country while they were clawing at the ore bodies? All supplies had to be brought in from "down below." That first year they built a shelter beside the Jackson mountain of ore and they got out before snow-fall, taking with them something less than three hundred pounds of ore, probably half of it iron and the other half worthless rock. This they had to pack on their backs about eleven miles down the Carp River to Lake Superior. Back home they succeeded, after several failures, in making in a blacksmith's forge a bar of pure iron, the first ever made from Lake Superior iron ore. Passing it from man to man in their smithy, they must have contemplated it with mingled enthusiasm and uncertainty: though unquestionably made from high-grade ore, this single bar represented a full season's toil and expense. But probably not even these men realized that by bringing iron ore to the East from a new Western ore field they had set in motion a revolution in the iron-making industry of the nation. In yet another way the expanding West was out-stripping the older East.

The Jackson Company's men went back to the range and found competitors busily exploring in the neighboring swamps and thickets. These were the Marquette Iron Company, formed by R. J. Graveraet acting for some New Englanders, and the Cleve-land Iron Mining Company, incorporated by a Cleveland syndi-cate that included Samuel Livingston Mather, who led it ulti-mately to unchallenged supremacy on the range.

Had Mather simply come to Upper Michigan in the early days, made a fortune, and gone back east, he would have been only one of many who did likewise. But he remained and founded an iron dynasty. One of his sons is today chairman of the board of the Cleveland-Cliffs Iron Company, which, growing out of the original Cleveland Company, is the leader on the Marquette Range; another son founded the partnership of Pickands-Mather, which became a power on the Gogebic and Mesaba Ranges. The leading hotel of Ishpeming is the Mather Inn; the Cleveland-Cliffs' new mine at Ishpeming, hailed as the finest underground iron mine in the world, is the Mather Mine. Mather is a name spoken reverently on the range.

Samuel Livingston Mather was born July 1, 1817, at Middle-town, Connecticut, the son of a well-to-do commission merchant. His is no Horatio Alger story: he was educated and traveled and he worked for his father. In 1843—Congress was concerned about the land question—he was sent to Cleveland to dispose of the family's holdings in the old long-controverted Western Reserve. He also acted as agent for other Eastern interests which owned claims to land in Ohio. He was admitted to the bar, though he never practiced law. He was simply a well-connected young man who decided on corporation law as a seemly, lucrative career. Before long he abandoned it. His connections led him to join in the incorporation of the Cleveland Iron Mining Company. In the beginning he was not particularly active in the struggling company's affairs; but in 1853 he became its secretary-treasurer; within a year the company was shipping ore, and from then on, it claimed all of Mather's time. Before he died, in 1890, he had replaced the crude equipment of the early days with modern railroads and steam ore-carriers; he had controlled the affairs of a half-dozen companies; he had heard independent authorities say, with justification, that his company contributed more than any other to the beginning of Cleveland's industrial prominence.

But in the 1850's success was only a dream to the men on the Marquette Range. Perversely, much of the richest ore seemed to lie in or near a swamp; mosquitoes assailed the miners. This low-lying ore bed was rimmed by steep cliffs; here the stubborn rock resisted successfully the crude attempts to blast it. Everybody knew there was iron here, but sometimes nobody could find it. The men would work in the pits for days, punching holes into the rock with hand drills, tamping powder carefully into the holes, lighting fuses and scrambling hastily up rickety ladders to safety —only to find no iron in the great chunks of rock torn loose by the blast. Why? What was wrong? Simply this: the ore was "pockety." It lay, not in vast compact beds as it later was discovered on the Mesaba Range in Minnesota, but in irregularly shaped masses locked deep within the convoluted folds of the rock formation. "Pockets" of ore the men called them, and pursued them desperately all over the range, scarring the countryside with test pits. One day you thought you had found the mother lode; the next day you had nothing but worthless rock under your drill bit: the tiny pocket was exhausted.

And the iron they did manage to find was sometimes disappointing stuff. Everybody knew what iron ought to look like: it ought to come in nice dark-gray, shiny chunks. But it didn't always, here. It ranged all the way from those gray shiny chunks of heavy specular hematite or magnetite to the soft hematite that looked like nothing but red sand or mud. Some of the ore was purple, some red, some yellow, some nearly black; some was magnetic, some was not. In short, iron was where you found it. And it might be outlandish stuff when you did manage to track it down.

Moreover, the early miners spent as much time struggling for existence as they spent mining. In 1850 barely 150 persons lived on the range and at the shipping point a dozen miles away called Marquette. Three mines were in operation: Everett's, Graveraet's, and Mather's. But so much snow fell during the winter of 1849 that it was impossible to move any ore from the Cleveland mine to the wharf. This iron country was as hard as the copper country in the early days; winters were long and lonely, and starvation was never out of men's minds; mails were uncertain, and so was existence itself. It is the story of privation and stubborn effort all over again. There was little of glory and much of disappointment. The silver and gold couldn't be found; the iron was nearly as bad. Many times the pioneers must have wondered if this country ever would amount to anything. The men lived in a boarding house and "trailed it" through the swamp to the mine. The boarding house became mining office as well as dwelling place; here at night, by candlelight, the six miners who worked the Lake Superior mine told their troubles to Captain G. D. Johnson, who had come up from Sandusky to run the mine; here Philo Everett may have lived when, in 1850, he moved permanently to the range.

Everett was troubled because, for five years, he could not get an Episcopal church started in the mining camp; he and his wife were the only communicants. But before he died, in 1892, he had served as senior warden of the church for many years, although his mine had not made him rich. The history of Everett's Jackson Mining Company is one of almost constant reorganization and financial difficulty. Not until 1862, some seventeen years after it was formed, did the company pay its first dividend. That same year it absorbed the struggling Peninsula Iron Company, whose incorporators eight years before had included William Austin Burt. Ultimately Everett's Jackson Company was absorbed by

Mather's Cleveland Company, as was the third early operator, Graveraet's Marquette Iron Company. The failure of the pioneers was due not so much to their crude mining methods—these improved gradually—as to problems of transportation and the sheer rugged cussedness of the country. They had no luck. Everything went wrong. Scarcely had Everett erected a forge on the Carp River and succeeded in making the first iron manufactured in the Lake Superior district when an unseasonable freshet carried the dam away. Patiently Everett rebuilt the dam and for a time, in 1848, some six blooms, or two-foot bars, of iron were made daily; but though various parties subsequently operated the forge, "but little iron was made and no money." Small wonder; the forge was completely uneconomical. It cost six times as much to forge a ton of iron blooms as it did to mine two tons of ore. For the forge charcoal was needed; that meant building a charcoal oven and cutting wood to feed it. Gradually the axmen were forced farther afield for timber, building expensive roads as they went. The water power on the tiny Carp River was inadequate and intermittent.

But the problem that almost defeated the pioneers was that of transportation. The men, having wrested the ore from the stubborn earth, had to haul it some three miles to the forge; thence the iron blooms had to be taken another nine miles to Lake Superior, where they were loaded on tiny wooden boats, taken to the Soo, unloaded, portaged around the rapids of the St. Mary's River, loaded on another boat and transported to the industrial East.

It cost nearly as much to transport ore those nine miles from the forge to the port as to send it nine hundred miles by water. The downgrade through the woods was so steep that "nothing that had wheels could stay upright on the rocky trails"; so a crude device called a travois was employed—a sort of skid or sleigh made from two sticks, curved upward and bolted together at the front and spread apart in the middle by a crosspiece. The roads were so wretched that usually ore could be hauled only in the winter.

In November 1851 Heman B. Ely contracted with the two mining companies to build a strap railroad from Marquette to the Cleveland and Jackson locations. His plans were grandiose; but

difficulties, chiefly financial, beset him. Tired of waiting, the mining companies built their own plank road, a highway paved with
rough-hewn boards. Soon this was outgrown; the strap railroad
was revived. Crossties, called sleepers, were laid across the roadbed at wide-spaced intervals; to them were bolted or spiked heavy
longitudinal timbers and atop these were fastened the rails: flat
pieces, or straps, of iron. The route skirted ravines, wound
tortuously around cliffs and swamps. Frequently the little flatcars got out of control and overran the mules and killed them,
an expensive disaster, for mules cost more than a thousand dollars
a team (and hay was worth fifty dollars a ton). Constant use
loosened the strap rails and the ends curved upwards, sometimes
punching through the floor of wooden cars and killing passengers
or derailing the trains.

None the less, progress was made. The strap rails were replaced
with lightweight T-shaped rails, not unlike the heavy flanged
I-rails used today. Heman Ely attempted feverishly to complete
a steam railroad before the long-discussed canal was opened at the
Soo, but he died prematurely and his brother, S. P. Ely, completed the steam road. Two engines weighing twenty-five tons
each and named the *Sebastopol* and *C. Donckersley* were imported; they were capable of hauling 1,200 tons of ore to the docks
in a day, compared with the single ton which a sleigh carried.

And now in 1855 the canal at the Soo became a reality; opening the locks was like uncorking a bottle. Suddenly iron ore was
released in a flood from the Upper Peninsula. Indeed, the canal
unlocked all of Upper Michigan; copper and iron and timber
went out; civilization came in.

POCKETFUL OF ORE

INCREDIBLY ENOUGH, not everybody in Upper Michigan wanted the canal. Its opponents included the men who had built up a profitable business in portaging merchandise around the rapids, the Soo tradesmen who feared they would suffer if ships were enabled to pass between the lakes without stopping, the politicians like Henry Clay, who scoffed at the idea of spending thousands of dollars in this "place beyond the remotest settlement of the United States, if not in the moon."

Their objections were overcome by the arguments of men like William Austin Burt. The mining companies, copper and iron, wanted the canal; so did leaders of public opinion like Burt and Peter White, one of the more remarkable of Upper Michigan pioneers. It was built as a land-grant project by a syndicate called the St. Mary's Falls Ship Canal Company, which was organized by Charles T. Harvey, a shrewd salesman of scales who had not found the demand for weighing-apparatus so brisk that it prevented him from looking about for greater opportunities in the wilderness. Having traveled through the iron, copper, and timber regions, he was in a position to select valuable lands; he now became active in lobbying for favorable legislation. As a result, his canal company secured lands worth millions, lands that included such diverse bonanzas as the fabulous Calumet & Hecla mine, some of the richest iron-ore beds near Ishpeming, and pine lands around Seney that made the Chicago Lumber Company great. Harvey, hard-bitten and realistic, fought a strike and a cholera epidemic with equal vigor and on April 19, 1855, after two years' labor, opened the sluice gates and watched the waters of Lake Superior rush into the canal. With equal speed he hastened from the scene to build a fortune on his lands.

When the first vessel laden with iron ore passed through the canal, a pattern had been fixed. Thenceforward the iron mining companies gradually abandoned their ill-conceived attempts at making iron near the mines and shipped the ore unrefined to the furnaces of the industrial East. Thus, unwittingly, they reverted to the first effort of Philo Everett. Everett's men later had easily fallen into error. Their first operation had demonstrated the difficulty of transporting iron ore to the East for refining. Why not, they argued, smelt the ore on the spot, near the mine? Thus the useless rock would be eliminated at the source. It was logical, in their day: the canal and railroad and docks were not yet built. But now the mining men realized they could not make iron profitably a thousand miles from any market. Fuel for the furnaces was inadequate (it has been said, with some truth, that a coal mine would be worth more than a gold mine in Upper Michigan). And when canal and railroad made bulk transport cheap, the companies started shipping ore itself to the East, a practice now used almost exclusively.

Before the canal opened, production was reckoned in pounds of iron ore or number of blooms; seven years after the canal was opened, 383,105 tons of ore and 29,341 tons of pig iron passed through it on the way down from the range to the East.

The records of clearances at the Soo provide a good index of the growth and activity of Upper Michigan. The burgeoning region imported from down below, only 13,616 pieces of furniture in 1871, but 44,768 pieces in 1872; 1,595 pieces of machinery in 1871 and 10,593 in 1872, 4,366 barrels of liquor in 1871 and 7,083 in 1872, and, similarly, 653,140 pounds of malt in 1871 and a whopping 1,545,875 pounds in 1872. That the country was far from self-sufficient is indicated by these imports: flour, pork, beef, bacon, lard, butter, cheese, tallow, soap, apples, sugar, tea, coffee, salt, tobacco, nails, dried fruit, vegetables, lime, window glass in boxes, cattle, horses, mules, hogs, brick, coarse grain.

In 1872 these items passed through the canal on their way down from the ranges: 1,709 tons of mass copper, 8,547 tons of ingot copper, 4,365 tons of stamp-work copper, and the iron already listed. In addition, 576,134 half barrels of fish, more than twice the production of the previous year, indicated a new booming industry. Farming was beginning in the Lakes region: 567,134 bushels of wheat were shipped, 94,270 barrels of flour, 898 bushels of barley, and 636 bushels of potatoes. Building stone and quartz also were mined and shipped through the Soo.

In a steadily increasing flow ships streamed up to Superior from the lower Lakes. Even before the canal was opened, of course, a few vessels had plied the coasts of Upper Michigan. In addition to such later ships as the *John Jacob Astor*, the fur companies had employed some ten schooners as early as 1800, including the *Recovery*, which was camouflaged with brush and hidden in a rocky cove of Isle Royale during the War of 1812. When the first men came to the mineral ranges, they received supplies and sent their ore out on a few boats which were hauled across the Soo portage into Superior. But not until the canal was dug did traffic on the upper Lakes become big business and a gaudy legend.

Veteran seamen swore they never had been buffeted about on salt water as they were on Superior. All the old tales of floating islands and Flying Dutchmen were revived, and new legends arose. Other ships joined the ghostly company of La Salle's *Griffon*. Fabled sunken vessels lured treasure-seekers. The *Rouse Simmons*, a 180-foot three-masted schooner, sailed bravely into a raging gale from Thompson Harbor near Manistique bound for Chicago with a load of Christmas trees; she was sighted near the harbor by the astonished crews of other vessels scurrying for shelter and again, flying distress signals and with her canvas in ribbons, by a Coast Guard rescue crew. Then the blizzard closed down; nobody ever saw the *Rouse Simmons* or any of her crew again, although the next spring fishermen hauled up branches of Christmas trees in their nets.

This was only one of many vessels which foundered in sudden storms near the opening or close of navigation, vessels which became legends. Gradually a folklore of Great Lakes shipping developed, comparable to the Mississippi River tales. The deckhands made songs about their labors reminiscent of the levee chanteys.

Theirs was a hard life. For a long time their vessels were years behind the more modern salt-water ships. In the main the men were on the boats from the opening of navigation in April till its close in December, with perhaps a day or so ashore while their vessels were loading or unloading. They were scorned by salt-water seamen as fresh-water men never out of sight of land, but any sailor knows that danger lies near land, that long stretches of open ocean provide a time for relaxation. So close-spaced are the rocks and reefs, the narrow rivers and canals and harbor entrances which the lake boats thread, that master and crew alike must be constantly vigilant.

Many of the Lakes sailors were, naturally, Scandinavians, like Captain Hans Simensen. Born near Oslo fjord in 1868, he went to sea when he was fourteen, sailing European waters for some twenty years until, completing a voyage at New York, he drifted inland to Milwaukee, where he shipped on a Lakes boat. After a time he bought an interest in the *Lucia A. Simpson*, which became a familiar hull in the Escanaba lumber trade. Captain Simensen sailed her more than a quarter of a century. In 1929, bound for Keweenaw to undertake salvaging operations, she ran into a summer squall off Algoma, her mizzenmast crashed to the deck, and she began to leak. The old girl managed to reach the car-ferry lanes, where Coast Guardsmen in a power boat towed her to safety. A few years later she was destroyed in a shipyard fire. She was the last of her type to visit the waters of Little Bay de Noc. (The car ferries, which today carry loaded railroad cars across Lake Michigan and the Straits of Mackinac daily, were conceived by a railroad man in 1891 and promptly labeled "Ashley's folly.")

One of the toughest jobs was that of the trimmer, who trimmed, or leveled, the cargo of iron ore to keep the little wooden sailing vessels on even keel. The trimmer was paid well—as much as $35 a day in some instances—but he worked long hours stripped to the waist, shoveling the heavy ore in the hold in sweltering heat below decks. When the harbor was filled with a score of vessels, the boss trimmer, a brawny rock-fisted contractor, would rush from ship to ship, lowering his plumb-bob, profanely directing the labor of his men, and, when they had finished, doling out their pay. In later years the trimmers were superseded by a mechanical iron beam which leveled the cargoes, and the old boss trimmers sang mournfully:

Then I was king of the trimmer crew
And I ruled with an iron grip
And never a slob on the whole damned job
Dared give me any lip.

But now, alas! my days are past;
The trimmer is no more,
They use a beam to guide the stream
Of bloody iron ore.

They took my crew of huskies, who
Knew pick and shovel's feel
And now a stick just does the trick
To ship an even keel.

Some of the captains on the Lakes boats became legendary. Among them was Captain Bundy, a hell-roaring master of the late seventies and early eighties who feared no man nor god on or above the Lakes. Laid up in Chicago, he attended a revival meeting to jeer at the parson, but ended by being converted. Thereafter he forswore profanity and rough sailor's clothes for gentle speech and broadcloth, and he rechristened his two-masted hooker the *Glad Tidings*. Of her it was said in reverence that her only cargo was the gospel. This she carried up and down the Lakes, and Captain Bundy trod her bridge, stocky, square-jawed, white-whiskered, bright of eye. He sailed from port to port, tying up at the dock and preaching from the deck; his wife accompanied him on the melodeon. His was the old-time gospel of hell-fire and brimstone, and it has been written that when he spoke, sinners died of fright, children screamed, and women wept. One of his favorite themes was the heathen practice of murdering pigeons and quail. He also foretold plagues. Once when, parched by his long harangue, he dispatched a boy to Dave O'Connor's saloon for a bucket of beer, O'Connor sent the empty pail back with the message that he considered the captain an old hypocrite who spent poor folks' collection money on booze. He also offered to lick the captain. Bundy strode to the saloon followed by a goodly crowd of spectators, who judiciously waited outside. They heard horrendous oaths, the crash of furniture and glassware. Presently the captain emerged, his ministerial cloth disordered and one eye rapidly turning black. Saying only: "The Lord be praised!" he went back to his gospel ship. Inside, O'Connor lay senseless on the floor of his wrecked saloon.

Nearly every port of call had its waterfront saloons where the sailors congregated. They achieved a reputation not unlike that of seamen everywhere, and some of the brawls in which they tangled with lumberjacks or miners became legendary, for all three groups were clannish and belligerent. The boats carried iron and copper down below and came back laden with supplies and, later almost exclusively, coal. All summer long the harbors were white with sails and thick with spars, and sailors roamed the streets. Sailing on the Great Lakes became a way of living, a seaman's life on the mid-continent inland sea.

About the time that shipping became important a new group rose to prominence in Upper Michigan: the men who go out on the Lakes to cast their nets for fish. Since the time of the Indians and Jesuits fish had been a staple of diet, and not long after the real opening of the country in the forties commercial fishermen began to ply their trade. Some of the earliest settlers of Escanaba were fishermen, and the intricate pound net, a rather high development, was introduced to Lake Superior as early as 1864, in White-fish Bay. The fishing steamer was introduced on Lake Michigan about 1869 and on Lake Superior about 1871. In 1899 Peter Anderson & Sons fitted a sailboat with a twelve-horse-power naphtha engine at Marquette and thus inaugurated the era of motorboats, which more than doubled the number of nets cast by the old-style sailboats. Fishing had become big business.

Long before dawn, lights could be seen along the waterfronts of towns or in little cottages built on sand dunes on the remote coasts of Lake Superior and Lake Michigan. Before the sun was up, the fleet of frail boats put out on the waters. Sometimes the fishermen sailed miles from shore to unreel and lay their nets. They knew the sky and the sweet-water sea, the invisible reefs and sandbars as other men knew ore formation. Their shanty homes were cluttered with hooks and lines and calking tools. The beaches were their front yards, and their children played there among the nets that were drying like great spider webs in the sun. It was hard work, but work which gripped men tenaciously so that son followed father into it.

Various types of nets were used, depending on such factors as the type of fish sought, the depth of water, the type of bottom. Nearly a score of food species have been found in Superior and Michigan. Among the more important commercially have been lake herring, lake trout, yellow perch, chubs, suckers, yellow pike, whitefish, and smelt.

Though the upper Lakes teemed with fish in the earliest days, shortly after the Civil War, with the introduction of the efficient pound nets, the catch began to decline, a process which has not been arrested. Among the more important Upper Michigan fishing centers on Lake Michigan have been Manistique and St. James (Beaver Island area), and on Lake Superior the Whitefish Bay area, Grand Marais, Munising, Marquette, the Keweenaw Bay area including L'Anse and Baraga, Ontonagon, and Washington Harbor on Isle Royale.

The Soo canal may not be what Peter White thought it was, the best thing for the whole United States that ever happened; iron ore may not be what Peter White claimed it was: "the key of the commercial supremacy of the world." But the two, linked inextricably, did much to shape twentieth-century American industry.

The careers of few men have been so varied as that of white-bearded Peter White. He arrived on the range as a boy in Graveraet's party. Truly he grew up with the country, and in the process he got his hand into nearly everything. At one time or another he was postmaster, legislator, storekeeper, lawyer, land agent, university regent, church official, insurance man, banker, mine executive. Raconteur, persuasive speaker, self-conscious maker of history, he became, in the view of some residents, Marquette's first citizen.

During his time Marquette grew from nothing to the leading iron-ore shipping port of the Lake Superior region (a pinnacle

from which it since has slipped). In the beginning the sailing vessels that brought provisions refused to enter the bay, which was
believed to be sown with rocks; anchoring out, they sent their
supplies and passengers ashore in lighters. At least once a herd of
cattle was shoved overboard and forced to swim ashore, and when
the first boiler was imported, it was corked and tossed into Lake
Superior and towed ashore. Soon a dock was built; the waves
washed it away that same night; another was built and it burnt;
gradually the towering modern ore dock was developed. In the
early days the docks were simply platforms built on piling twelve
feet above the water; ore was trundled onto them in wheelbarrows and shoveled into the small lake boats by hand. Five or six
days were required to load a 300-ton boat, compared to the few
hours now needed to load, mechanically, a block-long vessel
carrying 10,000 tons of ore.

Peter White was one of the men who founded and named Marquette, originally called Iron Bay and Worcester; likewise he had
a hand in the naming of the twin inland cities on the range,
Ishpeming and Negaunee. Both are Indian names; Ishpeming,
built on a swamp, means "high place," or "heaven"; Negaunee
has been translated by detractors as "hell," though a more literal
translation is "pioneer." Between these two, but closer to Negaunee than to Ishpeming, iron ore was first found by Philo Everett.
Like so many other towns of Upper Michigan, neither of these
places was founded with conscious design; it simply grew. A hole
in the ground, some houses around it for the miners to live in,
presently town government, and a name—that is the story. Ishpeming developed out of the Lake Superior Mine location and
was named in 1856; Negaunee resulted from the mining at the
Jackson location.

Both towns, boisterous mining camps in the beginning, grew
rapidly. Early difficulties had been surmounted; the Civil War
and the first real boom lay ahead, and visions of greatness rose
above the broad-shouldered clamor of the towns. In 1858 Captain Johnson and his twenty men shipped 4,685 tons of ore from
the Lake Superior Mine, a prodigious amount, and the reputation
of the mine was established. That same year the first birth of a
child was recorded at Ishpeming. The town then had seven houses

besides the miners' boarding house—a house and two log shanties at the Cleveland location, a house at the Jackson location near Negaunee, a log house at Negaunee, and two shanties at the Pioneer furnace, which, under construction, was the latest marvel of the range. In their spare time the miners could fish on the Carp River for trout or float down the stream at night with a lantern, shooting deer wantonly. Soon, with the coming of a saloon, they could brawl on payday to their hearts' content. Mining men were in the saddle and they would stay there; they built the houses, platted the towns, ran the local government, became the church elders and the oracles.

Furnaces had sprung up everywhere that men could find fuel, water power, limestone, and iron ore. The men who worked them were boomers, roving Irishmen and Scotchmen and French Canadians from the Champlain district of New York. They delighted in such pastimes as slinging a bucket of whitewash at a visiting minister, or victimizing a fellow worker who understood English ill, or, in the long winter, importing an orchestra for a dance, then, by brawling over the iron-making championship, breaking up the dance in a general melee.

Privation was not ended. One November two men set out in an open boat for the Soo to register a claim to lands on the range; they were drowned or frozen on the way. Money shortage was chronic; in 1857 cash became so scarce that one of the mining companies issued "iron money," token currency of its own.

But now the country was booming, the railroads were coming, the mining companies were sending explorers to search out the full extent of the range. The Chicago & Northwestern Railroad built its tracks into Ishpeming on a Sunday when the courts were closed so that the competitive Marquette, Houghton & Ontonagon couldn't get a restraining injunction. In 1864 the Peninsular Railroad reached Negaunee from Escanaba, providing a Lake Michigan outlet for iron ore; eight years later connection was established with the Chicago & Northwestern. Railroad surveyors performed all over again the prodigious labors of the men of William Burt's time, fording rivers and plunging through the wilderness to plot for the roadbed a course which never would be improved. As a railroad attorney Samuel Tilden had launched a career which would carry him as close to the White House as any man ever got without actually being inaugurated President. He came to Upper Michigan first because of his railroad connections; almost immediately he and two associates, William B. Ogden and John W. Foster of Chicago, incorporated, September 15, 1864, the Iron Cliffs Company and, on land bought from the St. Mary's Ship Canal and Mineral Land Company, opened the Foster and the fabulous Barnum Mines. Before long William H. Barnum became associated with them. Later Iron Cliffs was absorbed into Sam Mather's company to form the Cleveland-Cliffs. Other great men were coming now to Upper Michigan—John M. Longyear, who would build a landed empire, and Henry W. Oliver, who would play poker with Carnegie and Mellon for control of iron ore, and Raphael Pumpelly, an effete cosmopolite who took his wife on a canoe trip that ended with the opening of the Gogebic Range, and James Pickands, who sold enough coal and iron to become one of the giants of all the Lake Superior region. Mather, Pickands, Longyear, Oliver—they all gathered hungrily on the range when the Civil War had ended. War took away labor, but boomed iron; the Soo canal had been built none too soon.

In the midst of the wartime boom, prospectors found the "silver-lead range" up in the Dead River country north of Ishpeming. They opened a mine on the shores of Silver Lake and another, the Holyoke, closer to Ishpeming. Feverish excitement resulted, fanned by stories of silver in the Porcupine Mountains near Ontonagon and tales of the fabulous Comstock Lode discovered in Nevada in the fifties. Prospectors flocked to the region as they never had flocked to the iron fields alone. (Early realization of the difficulty and expense of mining iron ore spared the range much of the anguish suffered by other mining regions where fly-by-night speculations and shoestring explorations flourished.) About the time that people were willing to admit that nobody ever would make any money out of the silver veins near Ishpeming, prospectors found gold in the hills near the Dead River.

And all the time men were exploring the iron-ore body. They would discover that the range extended like a forked tongue westward from Negaunee, ending near the Baraga County line beyond Lake Michigamme, some thirty miles west of Ishpeming. But in those days the prospectors thought it might run almost forever through the wilderness. By canoe and on foot they explored it, sinking test pits and shafts everywhere. A pit, a shaft house, a few homes, a location, a boom town, ultimate disintegration—the story became familiar. But in those days disintegration was unimportant. There was plenty of ore. True, the iron was pockety, the range difficult to follow. But what of it? One authority declared that all you needed to become an iron king was a donkey engine, which, when one pocket was exhausted, could be moved to another. Deep in the woods the mining men built their shaft houses of crude logs, like blockhouses, and they raised the ore in buckets the size of garbage pails. They might not be accurate, but they were enthusiastic. One explorer near Champion tested the length of a vein when he thought he was testing its breadth and excitedly wired his employer: "Vein quarter of a mile wide, can't find the walls." In a few years, they would open the Marquette Range all the way from Negaunee to Humboldt and Michigamme and beyond; they would trace its tortuous course down the banks of the winding rock-walled Michigamme River; they would open the great Republic Mine and go on south to develop the vast Menominee Range and, finally, westward to the Gogebic Range.

They knew there was greatness in it. Somehow, out of the tangle of blunders and failures and disappointments, these men were fashioning something that would endure. Ore shipments zoomed upward in an almost unbroken progression. The Jackson Mine moved less than 13,000 tons in 1861, but a year later it sent 46,096 tons of ore to appease the wartime hunger of the furnaces; when the roaring seventies began, 127,642 tons went down below from the Jackson, 132,884 from the Cleveland, 166,582 from the Lake Superior group, and 177,155 from the new mines out near the western end of the range around Humboldt and Champion.

Marquette Range iron was setting the standard for iron the world over; it was making history; its supply was inexhaustible. These were the golden years. Even when the vast Mesaba fields opened, mining men at Ishpeming smiled tolerantly: you'll always need Marquette Range ore to make good iron. This was the mother of Lake Superior iron. Cleveland-Cliffs invented a slogan: "There is no section of the country where intelligent work is sure of better success than the Upper Peninsula of Michigan." Everybody believed it. Nothing could stop this country.

And it grew not only in terms of iron ore and copper but in terms of lumbering. In the sixties and seventies logging became the new giant of Upper Michigan. The loggers had cut the white pine down below; now they were moving northward, bringing with them a hell-roaring band of booted men whose Bunyanesque capacity for liquor, brawling, and women became an undying legend in the northland.

~~§ 9 §~~

DRIVE 'ER BOYS—SHE'S WHEELIN'

"I LIKE PINE TIMBER," the old lumberjack says as he sits with a beer in the back room of the saloon and remembers the brave days. "I don't know why; I just like pine timber."

The lumberjacks who cut a swath across the continent from Maine to Oregon scorned all the trees but the lordly white pine. In truth, their companies found no ready market for any other. But presently these rough brutal men came to feel the majesty of the pine towering darkly in the forest above the snow, above the hardwoods, the maples and birches, above the softwoods they called scrubby, the poplar and spruce and balsam and cedar and tamarack. And in the end the true jacks wouldn't even cross a rough-hewn bridge or sleep in a camp that contained a stick of "popple." They wanted nothing in the woods but white pine. And in the spring, when they came roaring down the rivers driving thundering logs, they wanted nothing in the towns but women and raw red liquor.

Today the white pine is nearly gone in Upper Michigan, and the lumberjack, old-style, though he persists in the more remote districts, is being replaced by part-time farmers with Ford automobiles and wives and children. In his day he lived a rip-roaring story, and his legend endures.

To "follow the pine" was a noble profession. Men went into the woods in Maine and Nova Scotia, cut out the pine, broke camp, and moved westward to the vast pine tracts along the Saginaw in lower Michigan; there they "cut out and got out" and went on to the Upper Peninsula and to northern Wisconsin and Minnesota; finally they moved on to the Pacific Northwest, always following the pine as other men follow gold strikes or the flag. In each of the sections they abandoned there would be other harvests, first of hardwood, then of softwoods for paper pulp, then of second-growth timber. But the lumberjacks of the old days couldn't wait; they had to follow the pine. They, like the fur traders who preceded them, were the great prodigals of Upper Michigan. When they came, pine covered the land like a soft green mantle; when they left, little remained but scrub timber, slashings, and the great rotting trees that lay where the jacks felled them too late in the spring to get them out of the woods.

Though pine grew everywhere in Upper Michigan, it liked best not the rocky mineral ranges but the low, flat sand plains and the edges of swamps that lay farther south and east. Upper Michigan can be split by a line drawn north and south through Marquette (extended, the line would hit Chicago). In general, the western half means minerals, the eastern half means timber. Inevitably, as Ishpeming and Marquette, Houghton and Calumet, Crystal Falls and Iron River and Ironwood became mining towns, the destiny of towns like Escanaba and Menominee and Manistique was shaped by timber. There sawmills buzzed from dawn to nightfall, the talk was of river drives and timber pirates and millions of board feet, the great men were pine barons, the brawlers lumberjacks.

As early as 1832 there was a sawmill on the Menominee River, and in the forties William Austin Burt found another at the mouth of the Escanaba; here a town called Flatrock sprang up and grew into the city of Escanaba, boisterous lumber and iron port of the eighties on an arm of Lake Michigan called Little Bay de Nocquet. In 1850 Ike Stephenson, one of the earliest pine barons and later a millionaire Senator, entered the lumbering business. A year after that the great N. Ludington Company was formed; in 1852 a sawmill was built at Ontonagon, and by 1865 there were five log buildings, most of them abandoned during the winter, at Manistique, which became the seat of Schoolcraft County and nerve-center of the lustiest, bawdiest logging operations in Upper Michigan.

In the seventies the real boom started. The first jacks roared up from the cutover country down below, certain the pine up here would last forever (it lasted thirty years). The lumber kings were coming from Chicago and New York, their pockets bulging with greenbacks, their eyes agleam with visions of millions of board feet and millions of dollars. Samuel Tilden was on the iron ranges with his Iron Cliffs Company, and Escanaba had its gilt-bedecked Tilden House. 'Bijah Weston came from New York with his Weston Lumber Company, and George Orr formed his powerful Chicago Lumber Company; they battled sin together and made fortunes. The Jamestown men came in from New York, and Robert Dollar logged without notable success, gave his name to the town of Dollarville, and went on to the coast and a fortune in shipping. Unlike the iron giants, great lumbering companies sprang up almost overnight. They traded in hundreds of thousands of acres, they controlled the destinies of fifty thousand lumberjacks and scores of towns, they cut out and got out, leaving desolation behind them, and they cared not a damn for legalistic hairsplitting ("to log a round forty" meant to cut the timber all around a forty-acre tract, and might involve cutting a lot of acres that belonged to somebody else). Among the great companies were the I. Stephenson Company, the Bay de Noc Company, the Von Platen Fox Company, the J. W. Wells Company, which once had sixty sawmills on the river, the Alger, Smith Company, and the Wisconsin Land and Lumber Company, which built Hermansville. While these giants were making farmland out of forests in the eastern part of Upper Michigan, far to the west the huge Diamond Match Company was moving into Ontonagon, where, as has been said, it flourished until, ironically, a great fire burned it out in 1896. All over the peninsula the woods rocked from daybreak to dark with the crash of falling timber, the thunder of breaking rollways, the ring of axes and hum of saws, and the deep long cries of "Timber-r-r-r!" The expanding United States empire simply could not get enough lumber for telegraph poles, for fencing in the new West, for farm buildings and railroad ties that marched across the continent. Softwood from Upper Michigan built a new empire's houses; its hardwood put new furniture into them.

The companies sent their men into the woods, where they cut

a little clearing and built a cluster of rough shanties overnight; presently a store and post office appeared, a lumber company's office, a hotel, and saloons and gambling joints and whorehouses; wagon roads came, and the railroad, plunging through the swamps and thickets. For a few years the muddy streets and board sidewalks were thronged with lumberjacks and gambling men and fancy women in silks and satins, with frock-coated gentlemen from down below visiting their baronies, and with frightened travelers glimpsing hell for the first time. Around the town the lumber camps sprang up; the lumberjacks were widening the clearing they had cut for the town; they moved deeper and deeper into the woods. Then all at once it didn't pay any longer to drag the logs across that widened clearing: the area was all cut out, and as suddenly as it had appeared, the town vanished. Its buildings might remain, but they would be overrun with rats, and bats would fly in and out of the broken windows; the barrooms would be covered with dust and cobwebs, and snow would fall through the caved-in roofs of the gaudy palaces of joy. Presently the buildings would collapse; the now priceless pine planks, two and three feet wide, of which they were built would rot into dust; in the end, weeds would overgrow even the foundations. Then, perhaps, somebody would erect a filling station at the crossroads, and puzzled tourists would pause on the concrete highway to inquire about that town on the map that everybody says used to be such a hell of a place. Such a town is Seney.

In its day Seney was probably as tough, two-fisted a town as any on earth. Old-timers vigorously dispute the question of which was the toughest town in Upper Michigan. Some say Seney, some say Hurley (which is in Wisconsin but owes its infamy to Upper Michigan miners), some even claim that the tiny shingle-mill hamlet of Shingleton was tougher than either. From the distance of fifty-odd years it is difficult to separate legend from fact; it is equally difficult to see how any place in the pineries could have come closer to hell than Seney.

Named for one of the contractors who helped build the predecessor of the D. S. S. & A. railroad—Duluth, South Shore & Atlantic—from St. Ignace to Marquette, Seney came into being about 1882 when the Alger, Smith Company began logging in the vicinity. Into its brief fifteen years of existence it compressed a hundred years' sin and hell-raising. Seney lies about midway be-tween Lake Superior and Lake Michigan on the long narrow eastern portion of the Upper Peninsula; it is situated north of Manistique on the Fox River, a tributary of the Manistique River, and it is in the heart of the great pine plains.

In 1882, when a Canadian named Phil Grondin came up from the Lower Peninsula to cook in one of the Alger, Smith camps, Seney wasn't much—a cluster of buildings along the railroad tracks, with mud and water in the wretched streets, nothing but a footpath north through the woods toward Grand Marais on Lake Superior, and only one boarding house, that of a man named Carlson who had run a similar establishment at Robert Dollar's Dollarville, twenty-five miles east. The snows were six feet deep on the level that winter of 1882–3, and in the spring the little Fox River was so high that the logs jammed almost daily on the drive down to the mills at Manistique. The townspeople walked through mud and water all spring though they built board side-walks on posts a foot above the street level. The next year Grondin put up the hotel that became a focal point in the Seney legend. Soon he opened a retail store and a bar. The whole shebang burned down in 1891, but he rebuilt, only to be burned out again about the time the town collapsed. One time he had no insurance, for fires were so common a peril in the pineries that the insurance rate was seven and a half per cent of the property's value.

By the time Grondin's hotel opened, Seney was really boom-ing. Here it was, just a collection of huts in the woods miles from nowhere; overnight it became a broad-shouldered little city. It reached its peak around 1890, with a population estimated—the population wouldn't hold still for a proper census—at 3,000. First, before there was any town, had come the timber cruisers, land-lookers whose job it was to cruise through the woods and esti-mate the amount and accessibility of standing timber. Then had come the wood butchers, carpenters who built the town and the camps around it. In the early eighties came the lumberjacks and the camp-followers, a motley horde. To work in the woods came French Canadians and Swedes, "with just enough Irish for spice." Poles and Finns and a few Cousin Jacks and Italians came too, but they stayed mainly in town or worked in the railroad section gangs. By 1893 Seney had ten hotels, a dozen saloons, two enormous "hoodlums" (the local euphemism for bawdy houses) and uncounted smaller ones, a single church, two big general merchandise stores, and a respectable collection of drug stores, meat markets, and, of all things, jewelry stores. The only hotel that didn't sell liquor was the White House, which had been built by the railroad company.

Above all else, this God-forsaken hamlet in the pines housed the offices of a half-dozen of the largest lumbering companies then operating in Upper Michigan, including the famed "C. L. Company" (Chicago Lumber Company) and the Alger, Smith. It was these companies that supported the town on their shoulders. How did they go about it? How, precisely, was logging done, and how did the lumberjacks live?

After the timber cruiser (of whom more later) had turned in his report, the companies sent wood butchers into the pine and they built the logging camp with logs cut and hewn on the spot. First they put up a cook camp, a one-room building combining kitchen and dining-room and capable of seating at the long wooden tables a hundred hungry men. ("But always remember, no matter what you're buildin', twenty-four by fifty-six is the best size.") Then they built the men's camp, or bunkhouse, and an office camp, tool shed, perhaps a smithy, and the wanagan. Wanagan, spelled variously, properly meant a flatboat carrying a cook stove and supplies which floated down the rivers behind the log drives, but by extension it came to mean the supply shed in camp—a sort of company store that stocked the wool socks and wool shirts and boots and "Peerless" chew tobacco and the numerous other items a jack needed to carry him through the long winter.

During the summer, while all this construction was going on, a crew was going down the river, cleaning from its channel and banks protruding logs or boulders that might start a jam during next spring's drive. The swampers, usually inexperienced woodsmen, were threading the woods with a network of tote roads for hauling supplies from town and skid roads for dragging the logs to the riverbank.

Finally in the fall all was ready, and the lordly jacks came into camp. All these preparations had been made for them; now, as snow fell, they went to work in pairs. Carefully one notched a pine; that is, cut a wedge-shaped notch with an ax on the side of the tree facing the direction in which he wanted it to fall. Then on the opposite side he and his partner began sawing toward the notch with their great crosscut saw, which was more than six feet long and had teeth sharp as needles. As the saw buried itself in the tree, the jacks drove wedges behind it to keep the saw from buckling and to direct the course of the tree's fall. They bragged that they could fall a tree so accurately it would drive a nail. Many of the trees were five and six feet in diameter and three men could scarcely reach around them, for these were the days of five-log pine: you only needed five logs to make a thousand board feet of sawed lumber. (Today you are lucky if your cut averages thirty or forty board feet per log instead of two hundred.) The saw bit through the enormous pitch-smelling butt like a hot knife in butter, and then suddenly came the sharp warning crack of the great tree; looking up, the jack could see the towering top shudder, and he cried: "Timber-r-r-r!" and got to hell out of the way as, with a splintering crash, the giant smashed its way to the snow-covered earth through the branches of lesser trees. And all around, other teams of jacks within earshot who had stopped work at the long warning cry took hold of their saws and went back to work.

They always did their cutting in the winter, sometimes standing in four feet or more of snow as they sawed away. Winter was the only time for lumbering; the temperature might go to forty below zero, the snow might drift over the camp roofs; but winter was the time for lumbering. The woods were free of deer-flies and mosquitoes, and the roads could be kept in shape. As soon as freezing weather set in, the camp boss ordered out the road icer, an ungainly but effective sprinkling wagon on runners which spread water evenly on the road; over this frozen surface the icer sprinkled more water throughout the winter, keeping the ice road grooved and slick as glass for the skidders.

When the fallen logs had been "limbed" and then "bucked" into suitable lengths, the skidders loaded them on sleighs or hitched them beneath the axle of a pair of "big wheels," enormous wagon wheels fifteen feet high, so built in order that the axle might be high enough above the ground to clear small stumps and rocks that obstructed the path through the forest to the skid road. Down the road the logs went to the riverbank, where they were piled on rollways, or landings, to await the spring drive. Oxen in the early days and later horses or mules pulled the big wheels and sleighs, and the loads they hauled were fantastic mountains of logs. Hell, they could pull anything that had two ends.

The jack ranked above the skidders, the swampers, the buckers. And, of course, above him was the bull of the woods, the camp boss or woods foreman. And above him was the walking boss, the company's overseer who went from one camp to another, supervising the whole operation. But the real king of the camp was the cook. None dared dispute him; in all the tumbling chaos of logging he was a symbol of discipline. If a man didn't come to dinner when the cook rang the gong, the cook literally threw the food out and the jack went hungry. If an expansive hard-boiled jack talked while eating, it was the cook, armed with a butcher knife like a machete, who told him to shut up and made it stick; no talking at meals was a never-broken rule, for the cook had no time to waste while playboys dallied at their food over light con- versation. When the gong rang, the jacks filed silently into the cook camp and sat down on benches at the long wooden table. Their tin or graniteware plates were before them upside down; on the table were great steaming pots of stew meat and boiled potatoes and cooked vegetables, huge pies, and enormous stacks of bread fresh-baked in camp. First there was a clatter as the jacks turned their plates right side up, and after that there was no sound in the big bare room but the noise of rough men eating. And all the time the cook marched slowly up and down, hovering over the men like a watchful turnkey.

Camp staples included blackstrap molasses, dried apples, small wormy prunes, bread, and bean soup. The meat more often than not was deer meat. Many camps hired a man whose illegal full- time job was to kill deer. He would average perhaps five a day, and so plentiful were the deer that he could pick his spot where he wanted them to fall: near the tote road, so the chuck wagon coming in from taking the men's lunch to them in the woods could drag the carcasses to camp for him.

Nevertheless, sometimes fresh meat got scarce and the jacks were reduced to a diet of the hated sowbelly. On one such occasion two jacks held a horseshoe against the head of the camp's prize bull and smashed it with a sledge; their attempt to convince the boss that a horse had kicked the bull to death failed because, inadvertently, they had held the horseshoe upside down.

After supper the jacks were free to do what they pleased. But by then it was past dark, and there was not much to do except go to bed. Bed meant the wooden cots without mattress or pillow, standing row on row in the men's camp. For ease and for warmth in the sub-zero temperature there were thin horsehair blankets and dirty straw; for a pillow, the jack's boots rolled up in one of his outer shirts (he invariably donned extra shirts one over another as cold weather set in). Sometimes, though it was strictly against rules, a jack brought a bottle of booze back to camp from his last jag in town. Sometimes on Saturday nights men danced with one another. They played cribbage or pinochle or smear with a pack of sticky dog-eared cards. They loved to gamble, and some ended the long winter's work without a cent and in debt. Sometimes they sat by the white-hot round stove and told lies to each other, and a few read the *Police Gazette*. Some invented jokes to play on the camp greenhorn; a favorite was for his partner to frighten him by exaggerating the perils of logging, chief among which was being smashed by a falling tree. One time a jack led his scared new Finnish partner in a mad race a full mile down the tote road from a toppling pine, and when they finally pulled up, the breathless Finn said he was going to quit; the sawing wasn't so bad, but the running was too much.

There was little enough joy in the lives of the jacks during the long winter. Mostly they worked. They rolled out of bed at four a.m. in the dark cold bunkhouse; by sunup they had finished breakfast and had walked through the dark eerie snow-lit forest to the quiet trees they were to cut. It was hard lonely work, dawn to dusk in numbing cold, often with a partner who didn't speak English. Small wonder that when the thaws came in spring, the jack threw aside his crosscut with relief, grabbed his peavey, and headed for the rollways on the riverbank. It was time for the drive.

For days while the sky turned blue, the bull of the woods had been watching the river. You had to catch it just right. You had to wait till the river had a driving head on—that is, till the snows had thawed sufficiently to give the river adequate depth. But if you waited too long, the later spring floodwaters would sweep your logs high into the woods. Often, if the stream was small, the boss would build a dam above the rollways; when enough water had backed up behind it, he would blow the dam and unloose the flood to carry his cut down to the mill. Sometimes he had to build a whole series of dams, intricate as any hydroelectric system, blowing them according to a careful plan; in such manner streams were diverted and as a consequence flow, to this day, in unnatural channels. Contrary to common belief, the "rivers" that the loggers drove were not large streams; you could jump across many of them in dry weather.

All winter the logs (which the jacks with studied carelessness called sticks) had been stacked on the great heaped-up rollways; now in the spring they were encrusted with snow and ice. Breaking them was a nice feat. The jacks peered long and carefully at them. They picked out the key log. With a sudden flip they broke it loose. And then the whole pile of logs came whirling thunderously down into the water, spinning and leaping like things alive. Two jacks, one on either end of the pile, cut the logs, checking the larger butt ends to give the tips a chance to catch up in the crashing surge to the water. The rollways were broken. The drive was on.

Down-river it went, and the swollen torrent became a highway paved from bank to bank with timber. In the van rode the veteran river-hogs, pick of the camp; balanced precariously on the plunging logs, they had the job of spotting and breaking up a jam before it got tight. Theirs was split-second work. Seconds after a log hung up on a boulder, others piled into it; in another minute the whole vast float of logs was pounding down on it; logs were upending, grinding into one another, wedging together so tightly that sometimes dynamite had to be employed to break the jam. When a jam started, the river-hogs in the vanguard would signal to the men farther back, who would try to string across the river the flyboom—logs chained together in a long row—to hold back the descending flood. If they failed, the jam-up was complete. Sometimes the expert river-hogs were able to spot the single key log that was holding up the entire drive and to free it. Once the jam was broken, the sullen river current flung the great flood of logs down on top of the men. A man had to be quick and nimble to skip from log to log to shore and safety.

Danger was everywhere on the drive. Sometimes, even when the timber flowed smoothly down a comparatively straight river, men were drowned or crushed. One time Red Jack Smith, a big red-haired Scotchman who bossed Camp 54, took on a young kid named Johnny Horn just before the drive. Nobody knows much about Johnny Horn; the man who tells the story today explains that in those days you didn't ask questions of a newcomer at camp. Well, they started driving Big Duck Creek. Now, the Big Duck is narrow, but "she's really wheelin' when she's got a drivin' head on." So they were coming down past the swamps and Johnny Horn was doing all right. But the boys kept telling him he'd ought to get him a pair of real Chippewa boots, boots with steel calks driven into the soles, for all that Johnny was wearing was a pair of baldheaded shoepacks. The pine logs were slippery, the river-hogs kept telling Johnny, and he sure did need a pair of cork boots, so finally Johnny went back to the wanagan and bought himself a pair of Chippewas. And, by God, next day he was riding a pine log slick as you please when all at once the bark slipped off. And that was the end of Johnny Horn. When the jam had passed next day, they found his body on the sandbar; they made a coffin of jack pine and buried him there on the sandbar.

You had to be a pretty good man to drive timber. Lots of the jacks who were good in the woods weren't worth a damn on a drive. Like Roaring Jimmy. He was one of the most famous of the old-timers, but he never could be a white-water man, though he cut down trees for forty years. As Roy MacGregor said, "Jimmy ain't a lumberjack, I wouldn't say. Jimmy is a stone-cutter by trade."

An old jack named Paddy, an albino, legend says, without a hair on his body, couldn't swim, and on the drive he was scared to death. Every minute he was out on the logs he kept so busy crossing himself that he hardly had time to use his peavey. But the minute he got ashore, he'd turn to the river and shake his fist and say: "You old son of a bitch, you couldn't drown me anyway." And the next day he'd start crossing himself again soon as he got out on the white water.

Drowning your peavey—losing it in the water—was the crowning disgrace. A peavey was a long heavy wooden club not unlike a giant's baseball bat with a spike on its end and a long free-swinging hook. With this heavy, dangerous weapon the jacks controlled the plunging logs, and sometimes, when the drive was done, they split skulls with it too.

On the drive the jacks rolled out at four a.m., worked hip-deep in water all day while dirty snow still lingered ashore, walked eight or ten miles back to the wanagan for grub at night, then lay down to sleep in damp straw. "And all for $1.75 a day and chuck." But sometimes the logs were not plunging devils; sometimes they went docilely down to the mill. Then the jacks could walk along the driver's trails on the bank, like policemen patrolling a parade. Some of them were stationed at anticipated trouble spots, narrow sharp bends in the river where a jam might form. Hour upon hour they sat and watched the logs go past. It was cold, and the jack brewed hot tea while he watched. He always carried a number-two size tomato can hooked onto his rear suspender button; in it he made tea, suspending the pail over the fire on a crotched stick, and to this day, you can see the old tea-sticks on the rocky points at the river bends. At night the jacks might lie down to sleep by their tiny campfires, for, superstition has it, jams never formed at night.

Perhaps the toughest dirtiest job on a drive was sacking and rearing. That was "some bull work," not spectacular, but back-breaking and nasty. The rearing crew followed at the tail end of the drive, collecting stray logs that the flood had carried out of the proper river channel. They started sacking when they found the logs stuck deep in the mud and brush ashore. Often they were stuck in quicksand; the suction then was terrific. "You take a dead lift on 'er, ' the old jack says in the pinetown saloon, "and when she starts to suckin', she's easin'." (A big man with shoulders like a circus strong man's, he always pushes his beer far away from him and stands back a foot or so from the bar to leave room for his gestures.) Frequently logs on the drive would be driven deep into the clay bank, "drove in down under that water like a spile driver had done it." Pine'll never rot there, under water; pine logs have been recovered sixty years later, sound as the day they roared down the rollway. And twenty, thirty years ago you used to catch grayling two feet long under them spiles. There's a difference of millions of board feet of timber between what the scalers measured in the woods of Michigan and what reached the sorting boom at the mills at the end of the drives. Much of it was scattered so deep in the woods that even the rearing crew couldn't loosen it; more remained in floodwoods—that is, narrow necks of land at river bends which the river, in flood stage, cut across, then, receding, littered with stranded logs. The rest was stolen by timber pirates.

These were unscrupulous thieves of the woods. Their fair game was unmarked logs—logs which the scaler neglected to stamp with the company's own brand-mark when he measured the logs at the rollways. But sometimes the pirate preyed even on marked timber. One time some 45,000 board feet disappeared in the course of a drive. Weeks later the walking boss found, at a small portable sawmill in the woods, a great pile of butt ends, each marked with his company's brand, and, near by, a big stack of new-sawed lumber and a smaller pile of bright-ended unmarked logs waiting for the saw. He took one log to town and when he put it under steam, the brand-mark came out clear as a latent fingerprint. Investigation disclosed that the owner of the portable mill had stolen the timber. Each night during the drive he had opened up the boom-sticks that closed the mouth of a branch stream, permitting hundreds of logs to flow up into a pond hidden deep in the woods; in the morning the company's river-hogs found the boom-sticks closed properly. Discovery of the theft broke the pirate; under threat of prosecution, he was forced by the company to hand over the lumber which he had sawed from the company's logs at great expense.

The log marks of the various companies, serving the same purpose as the Western cowboys' brand-marks, included such colorful symbols as a pair of legs and a "flying K" as well as the more prosaic diamond of the Diamond Match Company and the

CCICo of the Cleveland-Cliffs Iron Company. The marks were all-important at the end of the drive. In the early days competing companies sharing a common river raced to beat each other in using the water's driving head, and frequent battles resulted; before long they began to send their logs down-river together, pooling their manpower on the drive or even employing "boom companies" which did no actual cutting but only conducted drives. All this necessitated sorting the logs at the millpond at the mouth of the river or at the "pull-up" where the drive ended and the logs were pulled up out of the river and loaded on railroad cars. A sorting boom was constructed; as the logs whizzed into its narrow confines, sorters with prodigious memories spotted the symbols stamped on the butts and cried out the owner to the pin-whacker who was gathering into a raft logs destined for a certain mill. Sometimes these rafts, enormous cumbersome contraptions, were towed hundreds of miles across lakes and down rivers to mills.

A boom company on the Menominee River in 1872 passed through its sorting booms more than 142 million feet of logs; by 1889 this figure had reached 642 million feet, and when pine lumbering reached its peak, Michigan produced in all four and a quarter billion feet of lumber, more than any other state. Small wonder, when the drives came roaring down the Menominee and the Manistique Rivers, down the Brule and the Paint and the Michigamme and the Presque Isle and the Tahquamenon and all the other streams, small wonder that the sawmills began to buzz hungrily and that the jacks, equally starved for liquor and women, overran the sawmill towns like pillaging conquerors.

Manistique, Escanaba, Menominee—the cities were abandoned to them. The "good people" stayed indoors for days, from the first onslaught till the last drunk was plucked from the gutter. Merchants were nervous, but eager: some of the jacks might have as much as four hundred dollars burning holes in their pockets. Up and down Ludington Street in Escanaba they swaggered, in and out of its hundred and two saloons, their steel-calked boots punching holes in the board sidewalks and, later, striking sparks from the concrete. They wore their best plaid shirts, but they still had on their jack pants—Soo woolens hacked off at the bottoms with a broadax so the flapping cuffs wouldn't trip a man on the drive. Like the logs they drove down-river, they jammed the broad straight streets from sidewalk to sidewalk, a surging flood of bearded men, fighting, drinking, swearing, whoring. On down to the red-light district by the railroad yards they went, down to the old Thomas Street region, famed in northland legend. Here the girls were waiting, and twenty-four hours a day the drab buildings bulged with ribald song and brawling. (The whorehouses stayed open until 1942, when the police closed them because the Government moved into town to build a big ore dock.) The old tenderloin on Thomas Street was only two blocks long, but it contained a concentration of sin unsurpassed in the sawmill towns. One house on the corner harbored ten or twelve girls whose fee invariably was two dollars ("we didn't have none of that half-dollar stuff in this town," one old-timer recalls), and one fancy madame bade her beauties charge five dollars. A dollar, two dollars—what the hell? The jacks had worked all winter alone in the woods; what was a dollar now? And so they drank and whored until the woods bosses started rounding them up, dragging them out of dives and brothels and sobering them up and taking them back into the woods to prepare for the next season's cut.

George Orr was a lumber king who was determined that evil should not flourish in his realm. To that end he and his company bought up most of the land in and near Manistique. Saloons and bagnios were denied housing; Manistique would be an island of purity amidst the hell towns in the pines. But Orr's agents overlooked a single small parcel of land in the west end. Canny Dan Heffron snapped it up and opened a saloon, and over his saloon he maintained what have been called clubrooms. Embattled he stood against the forces of righteousness, fighting the good fight for man's inalienable right to drink enough liquor to fall on his face. Other free spirits joined him; soon the land that Dan Heffron had grabbed became the chief business section of Manistique. George Orr and his do-gooders were undone.

The Heffron boys—some spell it Heffernan—were powers to be reckoned with. Dan came to the Upper Peninsula first and sent for his younger brother, Denis, who became, during the height of the

Heffron power, the county sheriff. In this capacity he figured prominently in various enterprises in Manistique and the hell town Seney, serving his friends well and putting down upstart lawbreakers with a firm hand. True or not, one story concerning Dan is worth repeating. According to the legend, he was arrested in connection with one of his various enterprises, possibly one involving the use to which his "clubrooms" were put. On trial, he waited outside the courthouse in a sleigh while the jury deliberated. Came the verdict, and, by prearranged signal, a red bandanna fluttered out of the window of the jury room. Instantly Dan dived under a buffalo robe in the sleigh and the driver, an experienced stage-driver, whipped up the horses and down the street the sleigh raced, its runners singing in the frosty air. But what ho? Behind it sped a second sleigh, manned by bearded stalwarts sworn to uphold the law. The Mack Sennett cop-and-robber chase continued, with the betting on the cops, to the edge of town, where the fugitive's sleigh skimmed across the railroad tracks inches from the cowcatcher of an onrushing locomotive; the cops were barely able to stop in time to avoid crashing into the train. Thus aided, Heffron escaped, and the legend ends variously: some say he went to Chicago and opened a saloon, some say he fled to the new lumber districts of Washington in the Pacific Northwest, others swear he went on to the Klondike, where he struck it rich and died.

If Manistique and the other sawmill towns caught hell once a year, Seney caught hell the year round. To reach it, you went up the old tote road from Manistique, through Germfask, named magnificently by combining the initials of its founders, but called ignobly "the dump" because here logs were dumped into the Manistique River, and on up the river to Seney, the true hell town. Here, legend says, any traveler who got off the train wearing a white collar was seized by the heels and shaken till his money tumbled from his pockets into the hands of his tormentors, who promptly spent it on liquor at one of the dozen saloons. "I'm from Seney" may not have been quite enough to frighten any man in Upper Michigan into a stupor, as legend says, but the statement probably had quite an impact at that. Seney and the Seney boys were tough.

✺ 10 ✺

HELL TOWN IN THE PINE

✹

IN WINTERTIME the respectable citizens of Seney emptied the
watertank onto the frozen Fox River near the railroad tracks and,
having frozen a smooth fresh sheet of ice, went skating by moon-
light. This was just about the only innocent diversion which anyone can remember from Seney's past. The town was close enough
to the lumber camps so that the jacks could get in for a few days'
drinking when they couldn't wait till spring. And sometimes they
skidded the logs to Seney on ice roads and decked them in rollways on the bank of the Fox; and naturally, before going back
to camp, a man had to stop for a warmer. Seney was a hell town
even in winter.

But the saloons and drinking and fighting weren't what bothered
the good people most. The real scandal was the ladies of pleasure.
The Seney girls do not appear to have enjoyed the comforts of
their sisters in Houghton and Hurley and other more civilized
places where, the story goes, they drove through town elegantly
gowned in black brocaded silk, holding toy poodles on their laps
and parasols over their heads. The Seney girls were perhaps more
earthy. Many of them chewed "Peerless." One was called Razor-
back; her peculiar forte, perfected at bagnio dances, was to waltz
her partner near the door so the pimps could seize him and drag
him outside and beat and rob him.

Another was more picturesque. Every Christmas she came into
the Hargraves or the Morse & Schneider store and bought a hundred dollars' worth of fine ladies' clothing and sent it to Houghton,
mysteriously enough. To discover its destination, and also on

141

general principles, a mob of lumberjacks beat her up during a drunken brawl and, having forgotten in the joys of brawling their original purpose, continued the carnage until they had knocked out one of her eyes, kicked her unconscious, poured turpentine into her mouth and whisky into her vagina, dragged her out into the snow, and left her in the woods for dead. When she reappeared bloody and naked, they thought she was a ghost and leaped through the windows and fled. Her wounds had not fully healed when a little old lady came to the Hargraves store and inquired for her. The clerk sent word by a boy to the whorehouse that the girl had an out-of-town caller; she showed up in all her finery, expecting, naturally, a gentleman friend. The caller was her mother, come to take her home to Houghton.

The respectable wife of one of Seney's respectable citizens, Morse, of Morse & Schneider, cooked one season in a lumber camp to help out during a manpower shortage. But the work became too much for her, and her husband imported a strong-backed woman to help. When she arrived, husky and wholesome, Morse was on hand to ward off the mob of drunks which always met the trains. He personally conducted her out to the logging camp. On the way, they had to pass one of the town's two big bawdy houses; chancing to glance that way, Morse and his woman companion saw a prostitute standing in stark naked invitation in the doorway. Embarrassed and angry, Morse hustled the cook to camp, then hurried back to town, sought out the keeper of the bawdy house, and lodged a complaint. Immediately the whoremaster became indignant too. That wasn't any way for a decent whore to act. He stomped into Hughie Logan's saloon, tossed down three or four hookers of fortification, and went out to his bawdy house. There he interviewed each of the ladies, demanding to know which one had offended the proprieties. None confessed. So he went back down to the first floor and again worked his way upstairs, this time blacking the eye of every cutie in the joint. Finally one girl in an upstairs room admitted her guilt. Her boss knocked her down, kicked hell out of her, and threw her, half-dead, out of the window into a snowbank. He threw her trunk after her. She limped off to the depot and, having sent a drayman for her trunk, departed on the next train. Thereafter, the legend ends, you never saw bodies at the windows, only faces.

Both prostitutes and lumberjacks used the two big stores in Seney as banks. The stores would handle a jack's mail, sell him anything from dry goods to liniment, and cash his time slip, a piece of paper on which the woods boss recorded the amount the jack had earned, the amount he had drawn in advance, and the balance due him. Frequently a jack, come to town on a tear, would deposit all but five or ten dollars at the store, where it drew six per cent interest if left thirty days; sometimes he would deposit his roll at a saloon, where it was handier but also in greater jeopardy: five cents went as far as five dollars, for five dollars bought their owner only one beer since all the barflies in the house drank on a man with a fiver.

The prostitutes usually favored the stores as banks; they wanted security rather than conviviality. One pretty wench deposited $1,500 in a single month, showing up every now and then with great wads of bills. Everybody knew she was rolling the jacks—that is, catching them with their pants down and picking their pockets. When she had accumulated a vast sum, she drew out the entire amount. Surprised, the clerk inquired whether she was leaving town. Yes, she was leaving that very day for Benton Harbor. She added that she was to be married there on the 15th. The clerk was shocked. Sure, she said, she was engaged. Why not? Back home she and her fiancé had separated, each to make a stake; "And I guess I beat him to it," she added archly.

The lumberjacks, despite their carefree hell-raising, were lonely men. Secretly some of them spent long tortured hours composing love letters to ladies whom they met through such doleful agencies as the *Heart and Hand* matrimonial newspaper. One, a powerful illiterate Pole, prevailed on some of his fellow jacks to write letters for him to a damsel whose name and address he had obtained in this manner. Came the time when the dream girl requested his photo. Having on hand no likeness of himself, he sought the aid of John Bellaire, a man of letters who clerked for a time in Morse & Schneider's store and later worked in the post office. Bellaire, fearing that the man's fierce and ugly visage would frighten away the girl, urged him to substitute a photo of one of his more handsome fellow jacks. Of this chicanery the

Pole would have none. Resignedly Bellaire photographed him. Sure enough, the girl wrote back: "You look as if you have killed a dozen men. We are through." Believing himself duped, the wrathful Pole loaded up on whisky, got a gun, and went into the post office after Bellaire, who was able to talk him out of murder only after long nervous minutes of argument.

Many of the jacks who drifted in and out of Seney had unpronounceable foreign names, and Bellaire, for example, knew Tony Murphy a long time before he knew his name had been Antoni Krzyminiski back in Poland. The company clerks, harassed fellows who had troubles enough, tagged foreigners with American names whether they wanted them or not. The immigrants thought it was only another new custom of this strange new land. It was said that the Detroit post office forwarded to Seney all undeliverable letters from foreign countries.

Postal affairs in general mystified many of the jacks. One came into the post office, bought a stamp, mailed his letter, stood around a few minutes, then inquired: "No answer yet from down below?" Old-timers tell of a gnarled Finnish lumberjack who frequently came into the Seney post office and, borrowing pen and ink, retired to a corner where he shouted loudly at the paper in his hand, gesturing violently all the while and pausing now and then to scratch a vigorous "X" or other meaningless mark on the paper. After perhaps a half-hour of this he would fold the paper, place it in the envelope, seal it, and ask someone to address it for him to his wife in Finland. The letter mailed, he would depart content. His actions aroused much speculation; obviously he was not writing anything in these letters. The truth came out: when he got a letter from home, he had one of the other jacks at camp read it to him, and thus he fell under the impression that the paper talked to him; with incontestable logic, he assumed the paper which he talked at and mailed to Finland would talk to his wife there. Counsel was taken over this. Since explaining matters to the old man seemed too difficult, the other jacks wrote to his wife and, with his permission, enclosed the letter with his talked-at scratch-paper.

The Finns who came direct from Finland in the eighties worked on the Manistique railroad at first. Later they were suffered to go into the woods, where, though they rarely became true jacks, they were allowed to serve as swampers, teamsters, canthook men, and, ultimately, peacemakers between the Irish and the French or the Irish and the Swedes. Today lumberjacks may be Finns, Austrians, Poles, Scandinavians, almost anything; of them, only the Swedes resemble the true jacks, according to old-timers.

The bar in Dan Dunn's saloon was at least forty feet long. Dunn was standing near the rear when Steve Harcourt came in and took a shot at him. The bullet whizzed past him and cracked the enormous beveled mirror behind the bar, and as the customers dived for cover, Dunn snatched up his revolver from under the bar and shot Steve Harcourt in the mouth. Steve Harcourt ran out, but on the way he caught another bullet, this one in the belly. He fell on the board sidewalk. He was carried home and Dan Dunn was arrested and taken down to the county seat, Manistique. While he was there making a peace bond and awaiting the outcome of Steve Harcourt's injuries, all Seney seethed with excitement, for this was the biggest thing that ever had happened in a town that yawned at bloodshed.

Just what the trouble was between Dunn and the Harcourts has often been rumored. Dunn and the Harcourt boys probably were the two most powerful forces in Seney. They kept rival saloons, among their other enterprises. Their rivalry in one field or another undoubtedly led to the feud between them. (It should be noted that not all the Harcourts were in the saloon or kindred businesses: some were simply lumbermen.) It was said that Dunn was allied with the Heffrons, Dinny the sheriff and Dan the Manistique saloonkeeper supposed to have fled in a sleigh.

Dan Dunn came to Seney from Roscommon, Michigan, down below. There he had kept saloon and, the legend goes, when he was ready to move north, he gave a down-and-out jack fifty dollars to set fire to the place. With money from the insurance and other sources he had made a place of power for himself in Seney when the jack appeared demanding blackmail. Dunn took him out to an island in the river near Seney; the jack was not seen again. Not long afterward a druggist came to Seney to see Dunn about some money Dunn had borrowed. Dunn took the druggist to the same island. Years later the bleached skeletons of two men were found on the island, according to John Bellaire. Legend says a section in the Seney graveyard was reserved for unidentified corpses.

Dunn was married to a thoroughly respectable woman and he was gentle-voiced and reputedly a total abstainer from both liquor and tobacco. His feud with the Harcourts had been brewing quite a while before that spring day in 1893 when he shot Steve Harcourt. Politics was somehow mixed up in it, just as it was in some of the more famous Kentucky feuds (on election day in Seney votes and smashed skulls and stolen ballots were a drink a dozen). Involved also in the feud were various rumored items concerning illicit traffic and a tie-in with the authorities. It seems to have summed up to the old saw about this place not being big enough for the two of us, curse you. At any rate, Steve Harcourt died of his wounds, and thenceforward in Seney either you were a Harcourt man or a Dunn man, and you fought about it nightly.

While the feud boiled, Dan Dunn started back up to Seney from Manistique under a bond to keep the peace. On the way, changing trains at Trout Lake, he stepped into a saloon (just why he did this is not explained by his champions who claim he was a teetotaler). Into the same saloon came Jim Harcourt, brother of the dead Steve and, like Dunn, it is said, also under the persuasion of the sore-beset authorities who were trying to keep the peace. Precisely what happened then is not clear, although the saloon would have been a crowded place if all the persons who claim to have been present actually had been. Some witnesses later recalled that Dunn reached into his pocket for his "pocketbook," as a wallet frequently is called in Upper Michigan; the defense witnesses testified that they, presumably like Jim Harcourt, thought Dunn was reaching for his gun. At any rate, Jim Harcourt shot Dan Dunn dead. Though he pleaded self-defense, Jim Harcourt was convicted of manslaughter and sentenced to the prison at Marquette. At least one of his brothers spent a lot of money trying to get him out, legend says, but in the end, just as the old song runs, it was Jim's lovely red-haired wife who got him a parole. A long petition signed by many residents of School-craft County may have had something to do with it too. Subsequently Jim was elected clerk of Seney Township and then township supervisor, an office he filled with distinction.

Seney's other famous crime was the murder of Tim Kaine. Kaine already had won fame as one of the great rough-and-tumble fighters in the pineries. Years earlier John Dugan, reputedly a slave-driving camp boss, had knocked him down with a canthook when he asked for time off. Kaine swore vengeance, but Dugan went home to Canada. Kaine became boss. Four years passed. Then one day Kaine saw Dugan alight from the noon train in Seney. Theirs has been described as the greatest jack battle of all. A crowd gathered quickly around them as they fought up and down the muddy street, for everybody knew Tim Kaine had waited four years for this. It was toe-to-toe slugging, granite fists hammering like ax bits, and when a man went down, he scrambled to his feet quickly no matter how badly he was hurt, for every jack in the woods feared the sharp steel calks of boots in his face. More than an hour, the legend says, they fought until both were bloody and exhausted. Finally Kaine finished the battle with a single blow. His friends had to drag him off Dugan. He picked up his coat and led the crowd to a saloon, where, of course, he bought a drink around.

Thereafter he was a hero to all, apparently, but Isaac Stetcher, who worked in a logging camp that Kaine was running. The company rule was that a man who quit his job before the winter's work ended would be docked two dollars per month. This was designed to halt drifting from camp to camp. Stetcher quit the day before Christmas and resented being docked. Most of the men went to Seney that night, and, after dark, John Bellaire donned a Santa Claus suit and, in a sleigh bedecked with jangling bells, drove from house to house. He saw the bartender throw Isaac Stetcher out of Hugh Logan's saloon. Stetcher disappeared down the board sidewalk. In a moment Tim Kaine, apparently looking for Stetcher, stepped out of the saloon. Stetcher leaped from a dark alleyway and knifed him in the back. Kaine was carried into the saloon and died almost at once. The crowd muttered about lynching Stetcher, but Sheriff Tom McCann rescued him. Subsequently he was sentenced to serve seven and a half years in prison.

Brawling was chronic at Seney. But most of the jacks fought

just for the hell of it. They drank, they chased women, they fought; grown men, powerful men, they were like boys, boyishly proud of their great strength, boyishly loyal to their champions. Their amusements included playing poker and betting on cock fights and betting on who could carry the biggest log or who could buck a log faster; they even would watch a baseball game, and a few of them, their footsteps befogged by liquor no doubt, even found their way to Peterson's Opera House in Escanaba, where they hooted raucously when the villain chased Eliza across the ice. But their greatest pleasure lay in brawling.

One giant of a man who never had lost a fight hired a farmer's rig and drove the twenty-eight miles to Seney to pick a fight, taking a small boy with him for company. Arriving one Sunday morning—an auspicious time, since it was too early in the day for the jacks in town to be weakened overmuch by drink—he went into the main saloon and found fifteen or twenty men at the bar taking their morning facemakers, as the hair of the dog is called in Upper Michigan. Our hero bought a drink for the house, and the bartender came right back, and then our hero said loudly: "I hear you've got some tough men around here," and he wiped his mouth with his hand and said: "Hear you have to chain 'em up when a stranger comes to town." The bartender put down his bar cloth, leaned on the bar, and fixed the stranger with his gaze, saying: "I don't know about that, but we've got some pretty good men around here."

By that time, recalls our hero's boy companion, now a middle-aged man, "a fellow in the crowd was dustin' the linen, you know, peelin' the coat." Up he stepped and said: "I guess you're lookin' for trouble, stranger," and our hero replied: "That's what I druv twenty-eight miles for, but have a drink first." So each bought a drink and then they fought for twenty minutes, smashing furniture with their enormous tumbling, straining bodies. Our hero won, bought a drink for the house, then took on a second challenger, whom he licked in ten minutes; then, after appropriate fortification, a third, whom he licked in five. By this time he was getting warmed up and wanted some real action. But no matter how he taunted the Seney boys, none would take him on. So, telling them to pick out their toughest pal "and send him over—

I'll hire a rig for him so he won't get tired walkin' the twenty-eight miles," he went back home, having proved his point, which was, as his boy companion now says, that "Seney wasn't so tough unless seven or eight jacks could gang up on a man or shoot him or crack him on the head with a canthook." The name of our hero, his friend adds with a mournful shake of the head, cannot now be revealed, for "I don't know what got into him. He's got religious and that's all you ever can get out of him. He used to be a good man, too."

One of Seney's great fighters was Silver Jack Driscoll, a man so legendary that it is almost impossible to separate the facts of his life from the fiction. Indeed, there were various Silver Jacks in the pineries at one time or another. The one generally assumed to be the original left Seney about 1893, having established an enduring reputation as a Bunyanesque brawler and lumberjack. He went to the western part of the Upper Peninsula, where he drove pine for a time on the Yellow Dog up north of Silver Lake, then went on to L'Anse. Here, it is said, he made periodic trips from L'Anse alone on foot into the wild inaccessible Huron Mountains, which, lying north of the Yellow Dog and the Marquette iron range, are not traversed even today by any road. After an absence of weeks he would return to L'Anse, his pack laden with huge nuggets of gold and silver. Men around L'Anse got him drunk whenever possible in an effort to learn where he had found the riches. They even attempted to follow him on the trail, but so great a woodsman was he that none could match his pace. When he died in bed in 1895—he had been ill, but was only pretending to be dead as a joke when his heart stopped—the location of his bonanza still was a secret and remains one to this day.

Black Jack McDonald, Roaring Jimmy Gleason, Tea Pot Kelly, Handsome Jack, Runaway Shea, Buck Pete, Blue Jay, Felix, Protestant Bob McGuire, Stuttering Jim Gallagher, Pump Handle Joe, Stub Foot O'Connell, Fighting Jim Morrison, Frying Pan Mag—they were some of the men who thronged Seney's streets and saloons. Old Light Heart slept in two sugar barrels placed end to end and lived on raw beef livers; his toes had been amputated because of frostbite, and when he got drunk, Seney's comedians nailed the toes of his shoes to the wooden sidewalk so he would pitch forward on his face when he tried to stand up. In Phil Grondin's hotel the drunken jacks slept off jags three to a bed; those who preferred the floor were crowded into a big bare room called the ram pasture. The town had its enigmatic cultured Southern colonel who, it was whispered, had left home because of some lurid scandal and who now, when in his cups, declaimed the *Iliad* and *Odyssey* in the original Greek, standing at Hugh Logan's bar and beating time with a bung starter. And it had, too, its angel of mercy, an optimistic young lady of uplift who ran a log-cabin mission in a near-by town and strove valiantly to save the damned souls of the roisterers.

It had also P. K. Small, a lumberjack who had retired permanently to the saloons, where, for a drink, he bit off the heads of snakes, toads, or frogs; overreaching himself, he bit off the head of Frank O'Brien's pet owl, and Frank knocked him senseless with a canthook when Small handed the headless bird back to him. Justice prevailed; his opponent in a saloon brawl bit off the end of Small's nose. For a couple of drinks Small and Paddy Joyce "held up" the noon passenger with useless pistols; forewarned of Seney's toughness, women fainted and traveling men dived under the seats, where they remained until trainmen disarmed the two pranksters.

It was Paddy Joyce who had the unhappy experience with the pump. Penniless and with a hangover, he had a great thirst and so, in his extremity, turned to the town pump. He forgot to prime it and, of course, it wouldn't work. After laboring futilely for a time, he stood back and, gazing mournfully at the pump, spoke these deathless lines: "I don't blame you for not giving me any water, you old bastard; I only come to you when I'm broke."

The harassed Seney bartenders had to scurry mightily to find the keys to their establishments when, during a political upheaval, the authorities ordered all saloons closed down. On the second day of the drought one of the logging bosses hammered on the door of Hughie Logan's saloon crying: "For God's sake open up; the boys'll ruin the drive; they're drinking the river dry."

Two stories, clouded by time, surround the arrival of William Jennings Bryan in Seney. One relates that, having heard the great man did not intend to stop at Seney, his admirers there placed torpedoes on the railroad track to halt the train; forewarned, the engineer roared right on through, and when a Negro porter stuck his head out of a vestibule window to see what all the excitement was about, the jubilant crowd mistook him for the Commoner and cheered riotously. The other version says that Bryan actually did stop and went through a rather trying experience due to the white collar which he sported innocently enough.

Perhaps Seney's most infamous resident was Leon Czolgosz. As a young man he came to the hell town from down below and worked a summer in a section gang on the Manistique railroad. He was not notably a roughneck; indeed, old-timers say scornfully that Seney was too tough for him. But he distinguished himself in a way none of them so much as dreamed of. He went down to Cleveland, listened to one of Emma Goldman's fiery speeches about the working classes, then, inflamed, proceeded to Buffalo, where, on September 6, 1901, he shot President McKinley dead.

As the years passed in riot and confusion, Seney's reputation spread across the country. Newspaper writers came to examine this Gomorrah in the pines, and one of them told a story that will not down. In Seney, she wrote, painted women were kept locked in an outdoor stockade, where huge mastiffs were constantly on guard. The story shocked right thinkers everywhere and resulted in numerous indignant demands for a cleanup, but nothing much happened. Today old-timers explain that the story was planted on the lady writer—that is, certain Seney pranksters, knowing she was hunting lurid copy, invented some for her. But this stockade story is troublesome; although it appears impossible to run to earth anyone who actually ever saw with his own eyes such an outré establishment, the story bobs up at various places in the north country.

Seney's red flame flickered out fast. About 1894, a dozen years after the town was built, the Alger, Smith Company extended its railroad up north to Grand Marais, on the shore of Lake Superior. The company moved its large mill from down below to Grand Marais. The logging camps near Seney were abandoned, for the pine was all cut out. New camps sprang up farther north; Grand Marais boomed, though it never became a second Seney. Gradually the homes and saloons, the stores and whorehouses at Seney gathered dust, the prostitutes and professional gamblers departed.

The wind whispered like a ghostly voice in the empty buildings. Forests that once rang with the roar of breaking rollways became still. Grass grew in the streets that had been thronged with drunken jacks and their women. Once, on this door that now swings idly on broken hinges, a lumberjack with a hangover hammered and bellowed: "Open the god-damn door and give us a drink" in a voice heard all the way to Germfask, eight miles south, startling a dozing bartender there and causing him to drag out a bottle hurriedly. Now the voices are stilled, the men and their women departed. A filling station, a little hotel, a railroad station, a portable sawmill handling second-growth timber, weed-grown building foundations—nothing more remains of the glory that was Seney. As a crowning blow, the Federal Government has a project to rehabilitate the place: it will make of Seney's hinterland a waterfowl refuge.

LIFE AND DEATH
OF A COMPANY TOWN

৺

AFTER CHURCH the lumberjacks and sawmill hands came into Joe's tavern and started arguing about who had the best victory garden. Few of them were young: "The Selective Service says it'd a damn sight sooner have lumberjacks from up here than soda jerks from Detroit." Many of the men who were left in Hermansville in the summer of 1943 were beyond draft age or had lost fingers in the buzzing saws of the mill. Mangled hands and stooped backs broken by falling trees or crashing ore are common throughout Upper Michigan. The town was not dead, but it was dying fast.

David Downey, who came to the company town and helped lay out its streets in 1887, said he'd never seen the place so deserted. The vast sprawling lumber yards were almost emptied; you could see right through them. The mills were shut down. The flooring factory was far from peak production. The sawmill pond was empty.

"You can't get no logs," one foreman complained. "You can't get nobody to work in the woods. There ain't much timber left anyway, but what there is, you can't get nobody to cut it."

The vast pine and hardwood forests had become, in sixty-odd years, farmland and wasteland. The Wisconsin Land & Lumber Company, a giant whose trademark IXL had been famed for years throughout the nation, was just about all cut out. Hermansville, the neat little clean little company town it built, was just about "all caught up."

The men and women in the tavern didn't talk about this much,

153

probably because it wasn't very real yet. Hermansville had been here so long, the houses and the hotel and the stores and post office seemed so permanent to these people, that not until the very day they were told to move would the death of the company town become real. Some of them had come here from the old country; this had been their only home in America. Here they had learned to speak English, here they had borne and reared their children, here they had become a part of America. That this should end was inconceivable.

They went to Joe St. Jiuliana's neat, clean tavern and drank beer—no hard liquor on Sundays in Michigan—and listened to the juke box play tunes like *Rosie the Riveter* and *By the Light of the Silvery Moon*. The music was jazz and cowboy ballads, about equally divided; despite the numerous foreign-born patrons, there were none of the schottisches and polkas here that were so common elsewhere in Upper Michigan; Hermansville was progressive. The tavern was light and airy, with cream-colored walls and a family room containing shiny-topped tables and red leather and chrome chairs. Venetian blinds covered the windows, and punch-boards and Kewpie dolls lay on the back bar. A poster above the bar urged the purchase of war bonds and a Northwest Airlines advertisement displayed an airplane flying over a logging camp. Beer cost a nickel a glass and ice cream for the kids also was five cents. The large crowd was orderly and included a number of wives and some children. There was no brawling and little rough talk. Definitely this was no lumberjacks' saloon, with pictures of nudes behind the bar, a poker table in the corner and drunks in the sawdust on the floor. Yet virtually every man in the place was a jack or a sawmill hand.

The explanation lies not wholly in the date—1943. Elsewhere in Upper Michigan old-time loggers' saloons survive little changed from the hell-roaring days. No, the explanation of the peace in Joe's tavern lies in the character of Hermansville itself.

If Seney was vicious and now is bedraggled, Hermansville was busy and now is quiet. It always has been neat and orderly. Its homes are well-painted, its streets broad, its hotel clean, its tempo even and unhurried. Apparently Hermansville never had a whore-house or an overabundance of saloons. It is a company town, owned lock, stock, and barrel by IXL. The career of its builder personifies the American dream. Somehow the town compressed its rough-handed lumberjacks into the same mold.

It is hard to realize that so orderly a place had a beginning similar to Seney's. A tract of pine, timber cruisers, a booming town, lonely tar-paper logging camps, skid roads, and river drives —all of them were here. One of Hermansville's pioneers was David Downey, a man whose life is curiously split into halves. He is part typical smug company man, part free-spirited woodsman.

Born in Canada, Downey calls himself a "Duke's Mixture" of Scotch and Irish. He started working in the woods when he was eleven years old. His father died and David went down to Michigan. He was hired as a teamster for "a dollar a day and board myself" when he hit Bay City, which with its twin, Saginaw, was the bawdiest place in the Lower Peninsula and probably in all of Michigan. (Seney was still wilderness.) Soon David Downey went on to Upper Michigan, where he worked at a furnace making pig iron. Presently he returned to Canada and was married at Barrie, Ontario, on St. Patrick's Day and the dust was flying in the street outside the church, but a few weeks later, when he brought his bride to Hermansville, two feet of snow lay on the streets.

Hermansville was less than ten years old when David Downey arrived and became a woods boss and cruised the timber that built the IXL empire. The great surveyors preceded Downey by only about forty years. As a timber cruiser he used their field notes constantly; above all men, he appreciates their greatness. He has been there. The job of a timber cruiser, or landlooker, is to go into the woods and estimate the kind and amount of timber on a given tract of land. This cannot be a rough estimate, for on it is based the price that the cruiser's employer pays for the land. It must be accurate beyond belief. That any man can go into a tangled, broken territory stretching for miles in each direction, part of it fine dense stands of virgin timber, part tamarack swamp, part cutover or burntover plains, part rocky wasteland and lake region—that any man can cruise through such an area, bedeviled by mosquitoes and cold and rain and natural obstacles, and come out with an estimate only a few hundred board feet off the final count is almost inconceivable. Yet it is done daily in Upper Michigan. In the

1940's the timber cruiser is the only living direct descendant of William Austin Burt.

On the basis of Downey's estimates the company has bought thousands of acres. Now as he goes over his plat books and field notes and maps and compasses, his face softens; he is remembering. Remembering the days when, alone or with a single compassman, he spent all summer of every year out in the woods. As soon as the ice was out in the spring, he assembled his outfit. It differed little from Burt's, except that the peas were canned. Never any mosquito dope for David Downey: "Them little things don't hurt." (But most cruisers carry mosquito repellent and argue loudly about the best brand; many prepare their own.) Into the woods he would go. Perhaps he had a tract of several square miles to cruise. His first task was to locate its corner. This, of course, involved finding the section-corner stake or tree marked in the surveyor's field notes. Sometimes the section corner had been inadequately marked, its landmark had long since disappeared. Or perhaps the original survey had been inaccurate. In these cases Downey had to pick up the township and range lines and rerun them to the corner.

Having located the corner, Downey sent his compassman precisely 177 paces northwest. This put him one tally (125 paces) in from each line of the corner forty. There are sixteen forties in a section. Then Downey started north on the line, counting the trees sixteen and a half feet into the forty. He walked north two tallies, which brought him to the northern boundary of the forty; he then walked two tallies west, which brought him to its west boundary; then two south, then two back east, to the starting point. And here he sat down with his back against a tree and did some figuring.

He had marked down the kind, number, and size of trees in his notebook as he walked along. (He didn't use a real notebook, but only a schoolboy's writing tablet tied together with string.) He had listed the height and d.b.h.—diameter at breast height, 4.5 feet —of each tree. Say he had found ten maples. They would cut perhaps two or two and a half logs to the tree, according to the tree's quality and size. Say they ran, in this forty, two to the tree. That's twenty maple logs, and it would take eleven logs to the thousand board feet. Now say he had eight basswood; being taller, they would cut three logs to the tree, a total of twenty-four logs; they would run ten logs to the thousand. He also had two elm trees which would make four logs. Now he figured it all up. Totaling his board feet, he divided by two, for he had estimated about two acres in the forty acres and, on this particular forty, the timber would not vary greatly. Having figured the board feet per acre, he multiplied by forty and arrived at the total board feet that could be cut out of this forty-acre tract—perhaps 300,000, which probably is, incidentally, above the average these days in Upper Michigan.

That took care of one forty. Then Downey went on to the next and repeated the process; and so on until he had taken a sampling of the entire tract of land. On some forties, of course, allowance must be made for lakes, swamps, burntover areas, while some forties were nearly uniform.

At the end of a day's work Downey selected his camp site. It must be on high ground so a sudden squall wouldn't soak him, and it must be among small trees in case of a windstorm. Having pitched his square tent, he built his fire in front of it (but not too close) and, while supper was cooking, collected balsam boughs for a bed. Usually he paused for a drink, half a teaspoonful of Jamaica ginger, strong with alcohol, and half a teaspoonful of sugar in a tin cup of water from a near-by stream, for the water might not be safe to drink. He had heard somewhere that Jamaica ginger kills germs; and, besides, it tasted good after a hard day's work in the woods.

Darkness came soon after supper. In the brief twilight Downey worked on his notes. They were not all statistics. He was mapping the country as he went, showing contours and topographical features. "I'd come to a swamp or a piece of high ground and I'd shade it on my map. God, I used to like that shading." It was the best part of the day in lots of ways, that hour or so after supper before dark.

If the next day was wet, he might spend it fishing. But if it was fine, he would go on with his cruising. Every two weeks or so, if he happened to be near a railroad, he would flag down a section gang's handcar, hop a ride to the nearest town, and go home for a day or two with his wife. Then back into the woods again.

In one respect his task was more difficult than Burt's. The early surveyors had worked in clean virgin forests, where often the foliage of the forest giants was so thick that it kept the sun from the earth, thus preventing undergrowth; but by the time Downey did his cruising, pine had been logged out of many sections and the slashings remained in enormous tangles, mingling with the under-brush to bar his way. In any event, his was hard work, cruising day after day with a hundred-pound pack on his back. And it was not always safe work. One calm, clear day Downey was cruising a rough hillside when he heard a high-pitched roar off to the south-west. Turning, he saw the trees by the swamp below bending to the earth before a furious freakish wind that was sweeping up the valley. Onward it came, and suddenly it turned and started to climb the hillside, wrenching enormous trees up by their roots, leveling everything in its path. Downey dived into a root hole be-neath an old pine and crouched there while the wind roared above him. He heard the warning crack of a falling tree, saw a giant maple toppling, covered his head, crouched deeper into the hole. Down came the great maple, and then another, atop the pine roots that protected him. But though earth showered him as in a shell-torn dugout, his shelter held. A moment later the wind was gone, howling farther away through the woods. Uninjured, Downey clambered out of his storm cellar. There was no more standing timber to cruise; the storm had cut a swath five hundred feet wide through the forest as neatly as a mowing machine cuts through wheat.

Rarely did Downey see any humans while he was cruising, for cruising was done more often than not in completely uninhabited regions. But now and then he ran across a squatter, and squatters in Upper Michigan, like squatters everywhere, are not altogether friendly. One such refused Downey and his compassman a drink of water from his well on the hottest day of the summer and drove them away from his lonely cabin at rifle-point.

Downey saw Hermansville grow from a collection of shacks in the woods into a neat modern town. Its founder was Charles J. L. Meyer. About 1878 pine was getting scarce in the Winnebago Valley in north central Wisconsin where he was lumbering, so

Meyer sent a timber cruiser to Upper Michigan. At that time the Hamilton & Merryman Company owned, in Menominee County, what was considered the best pine tract in the Lake Michigan country. Just as the pine kings were doing farther east near Seney, H. & M. was cutting the pine vigorously and driving it down the little streams that emptied into the Menominee and Escanaba Rivers. Into this boiling activity Meyer stepped, and bit by bit he pieced together the beginnings of a timber empire, making his first purchase on August 1, 1878, in Section 2, Town 38, Range 27, where he built a town and named it Hermansville after his younger son.

This still was wilderness. In 1872, the Chicago & Northwestern Railroad had started to clear a right-of-way west of Powers toward the Menominee Range, the new iron district that was opening up. But the Breen Mine, first lodestone, didn't pay out at first, and hard times hit the nation in 1873. Not until canny Charles Meyer, seeing the return of good times, entered Upper Michigan in 1878 was work on the railroad resumed. Spurred by improved prospects at the Breen and other mines on the Menominee Range, the railroad laid tracks to Hermansville and beyond, all the way to Quinnesec, a mining camp near Iron Mountain. Early in 1879 Meyer built a sawmill at Hermansville and shipped, on May 26, a carload of shingles down to a Wisconsin dealer, J. Weber & Sons, accompanying it with a letter expressing hope that this "first car of the Michigan Product will prove satisfactory." Apparently it did. Forty-six years later Weber & Sons still had an open account with Meyer's company.

Quickly Hermansville acquired a store, a meat market, and an icehouse. For the jacks and mill hands a boarding house was built, and subsequently private homes. Men came so fast there weren't enough houses, and some of them lived temporarily in abandoned charcoal ovens, huge conical masonry structures. Streets were laid out. Meyer bought land in huge chunks and tiny parcels throughout Upper Michigan. Ultimately his company's holdings approximated 100,000 acres spread over eight counties.

Hermansville was Meyer's first love and the capital of this vast lumber empire. To its mills came most of the hardwood this side of the Menominee. It was a company town in the purest sense.

The company owned the land, cleared it, pushed hills into ravines, filled the swamp, graded the roads. On the land it built the mills, built the houses and the school and the community center and the recreation hall and the office buildings and the post office and the hotel and the landscaped houses of the lumber barons. Charles Meyer created Hermansville.

After the winter's cut was finished, some of the jacks came back to staid, quiet Hermansville to live among the mill hands and their families, and some headed for the saloons and the girl beer-slingers of Menominee and Marinette, or maybe Escanaba. As the Menominee Range opened up, Iron River competed for the pleasure trade, as did other towns. But not Hermansville. Nor can Hermansville recall the brave days when there were sixty saloons on Main Street. George Orr, thwarted at Manistique, would have loved Hermansville. The good people got the upper hand in the beginning and they never let go.

They had great plans for Hermansville, in the early days. They laid out First Street a hundred feet wide. When the Spalding Township school board refused to build a school at the new town, Meyer forthwith built a school of his own, imported a teacher from down below and a few years later cut Meyer Township loose from Spalding.

Hermansville took care of its own. Paternalism appeared early. The grave of a faithful night watchman who died and was buried at Hermansville is still kept green. E. P. Radford bought cheaply from Meyer an eighty-acre tract he fancied and, having worked his way up from surveyor to vice-president of the company, re-tired to a 1,300-acre farm. As it should be in a feudal fief, justice at Hermansville was dispensed in a manner contrasting sharply with the tumultuous goings-on at Seney. One night, while the company blacksmith was reading in the boarding house on Park and First Streets, a vociferous drunk came in and wanted to talk. The blacksmith ignored him. The drunk persisted. The black-smith, a brawny but quiet and peaceable man, moved to another chair. The drunk followed. The blacksmith warned him, then hit him, breaking his neck with a single blow. Radford ordered the deputy sheriff to lock the body in the jail for the night and sent the blacksmith to his room. Subsequently a judge in Menominee discharged the blacksmith, enjoining him to remember that he was a blacksmith, accustomed to striking iron.

Except for a rutted wagon road through the woods, the railroad was Hermansville's only link with the outside world. This, of course, contributed to its insularity. In the early years it fought its numerous fires with its own volunteer fire department. The company ran its own dairy for two years because its "people had to have milk." Undaunted by the dairy's failure, Meyer, an exuberant experimenter and hard-headed believer in his own ideas, built a hog barn. He imported a carload of plump, well-bred hogs and turned them loose in the elaborately-appointed basement. But despite Meyer's loving care and the best provender that money could buy, they pined for the sunlight and sickened and died. This experiment cost Meyer $1,393.73.

Another was more expensive. An impatient man, Meyer never could find mill machinery that would chew up timber fast enough to suit him. So he designed his own machinery and mill for making railroad ties and built it, in 1883, at a cost of $10,676.90. After weeks of careful planning and construction under Meyer's personal supervision, the wheels were started turning. In a flash the first finished tie came whizzing through the rollers, flew through the air, smashed through the end of the mill and out into the swamp, where it buried itself several feet in the muck. Adjustments were made. But the difficulty remained; the trouble wasn't that the complicated contraption wouldn't work, but that it worked too well. Mill hands agile enough to dodge the flying timbers could not be hired. Known as Meyer's folly, the magnificent white elephant never was used.

But some of Meyer's other numerous inventions did prove valuable. He designed much of his own machinery, and when the pine was gone, he pioneered in the manufacture of hardwood flooring, the tongued-and-grooved and matched IXL brand which became famous in the lumber trade. More than anything else, this use of timber which had been scorned by the early lumberjacks sets Meyer and his successors apart from so many other lumbermen. Many of the early loggers, without big immovable investments, could afford to follow the pine. IXL was anchored to Hermansville by the money it had sunk there.

Meyer developed machinery for working the flinty Lake Superior rock maple. By the time David Downey arrived, the pine was nearly gone. You can't drive hardwood; it's not buoyant enough. So logging assumed new contours. Downey was in the thick of the change-over.

The jacks still cut their trees down with axes and, later, saws; they still inhabited, winter-long, tar-paper shacks lighted by kerosene lamps, still slept on board bunks cushioned with hemlock or balsam boughs. The difference came when it was time to get the logs to the mill. Instead of breaking rollways along the riverbanks, the jacks loaded the enormous hardwood logs on wagons or railroad flatcars. This they accomplished, in the early days, by "decking" the logs on a downhill grade above the roadbed so that, in effect, they broke the rollway and the logs tumbled down on the flatcar or wagon. But appropriate locations were not always available. Sometimes the logs were pulled up onto the cars by means of a chain and swamp-hook rigged to a stout team. This was slow, difficult work. So the Austrian loader was devised, a derrick that hoisted the logs from level ground to the cars. Other improvements were made later.

All this meant that wagon roads and railroads were needed. The company built the Hermansville & Western Railroad at a cost of nearly $50,000. Its standard-gauge tracks wandered more than ten miles south and west into the woods from Hermansville, an improbable Toonerville in the hills and thickets. When the jacks had finished cutting in a forty, they tore up the railroad and moved it to another stand of timber. One time they moved the whole shooting match clear over to Alger County. But nowadays the road only runs around the company's lumber yards at Hermansville.

The loads that the jacks piled on the wagons were almost frightening. The various camps tried to outdo each other in sending the biggest load to the mill. Once David Downey's camp sent in the biggest load of all, towering so high above the groaning wagon that they had to take down the telegraph wires to get it across the railroad tracks. That load scaled 13,362 board feet.

Downey, being a foreman, was able to leave camp nearly every Saturday night to spend the weekend with his bride in their new home at Hermansville. You can't get men today like those old-time jacks, Downey says. Time was when the boys'd stay in the woods all winter before they headed for Thomas Street in Escanaba. But nowadays you're lucky if your men'll stay in camp till Saturday night. Soon's they get a few dollars in their pockets, they head for a saloon. Now at least half of them around Hermansville own a little piece of land and do some farming or work on highway construction jobs in the summer and only go into the woods in the winter. The rest are mostly transients.

Downey ran camp for IXL for eight winters. Summers he was a foreman around the lumber yards. Out of his experiences he collected a set of pat ideas that symbolize Hermansville's smug success. "The cheaper you can do a job for your concern, the more they'll think of you, and the faster they'll advance you. That's why I been woods superintendent forty-nine years." He was good to his company; his company was good to him. He was one of three men who kept on working during the company's only major strike. He labored diligently for many years; now he can retire honorably whenever he wishes.

If ever a man lived the American dream, George Washington Earle did. Born to modest circumstances in 1849, he worked diligently, saved soberly, invested prudently, and fortune smiled on him. He married well and became a lumber baron. His mark is on the town.

Born in Truxton Valley, in central New York State, Earle was the youngest of twelve children. His grandfathers had fought in the Revolution under George Washington. When he was six, his father took him west, to Illinois, where he was building a railroad across the prairie. George worked for a hard-bitten, taciturn farmer, attending school four months out of the year, investing his meager chore-boy's pay in lands, and returning east to put himself through medical college at Buffalo by shearing sheep and haying during summer vacations. He also overcame the handicap of ill health. After practicing medicine successfully in a little York State town for fourteen years, he went on an extended trip to Europe, in the course of which he met the daughter of Charles J. L. Meyer. In 1888 Earle married her.

At his father-in-law's invitation, Earle went to Hermansville in August 1889. He intended only to rest there a year. But his son, G. Harold Earle, was less than a month old when, on December 13, 1889, a day remembered as Black Friday in Fond du Lac and Oshkosh and Hermansville, Meyer, overexpanded, was forced to make an assignment of all his holdings. Hard times were overtaking the nation. Meyer was squeezed. He sold his best remaining pine stumpage to raise cash. He was gratified to see the Mormons use his finished maple flooring in their famed temple at Salt Lake City, but he lacked the money to develop the product properly. On July 30, while driving from his office in Oshkosh to the Northwestern depot, his horse shied at a windblown scrap of paper; the buggy wheel struck the curb and Meyer was thrown to the pavement. He never recovered his health fully. Earle treated him and, not quite forty years old, took over the company's problems.

Interest on the company's bonds was past due; the trustee had been asked to foreclose. Earle succeeded in saving the old homestead, but not before a windstorm and fire had wrecked the Number One Mill, the pine lumber yard had burned, the bondholders had sold much of Meyer's vast domain, including 133 farms, and the trustee had offered to sell for $100,000 the whole outfit, which represented a million-dollar cash investment.

Earle, in buying the company from the trustees, formed a co-operative association and offered stock to the employees. Few wanted any. Things looked bad for IXL, for this whole bloody north country. The big operators all around were selling out their cutover land and heading for the west coast. Seney was finished, Grand Marais was just about all caught up. In a few years Hermansville too would be a ghost town. Who wanted to invest in its future?

Almost nobody except the New York physician. He settled his wife and their three sons—one died in infancy—at Hermansville and set out to try to maintain his father-in-law's dream of grandeur. Suddenly the capricious barometer of logging moved upward. Maple stumpage became scarce in the Lower Peninsula, and about the same time hardwood flooring and hardwood furniture became best sellers. A rush commenced to Upper Michigan. Earle, riding the wave, bought land. When land prices outstripped him, he bought logs from small jobbers who cut the timber. Thus he anticipated, in the early 1900's, the whole pattern of modern lumbering, for few giant companies today maintain lumberjack crews. They simply operate mills and hire small jobbers to do their cutting in the woods.

IXL prospered. Before he died, in 1908, Charles Meyer had seen his town of Hermansville undisturbed by the banking panic of 1907, had seen his IXL company become a leader in Upper Michigan.

One of Earle's large land acquisitions was that of the Blaney purchase, some 33,000 acres in Schoolcraft County not far south of Seney. By 1926, three years after Earle died and left control of the IXL company to his sons, G. Harold and Stewart Edward Earle, Blaney was all cut out. What to do with Blaney? Salvage what little could be sold for farmland and let the rest go tax-delinquent? This was the customary procedure. Or try some new scheme to make Blaney self-supporting?

Private reforestry was considered and rejected. By the time newly planted trees grew to marketable size on the cutover land, taxes and other expenses would long since have eaten up any potential lumbering profits. Cattle-raising had been tried unsuccessfully. But the area, like almost any area of comparable size in Upper Michigan, contained numerous lakes and streams, tracts of second-growth woodland, picturesque scenic spots. G. Harold Earle determined to develop Blaney into a resort.

The name of the place was changed to Blaney Park. Fresh scrubbed tourist cabins replaced old tar-paper lumberjack camps. The old-time saloon came down and a cocktail lounge was built in the new central lodge. A golf course, tennis courts, shuffleboard courts, a swimming pool with underwater lighting—all the paraphernalia of vacationing was provided. The management arranged touches of local color somewhat grimly: a road icer, an Austrian loading derrick, and other lumberjack equipment was parked in "Paul Bunyan's Camp." Streams and lakes were stocked with game fish, and deer were propagated; bridle paths were cut through the woods where the lumberjacks had cried "Timber-r-r-r!" There even was a Blaney Airport. Today Blaney is an established resort. It also is IXL's largest single remaining holding. The empire that Meyer built and George Washington Earle rescued has fallen apart, though Hermansville, its heart, survives.

The mill hands have moved from the company boarding house to company houses; many have bought their homes from the company. Those who still rent from the company pay from seven to fourteen dollars a month. The company houses are maintained better than many company houses in Upper Michigan. The company also owns a hotel, which is operated under lease by a private party. Single men living there pay $1.25 or $1.35 a day for room and board. The hotel, which appears scrubbed, is busy most of the time, especially during deer season, when hunters stop there, and around the Fourth of July, when men arrive to corral the foxes that are raised on a near-by fox farm. The hotel rooms are ordinary and are furnished with Gideon Bibles, pictures of babies in blue, washbowls but no private baths, and rocking-chairs and brass beds. The hotel is a remodeled boarding house and supplants a huge old brick hotel, now fallen into disuse, a ghost-haunted relic of Hermansville's boom days. In 1942–3 the vast community hall, built by a workers' co-operative, was not used either.

Mill hands at Hermansville were paid in 1943 from 47½ cents an hour for common labor up to $1.07½ an hour for a filer. Actual logging in the woods was done on a piece-work basis by lumberjacks working not for the IXL company but for small jobbers. A good jack could average, in 1943, around $7 a day and he might earn up to $18. In the old days they received $30 a month plus board. (But in the old days they didn't have to worry about rationed meat, which is a real problem to the camp cooks who have to feed voracious lumberjacks.)

By and large, Hermansville has not seen, so far, the hectic ups and downs that have afflicted so many company towns and other small Upper Michigan communities. Its population has not dropped from three thousand to three hundred, like that of Seney or Michigamme. Its residents have been home-owners, not transient pine followers. Many came to Hermansville direct from the old country. The French and Swedes worked in the woods, the Austrians and Italians in the mills. Each nationality had its own settlement. When one man came here from Italy, he couldn't speak English; now he is foreman of the factory. The father of Joe St. Jiuliana, proprietor of Joe's tavern, came from northern Italy, where the land was so crowded that the villagers had to take their cows up into the mountains to pasture. Joe's father came to Hermansville, where a friend had preceded him. He worked both in the woods and in the mill, and he ran a store, and Joe converted the store into a tavern.

It is hard to explain why the Italians came to Upper Michigan. In their homeland are neither mines nor forests of great extent. Indeed, having seen nothing more rugged than olive groves, the early Italians were frightened by the huge dark forests here. But somehow they stuck; today they comprise a large portion of the populations of such iron-mining centers as Loretto and Vulcan and Norway on the Menominee Range. Chances are the matter can be explained by the fact that Italians, like the Irish, seem to go wherever in the world there is heavy labor to be done.

Is Hermansville dying? The lawns and gardens of the lumber barons, the Earles, are green as ever. The paint on the homes of the workers is fresh. But the mill is closed down, the yards are empty, the company has cut out and sold most of its land, except for Blaney Park. Nor, apparently, can it buy more land: much of what remains near by is held by other big companies, like the Oliver Iron Mining Company, and they will not sell. This may be the end which was foreshadowed in 1901 when Earle had to plant trees in the cutover desert surrounding his home.

If Hermansville dies as a lumbering town, it conceivably may revive as a farming community. Not far from it is some of the best farmland in Upper Michigan. About a third of Menominee County has been farmed. Here, as elsewhere in Upper Michigan, the best soil seems to have been found where the hardwood forests grew. After the loggers cut the trees, the farmers moved in. Indeed, in some cases it may be said that lumbermen were permitted to gut the forests by politicians anxious to encourage the immigration of a settled farm population.

Menominee County is the southernmost county of the Upper Peninsula. In the late thirties its farmers earned some $1,500,000 annually. Of this, dairy products brought in 66⅔ per cent, potatoes 12 per cent, sale of cattle and other livestock 10 per cent, eggs and poultry 6 per cent, sugar beets 1 per cent, and miscellaneous crops and other farm products 4⅓ per cent. Elsewhere in Upper Michigan such crops as hay, oats, barley, wheat, and rye are more important.

But the rigorous climate and the predominantly rocky or sandy soil handicaps farmers everywhere in Upper Michigan. While some research has indicated that the best crops are produced nearest the northern extremity of, for example, the wheat belt, it cannot be disputed that, generally, the short growing season militates against agriculture in the Upper Peninsula. True, isolated small areas of Upper Michigan have been farmed successfully for years; farmers have sent seed from here to all parts of the nation and have won state and other prizes for their produce; the percentage of farm tenancy in Upper Michigan is lower than for the state as a whole. None the less this simply is not farming country. In the early days visions of a vast agricultural economy to replace the vanishing lumber industry led simple men to attempt farming in hopeless circumstances. Little but disaster resulted from their bitter struggle against the encroaching wilderness, the hard climate, the poor soil, and the frost-erupted boulders. In more recent years efforts to farm marginal land have been abandoned. State experiment stations and co-operatives have encouraged scientific methods. The better land is farmed intensively. The Resettlement Administration has been active. As a consequence, farming is emerging as a relatively small yet substantial part of the Upper Peninsula's economy.

If timber and copper are vanishing now from Upper Michigan, iron remains. Iron is truly the Upper Peninsula's giant. They had been taking ore out of the Marquette Range around Ishpeming and Negaunee for thirty years before they started shipping much from the other two ranges, the Menominee and Gogebic. The Menominee lies not far west of Hermansville. And beyond that, at the very western end of Michigan, below the beetling Porcupines, lies the vast Gogebic Range. Wrapped into its story are the stories of U. S. Steel and of beauteous Lottie Morgan, one of the girls of Silver Street.

⤐ 12 ⤏

WEST TO THE GOGEBIC

THE WESTERN END of the Upper Peninsula was far from civilized when the Menominee and Gogebic iron ranges were opened up. Railroads and wagon roads had been built only in the copper country and on the Marquette iron range, the two islands of civilization in the vast wilderness. Elsewhere rivers still were the only roads, as they had been from the beginning. Along the main streams were stations, or stopping places, isolated deep in the woods, one kept by a widow woman, another by a Frenchman, another by an Irishman who lived with an Indian squaw in a log house at the mouth of the Sturgeon River. A few towns had been built on the coast between the iron and copper range, but the interior was wilderness. So many deer roamed it that it "resembled a sheep ranch." It was covered with heavy stands of white and Norway pine. Except for a few squatters, station keepers, trappers, and Indian traders, the only human inhabitants were Indians, who still were numerous.

The Menominee Range, second to be exploited on Lake Superior, is broken into three segments. Between it and the Marquette Range lie scattered ore beds. That ore occurred here was known to the surveyors of the forties, and as early as 1850 Government geologists went down the Michigamme River to the Paint and thence down to the Menominee. (This river system, lacing the broken range together as it does, remained for a long time the highway of discovery.) But during the excitement of

169

opening the Marquette Range, the Menominee Range was neglected.

Then suddenly in the sixties the explorers, called bush-whackers, thronged to this remote region. Some came up to it from the Menominee pine country, hunting timber; others came down to it from Ishpeming and Negaunee, hunting iron ore. They met at improbable trail crossings in the wilderness, fifty miles from any settlement. Misled by rumor and the raptures of ill-informed journalists, many were babes in the woods, totally unprepared for the rigors of the country. They got lost, they starved, their feet swelled enormously because, city-bred, they wore only tourists' thin-soled moccasins.

Some, better equipped and woods-wise, were successful. Bartley Breen located the first mine to be opened on the Menominee Range. John Armstrong, having grown restless keeping books in a Negaunee store, went into the woods and became the first man to wield a pick among the iron slates at the Paint River Falls. Solomon Curry helped open the Gogebic Range. John Buell hit a large vein of blue hematite near the future site of Iron Mountain. N. P. Hulst pioneered the Crystal Falls and Iron River district of the Menominee Range, and H. D. Fisher discovered the Florence Mine in the Wisconsin portion.

Raphael Pumpelly was not the first man on the Gogebic and Menominee Ranges, but he was one of the most colorful. His genteel speech contrasted strangely with the brimstone vocabulary of his colleague, Major T. B. Brooks; similarly anomalous were his expensive boots and hats and the gloves he invariably wore to protect his hands from the ore he was forced to handle. Pumpelly was about thirty years old when he came to Upper Michigan. Tall, blue-eyed, red-bearded, born to wealth, he had traveled widely in Europe, studied geology at Freiburg, developed some copper mines and dodged the Apache terror in Arizona, served as a geologist for the Japanese Emperor, crossed the Gobi Desert, and prospected in Mongolia and Siberia. Returning to the United States about 1866, he went to Upper Michigan to help select the lands which the Government had granted to the company that built the Portage Lake canal across the base of Keweenaw Peninsula. With an assistant and four Indians, he followed the trail of Foster and Whitney down the Michigamme. His intent was to explore for iron ore while other men cruised timber for the canal company. They lived in tents of unbleached sheeting and subsisted on a diet similar to Burt's.

Pumpelly had read William Austin Burt's field notes but he could not locate the ore that Burt had observed near the Crystal Falls of the Paint. Moreover, he found the geological formation here entirely different from that of the Marquette Range, with which he had familiarized himself. But finally he ran into Jack Armstrong, the ex-bookkeeper from Negaunee, who, for a thousand dollars, led Pumpelly to a bed of magnetic ore.

Sophisticated though he was, Pumpelly was impressed with the vicissitudes of this country. In his *Reminiscences* he wrote at length of the nests of hornets which, concealed in windfalls everywhere, attacked the landlookers constantly; of the arborvitæ swamps and mosquitoes; of slow progress and quaking bogs and dense growths of bush and briers in the big blowdowns. An Indian shocked him by presenting him with a misshapen potato resembling a phallus. He described enthusiastically the abundant sturgeon which lay beneath the high picturesque falls of the Menominee River and the jagged blocks of white quartzite, an iron-ore indication, that he observed in the long white-water rapids. He paddled "two hundred miles" down the Menominee, passing up en route an inhospitable section where later one of the range's richest mines was located.

Pumpelly married in the autumn of 1869 and spent a winter lecturing at Harvard. At the invitation of the state of Michigan, he returned to make a geological survey in collaboration with Major Brooks and Dr. C. Rominger. This he combined with a private enterprise, locating more lands for Quincy Shaw and Alexander Agassiz of the famed Calumet & Hecla copper mine. Pumpelly took his bride with him on this trip into the wilds, and his Indian *voyageurs* carried her around portages in a hammock swung on a pole. They journeyed to the very western end of Upper Michigan, beyond Lake Gogebic (spelled and pronounced correctly, with the first "g" hard and the second "g" soft, A*go*gebic, meaning "smooth rock," but usually shortened and pronounced Go*ge*bic, with both "g's" hard). Here early Government geologists had reported iron ore on both sides of the Montreal River, which separated Wisconsin and Michigan south of Ontonagon.

Pumpelly was one of the first modern investigators to study this range, but nothing came of his work immediately. Pumpelly, who always enjoyed referring whimsically to himself as a luckless man, later wrote that he missed "the opportunity of a lifetime" on the Gogebic Range. Agassiz lost confidence in him; discouraged, Pumpelly made only small purchases on his own account. In a copy of his *Reminiscences* believed annotated by a luckier man, John M. Longyear, someone has penciled: "Wasn't this fortunate for me?" Captain Nat Moore, chancing to rest on a hill near Pumpelly's land, leaned against a huge overturned birch and found beneath its roots an outcrop of very rich Bessemer iron ore; almost from under Pumpelly's nose Moore bought the tract, Pumpelly wrote, and on it was developed the Colby Mine, the first shipper on the Gogebic Range and one of the greatest. Nevertheless, on the property Pumpelly did buy were located subsequently the Newport and Geneva mining properties, which have produced more than twenty-five million tons of ore, and with his profits Pumpelly built sumptuous houses at Newport and other places, which he furnished with *objets d'art* collected during his Oriental travels.

As a result of Pumpelly's explorations, the Keweenaw Land Association acquired most of the land on the range, and what it didn't grab, John M. Longyear did. Though Longyear did not arrive at Marquette till 1873, there still was no road to the new Menominee Range south of the Republic Mine, which had been opened the year before. He and his party lost their boat at the Grand Portage, about three miles above the mouth of the Michigamme, and were forced to proceed on foot through the woods to the Twin Falls of the Menominee River, where they found a tote road and the explorations which became the Vulcan and Emmett Mines. Here at the Emmett the village of Waucedah later was built, and N. P. Hulst developed the Breen exploration until, in 1877, when the railroad came through from Hermansville, the Breen and the Vulcan shipped 10,405 tons of ore, the first from the Menominee Range. And during the next year five mines shipped ore—the Breen, Vulcan, Cyclops, Norway, and Quinnesec.

All these were simply test pits, crude explorations when Longyear arrived. The road through the swamp beyond Hermansville was from six inches to three feet under water. S. S. Curry was following the somewhat bizarre but effective method of locating ore by digging beneath the roots of the largest pine trees. Other prospectors were scraping away a green scum in a swamp and uncovering the Aragon ore bed, necessitating the removal of the town of Norway. The loggers were moving north and west and people were asking why open a new range when the Marquette Range could produce all the ore the world could use for generations?

Undeterred, Longyear bought land everywhere, moving westward from the Iron Mountain region to the Crystal Falls and Iron River district and then on to the Gogebic Range in 1882. Here, after a trip by sailboat and horseback, he visited the Montreal Mine location, passed on to Sunday Lake, where a rich mine soon would be opened, and on to the beds of ore that underlie the city of Bessemer. Bessemer, Wakefield, Ironwood, Ramsey, and, across the river in Wisconsin, Hurley—those are the iron cities of the Gogebic Range, built atop minerals worth millions and famed for both iron ore and bawdy houses. Here Longyear met Brooks, who in 1882 still didn't think much of the Gogebic Range. In those days high-grade ore was so plentiful and accessible and mining and furnace methods were so crude that only the specular and magnetic ores were considered valuable. The soft hematites, which today comprise the bulk of the ore shipped from the Lake Superior district, were scornfully (but rather accurately) called Lake Superior mud. Dr. Rominger, then state geologist, was reported to have said that he could carry away all the iron ore on the Gogebic Range in his hat. Two years later the Colby Mine shipped the first ore from the range, 1,022 tons of it, a good-sized hatful. Longyear had ignored the scientists. He thought there were at least 150,000 tons of high-grade ore in the Colby location, which turned out to be almost a classic understatement. Five and a half million tons have been taken out of it. He became associated in development of the Colby about the time that A. Lanfear Norrie was exploring the lands on which the city of Ironwood is located. Norrie's father, legend says, had given him $25,000 with which to make his fortune. He had come to Upper Michigan to hunt iron ore; luckless, he had about exhausted his nest egg when he stumbled on the vast Norrie ore bed.

The boom came fast. When the railroad was built to the docks at Ashland, Wisconsin, in 1886, shipments from the range totaled nearly a million tons. Already Longyear had moved on. He had become interested in lands in Minnesota where, in 1889, the Mesaba Range, greatest of them all, would be opened up.

Like Philo Everett, pioneer of the Marquette Range, Longyear came to Upper Michigan partly because of ill health. He worked first for the state, examining lands in the mineral reserve, then was employed privately as a landlooker. Swiftly he built a fortune in lands. Upper Michigan and Minnesota were not enough for him; in association with Frederick Ayer of Boston, he purchased coal mines in Spitsbergen. Meanwhile he found time to dominate banking and civic affairs at Marquette and to found the Huron Mountain Club, a fenced retreat in the Huron Mountains accessible only to members. Nevertheless, he withdrew abruptly from the Upper Michigan scene. Incensed because a railroad built its tracks between his elaborate mansion and Lake Superior, he moved the house, stone by stone, from Marquette back to Brookline, Massachusetts.

The eighties and nineties were great days for Upper Michigan. Marcus A. Hanna went into the shipping business, sending his boats from Cleveland to the upper Lakes. Scientists reported that the ore from the new Minnesota ranges was inferior to Michigan ore. The railroads were coming now, and coming fast. And so were the real iron kings. Henry W. Oliver, his political ambitions thwarted despite the backing of Matt Quay's powerful Pennsylvania machine, would devote himself almost exclusively to his career as an ironmaster. From a Republican convention at Minneapolis, he went in a private railroad car to the Mesaba Range, which was wild with prospector's fever. A surveyor named George Stuntz had found the ore here in Minnesota years earlier, and now it was being exploited, and Oliver, the Eastern magnate in top hat and frock coat, had to sleep on a billiard table in one of the jam-packed mining towns. His company became the world's biggest producer of iron ore, largely as a result of its operations on the Gogebic and Mesaba Ranges, and, in 1901 its enormous power helped Andrew Carnegie to world supremacy in steel: Oliver sold out to Carnegie's new U. S. Steel Corporation. Sam Mather, whose brother's Cleveland company already was a leader on the Marquette Range, joined Jay C. Morse and James Pickands to form, in 1883, the partnership of Pickands, Mather & Company, which today still dominates the Gogebic Range and is the world's number-two ore-producer. Oglebay-Norton, of Cleveland, moved in. Betchamillion Gates, along with the Big Steel boys and Rockefeller, invaded the Lake Superior ore fields. Time after time the locks at the Soo were enlarged to accommodate the seam-busting ore trade. To the promised land came little people from all over the world—the Cornishmen and Irish now were joined by the Swedes and Finns, who would impart, somehow, a distinctive flavor to the region. Expansion was in the wind everywhere: new ore docks at Escanaba and L'Anse and Marquette and Ashland; new hotels and new streets in all the new cities and towns; new companies using new mining methods and new machinery and new steel-making processes; new railroads and highways to replace the tote roads and canoe portages.

There were dark spots, of course. Financial panics, though brief, hurt. Labor unrest began. Abandoning hope for the future of the Ontonagon country, 350 families began a trek in midwinter across the snow and ice to the Vermilion Range in Minnesota, and hardship and famine and death stalked them on the trail.

But by and large, these eighties and nineties were times for greatness. Suddenly the story of Upper Michigan had ceased to be a story of pioneers and *voyageurs* and log cabins and campfires; it became a story of illiterate prospectors uncomfortable in new frock coats, of big businessmen come to the ranges with retinues of courtiers, of gaslights and lurid "variety" shows and bawdy houses and elegant girls in parlor houses: the rip-snorting free-swinging story of a new mining camp in a gaudy era.

Though the older Marquette Range was more settled by now,

the Gogebic abandoned itself to a period of wild speculation. The tripods of diamond-drill rigs were thick as tamarack in the swamps. There were wildcat holes in the ground everywhere (even today they menace buildings in the centers of modern cities). There was claim-jumping, "salting" of claims, pyramiding of watered stock, all the customary chicanery. Legends arose. Old John Hanousek homesteaded forty acres of rocky, worthless pastureland that Longyear and the Keweenaw Association scorned; he tried to get rid of it but couldn't. And then one day somebody came along and found iron ore on it. Canny John Hanousek wouldn't sell, but he would lease. So all right; he leased, and they dug the vast Plymouth Mine, today one of the two largest, richest open-pit mines in Upper Michigan, and day after day, year after year, old John Hanousek used to sit and watch the steam shovels scoop the ore up out of the pit and load it into railroad cars, and with each scoop he'd mumble: "Fifty tons to a carload, twenty-five cents a ton—that's twelve dollars and a half more for old John Hanousek."

And legends of a different sort, concerned not with hematite or magnetite but with the gamblers and whores of the hell town, Hurley. Old-timers swear today that uncounted bodies of pleasure-seeking men who disappeared in Hurley's dark hidden places were dumped into the old water-filled Germania shaft. And they say the same thing of the Minnewawa. True? Who knows? The shafts are black and the shafts are deep, and they are filled with water and the slime and muck of years. Even the names of the men who disappeared have been forgotten.

Bessemer, not Ironwood, became the county seat of Gogebic County by herding unnumbered drunken lumberjacks to the polls on election day. Similarly, civic leaders of Crystal Falls engaged the Iron River politicos in a poker game while their accomplices stole the courthouse records, loaded them on a boxcar, shipped them to the Mastodon Mine, and hauled them in a wagon under heavy guard to Crystal Falls, which remains to this day the seat of Iron County.

But these shenanigans were the doings of Sunday-school cutups compared to the deeds of the boys and girls of Hurley. Situated in Wisconsin directly across the tiny Montreal River from Ironwood, Hurley was the hell-roaringest place west of Seney. Indeed, a careful investigator could argue that Hurley surpassed Seney. Though its population probably never exceeded 5,000, counting whores and barflies, the town supported (and supports today) eighty-odd saloons. In extenuation be it noted that, unlike Seney, Hurley must cater to a whole collection of other communities. In truth, Hurley's gaudy affluence was built by the miners from across the river in Michigan.

Hurley is a few years older than Ironwood and, in the beginning, grew faster because of the Montreal Mine group, still the biggest underground shipper in the entire Lake Superior district. By 1891, saloons occupied every building but two on Hurley's principal street. This was Silver Street, famed throughout the north country wherever lonely men wished they could go into town to get drunk and charmed. Silver Street was only a muddy thoroughfare straggling up from the river, but it boomed so rapidly that the sawmills couldn't cut lumber fast enough to build new saloons. Each arriving train was crowded with a new contingent of gamblers, charmers, and assorted camp-followers of pleasure, and on Saturday night, the board sidewalks were jampacked with drunken miners and their ladies.

⤙ 13 ⤚

THE GIRLS OF SILVER STREET

꠸

HURLEY'S DEBAUCHERY, which lowers miners' efficiency, always has been fought by the mining companies. They have suppressed vice in Ironwood, which they control, and Ironwood civic leaders have piously adopted their attitude, denouncing Hurley and speaking of it as an embarrassing poor relation. The newspaper of the nineties printed the town's name in lower case: hurley. To no avail. Hurley prospered, bawdy and unrestrained except by occasional token raids by the authorities. Even so, Marinette, across the river in Wisconsin from Menominee, and Florence, across the line from Crystal Falls, flourished. Indeed, it might almost be concluded that Wisconsin was a haven for the dissolute and the wicked.

Curiously, many of the girls of Silver Street did not ply their trade in bawdy houses but worked out of saloons, somewhat in the manner of today's call girls. There was something homey about it. Sometimes a saloonkeeper would import a beauty from down below and she would live with him and his wife and children, taking her meals at their table, spending her off nights at their home. She was accepted by his wife as an accouterment of his business and also as a friend of the family, much as a hired girl is accepted on a farm. This cut down the pimp population. Many of the girls supported boy friends on their hard-earned money, but this was voluntary. (However, it is said today that the girls are shipped in and out of town on an organized vice circuit.)

The old stockade story appears at Hurley. Legend describes a log pen with a single entrance guarded by savage dogs; inside the

178

pen was a house consisting of a single large room, its floor covered with close-spaced pallets, or workbenches. Here a dozen girls labored, and the dogs were trained to prevent them from escaping but not to prevent customers from entering. This story can no more be verified at Hurley than at Seney, and probably is not true. Nor is it possible to determine how many girls operated in Hurley at any given time. It is safe to assume that many of the eighty-odd saloons sheltered three or four hookers and that a few gave asylum to as many as a dozen. On this basis, there may have been at least two hundred girls active along Silver Street simultaneously, and perhaps many more. There were a lot of miners, and a girl can only do so much.

Hurley was as wide open to gambling as it was to vice. Roulette was available, but craps, poker, and faro were more popular. Today most of the saloons have slot machines as part of their equipment, and many have crap tables near the bar. Money is cheap. All together, the town today is a curiously down-at-the-heels place whose only apparent reason for existence is pleasure. By day it is quiet and deserted and ugly. But after eleven o'clock at night Silver Street lights suddenly with neon, poker chips click furiously, and so do glasses and, sometimes, skulls. It is a poor man's Monte Carlo, a Midwest Port Said.

In its later days Hurley became famed as a sportsman's town, haven for Battling Nelson and other fighters of some renown. Ralph Capone visited Hurley and went shopping in Ironwood from his near-by estate at Mercer, Wisconsin, while the Federals were hunting him in New York. Gambling on horse races is big business in Hurley, and so is the baseball pool.

By the summer of 1943 many of Hurley's whores had gone into war plants down below. In five blocks up from the river, there were exactly sixty saloons on Silver Street. Much chromium and red leather distinguished the décor of a few, but most were more old-fashioned. Nearly all had front windows painted black or a partition near the door to prevent passers-by from seeing who was inside. (This may be a hangover from the nineties or from the Prohibition era; Hurley never did go dry, really.) But despite the wartime drain on manpower and womanpower, the Fourth of July in 1943 was just like the old days, with lumberjacks and miners swaggering up and down the sidewalks for two solid days and nights. The bar of the respectable Burton House, a huge rambling hotel built during the eighties, was jammed as in the old days when, in its high-ceilinged rooms and ornate lobby, the iron kings made history on the range.

Of all the girls of Silver Street in the old days, the most celebrated was beauteous Lottie Morgan. She was, an admirer recalls, strictly a high-class girl. Like most of her sisters, she worked out of a saloon. Apparently her clients were men of means, for she accumulated a certain amount of expensive jewelry, which subsequently became the subject of much speculation. Her clothes were better than average for Hurley and were, of all things, rather demure. But a string of dully glinting ornaments attracted attention to her friendly bosom. Her hair was curly and dark brown, her mouth thin and wide, her eyes rather large and suggestive. She wore her hair upswept. In April 1890, when she was murdered, she probably was in her late twenties or early thirties, a sporting woman of the town.

About six a.m. on April 11 a passer-by discovered lovely Lottie prostrate in an alley behind Silver Street at the rear of Crocker's saloon. The passer-by saw, perhaps to his surprise, that she was not drunk, but dead. Her skull had been crushed. The police found an old ax, matted with hair and blood, in a near-by woodshed. There was a large gash at her temple and a second blow apparently had been dealt her after she had fallen; this had crushed her skull and scalped her. A post-mortem examination disclosed that she had also been shot. The press reported that the police had many clues and no doubt would bring the murderer to justice soon. But they never did bring him to justice, however diligently they worked.

Many theories were advanced concerning the murder. Indeed, the woman's life was so tangled and devious that almost any theory was plausible. One school of thought held that she "knew too much" about a recent bank robbery in Hurley. This was ridiculed by the editor of the *Interstate News-Record*. Other theories, inevitably, involved hypothetical husbands and lovers of Lottie, jilted admirers, jealous women, blackmailed men of prominence, and so on. Little, actually, was known of Lottie's past.

About eight years earlier, it was said, she had lived in Milwaukee, the "supposed wife" of a Pinkerton detective. Before that they had lived in Chicago. She stayed in Milwaukee but briefly, disappearing suddenly and reappearing in Hurley. She was said to have had an uncle connected with a variety theater in Chicago. And this was virtually everything that came to light about the woman's past.

The police found a witness who at about eleven o'clock on the night of the crime had seen a tall, well-dressed, beardless man standing in the alley where Lottie's body was found. But so many tall, well-dressed men went into Hurley's alleys for one reason or another that this aided the police little. They did arrest one Terry Day, alias Riley, a few days after the crime was committed but he produced an alibi and was released.

Perhaps the high point in the whole affair was reached at Lottie's funeral. That morning Hurley was flooded with small handbills proclaiming: "Died, in Hurley, on April 11, 1890, Lotta Morgan. Funeral at the Opera House this afternoon at 3 o'clock. Speaking by the Rev. C. C. Todd, W. P. Burrows, Father Gilbert. Everybody invited to attend." And just about everybody did attend. Hurley gathered to do honor to its own. Long before three o'clock the opera house was crowded to its doors. At least a third of the mourners were women. Promptly at curtain time, the casket containing the body of the slain beauty was carried into the opera house and placed near the stage. After a suitable prayer and a hymn, *Ashamed of Jesus*, which reportedly had impressed Lottie greatly at the funeral of the girls who perished in the variety-theater fire, the Reverend Mr. Todd rose and addressed to the house packed with the bereaved a remarkable sermon on immortality and immorality. He said, in part: "Lotta Morgan was no ordinary woman. She was ladylike, she was courteous, not only that she had a woman's heart, she had aspirations for something better, she could adorn a social position. Though her sins are as scarlet they may be made whiter than snow. Let no man judge Lotta Morgan, for evil comes upon us like a flood and we cannot resist. . . . I blush to say that in this town people say that houses of ill fame are a necessary evil—that they are good for the business of the community. But, oh my brethren, do you wish prosperity and business at such price as this? I think not. A necessity is it, that immorality should exist here? Do you want dollars to come into your place stamped with woman's honor, stamped with woman's blood? If a woman's life is precious, is not a woman's honor precious too? We shed tears over the remains of Lottie Morgan, but why not shed them before and she would not be in this position today? . . . The spirit of Lotta Morgan has gone to Jesus. I would not say, I dare not say, about her future. She is in God's hands—she is in Christ's hands today. Let no man judge her here, but let us in this hour join hands and do something for humanity that will make life better. Let us make this moment one of value to ourselves, so that this great price for our future advancement will not be in vain."

Following this, the Reverend F. A. McGaw offered a prayer, and then the Reverend Mr. Burrows said, in part: "The man we are pleased to reform. He ofttimes is steeped in the very depths of sin and licentiousness, and yet when he becomes sensible to his condition and wishes to reform, he is extended the ready hand of fellowship. We find men can reform—they are lifted to a high standard. But, how different with a woman. Once she diverts from the path of propriety and honor, she is scorned, held down, and no one speaks of her. No ready hand is extended to a fallen woman —she is overlooked, while an equally guilty man is shown every consideration. Is this right, is this as it should be?"

The service was marred only once: At the announcement: "We will all rise and sing Lotta's favorite hymn," one of the more ribald mourners called out: "Bet on the red," while another cried: "Keno." And indeed these may well have been poor Lottie's favorite hymns.

Following the funeral orations the choir sang "the beautiful hymn, 'Where Is My Girl Tonight,'" the Reverend Mr. Burrows pronounced the benediction, and, followed by "a goodly number of carriages," the mortal remains of lovely Lottie were taken to the Hurley cemetery. The newspaper observed: "It was a sad cortege, a sad ceremony—one that has undoubtedly left its lesson on the large number of fallen women who were in attendance."

A terrible howl was raised for the apprehension of the murderer. The editor of the Ironwood weekly wrote: "That Lotta Morgan was an abandoned woman of the town is no reason why her slayer should go unpunished," and hinted darkly that the Hurley authorities did not want to solve the crime. To no avail. A week later townspeople on their way to church were handed printed handbills announcing the death of a dog, Curley, Jr.: "Funeral at the Opera House, 4:30 o'clock next week. Preaching by celebrated sky-pilots from abroad. Mrs. McGinty will sing Curley's favorite hymn entitled 'Asleep In The Montreal River' composed by one of our police. Everybody invited. Refreshments can be had at the —— saloon. P. S. 'Any raffle pays 180 for 1.'" Disgusted, the Ironwood editor embarked on a bitter unrelenting attack on Hurley, which, he wrote, led a band of Hurley toughs to try to lure him across the river, where, he said, they could kill him with impunity.

The opera house was quite a place. It housed almost everything, from *Uncle Tom's Cabin* to Lottie's funeral to a Finnish wedding that ended in a brawl involving several hundred guests and spectators. About the same time, the International Literary Society was organized "to instruct its members in the English language" and kindred matters. Hurley beat Ironwood 9 to 6 in a rowdy baseball game, and the Sons of St. George descended on Ironwood for their convention. The Marshal raided Paddy O'Neil's "boarding house" down by the tracks in Hurley and arrested Fannie, Jennie, May, Kitty Lee, and Lola; the girls promptly pleaded guilty to charges of being inmates of a house of ill repute, were fined twenty-five dollars apiece and released, presumably unchastened. An arrest was made in connection with the Hurley bank robbery. And, above all, the townsfolk gathered 3,000 strong in Union Park to witness a wrestling tournament which attracted all the best Cornish-style wrestlers in the Lake Superior district and nearly ended in a riot when the local favorite was adjudged defeated.

Even when no such great event occurred, life was far from dull on the Gogebic Range. Come payday in the mines, all the boys "took on their monthly jag" and "Justice Murphy's court did a land office business." On a payday Saturday in August 1890 "Jack Burke came up from Bessemer to see the elephant," and was sentenced to thirty days for throwing half a watermelon at the promenading town midget. Two drunks hired a livery rig and raced about town till they ran over a child on East Aurora Street. Three men belabored each other with boulders and clubs on Ashland Avenue, and a prisoner knocked a hole in the roof of the jail and escaped. When a resident of the Italian settlement, which was called Bull Dog Alley, allegedly stole a keg of beer, Pat Hurley knocked him down, for which Hurley was sentenced to thirty days as "the guest of Sheriff Foley." (The jail was the "Hotel du Foley.") Two drunks failed in their attempt to drive their buggy across the new railroad tracks ahead of a locomotive and "there was not enough left of the buggy to mention."

The social scene was enlivened by news of the imminent marriage of the daughter of an iron king to an apparently indigent French count; the editor of the *Interstate News-Record* wrote: "Another title gone! Who's the next bidder?" A variety song-and-dance man, convicted of drunkenness and vagrancy, was seized with a violent attack of delirium tremens, shook off his several captors, ran up the jail steps, collapsed, and died. Eight tramps stole six kegs of beer, called "Milwaukee Champagne"; arrested after the crime was exposed by charred barrel staves in their campfire near the railroad yard, they entertained the ungrateful mayor and city council with "speeches and vocal solos" before being sentenced to three months in jail. A boarding-house keeper at the Montreal Mine was picked up in a gutter on Suffolk Street by the police, for "The Ironwood police have no particular use for people who get drunk in hurley and come over here to work it off." An ex-pugilist about town, "The Cockney," put in a pleasant half-hour smashing windows and glasses in Hanley's saloon before Officer Dan Sullivan commandeered a gravel wagon and hauled him to the jail.

Hot controversy raged over proposals to reopen the "variety theaters," which moralists had closed. When the righteous folk won, the *Republic Sun* rejoiced that this was "about the last act in the dive keepers career in the Upper Peninsula." The Methodist Temperance Society held weekly meetings every Friday night in the church at Ironwood. And a goodly crowd attended the offerings of the Ironwood Dramatic Company as well as the high-school commencement exercises at which orations on "The Battle of Gettysburg" and "General Sherman" were delivered.

But these were voices crying in the wilderness. They were drowned out by the unprintable language of an old French saloon-keeper in Hurley who ended fights with his wife by carrying her sewing machine on his back to the express office and sending it to Peshtigo, her home in Wisconsin. And drowned in the hubbub of the crowd at the two-story Alhambra Theater, where a variety show was run by Paddy O'Neil, who boasted that his head was so hard he could butt out the panel of any bar in Hurley. And drowned too in the excitement over the great stagecoach holdup.

This crime, which rivaled the murder of Lottie Morgan for public interest, had a more satisfactory outcome: the culprit got what moralists of the time called his just deserts. And before he was released from prison, Raymond Holzhey won a measure of fame as a literary man of "unusual mental gifts." On August 26, 1889, when the stage bearing A. G. Fleischman and four Chicago bankers was about two miles out of Gogebic Station, Holzhey stepped from the roadside bushes, pistol in hand, seized the horses' reins, and told the passengers: "Donate, I'm collecting." One of the Chicago men said: "Here's mine," and whipped out a revolver and fired. But he missed, and Holzhey emptied two guns. The team ran away, leaving Fleischman's body in the road. Holzhey rifled his pockets, taking thirty-seven dollars, a wallet and a watch and chain.

Immediately Sheriff Dave Foley organized a posse. The robber had hit for the woods. The posse trailed him as far east as the west fork of the Ontonagon River, about thirty miles from the scene of the crime, then lost the trail. By this time other depredations had been recalled and authorities decided that one man was responsible for holding "the entire Upper Peninsula in terror as much as ever did Jesse James or the Younger brothers in the West." He had operated in northern Wisconsin and the western end of Upper Michigan, committing, it was charged, train robberies, store holdups, burglaries, and at least one murder. But he was not above strongarming an old Indian. Now at bay, he was considered fearless and desperate, and it was generally believed that he would die rather than be captured.

The suspense continued for less than a week. Holzhey appeared at Republic, some 125 miles eastward on the Marquette Range, having walked most of the way. A hotel proprietor recognized him and notified Deputy Sheriff John Glode and Justice of the Peace E. E. Weiser, who kept an eye on him. Saturday morning Holzhey started for the train carrying a small valise. Deputy Glode and Justice Weiser approached him on the sidewalk; when he walked between them, they seized him, and though, they later recalled, he reached for his pistols and a wicked-looking knife, they managed to hang onto him until Constable Pat Whalen came up and knocked him senseless with a billy-club. He was sentenced to serve a life term in Marquette prison, where his literary efforts were prodigious and, some claimed, of high quality. He was paroled after serving about twenty years.

Life on the range was not all drinking and whoring and hell-raising. It was lived against a somber background of mining. Nearly every issue of the weekly newspaper recounted an accident in the mines, frequently fatal. Much of the mining was done by the open-stope method, in which the galleries were not timbered but depended for support on the naked rock. Frequently the rock collapsed in the stope and killed or injured the men. In the timbered soft-ore mines, fire was the nightmare. Five men were suffocated when the Germania caught fire, among them "an unknown Polander." Legends of miraculous escapes from death arose. A cave-in at the Aurora Mine in June 1890 sent such a blast of air roaring through the shaft and drifts that miners were lifted thirty-five feet into the air and slowly let back down to the floor of the drift, uninjured. Some of the accidents were due more to the hell-roaring spirit of the times than to the normal hazards of mining. James Oram, descending the ladder in the shaft of the Superior Mine, was impatient of the slow progress of his partner below him on the ladder. Bored, he paused and then sought to display his agility by dropping and catching the rounds, thus stopping himself. His partner, fearing he would be knocked off, remonstrated with Oram and finally stepped aside to let him pass. A second later Oram's body hurtled through the air and fell into the water at the bottom of the pit, some seventy feet below. The tart editor of the paper saw in this a lesson to show-offs.

An advertisement ran: "The Range is booming and so is Mark-strum's Store (groceries, provisions, dry goods, boots and shoes, clothing, furnishings, goods, etc. etc.)" John M. Longyear, agent for landed empires, offered some 700,000 acres for sale or lease. Frederick Weyerhauser, the lumber baron from the Chippewa and Mississippi Rivers who made his real fortune on the west coast, bought an interest in a mine near Hurley. Carnegie told Oliver: "Your genius as a negotiator is unequalled." The days of prospectors were ended. Towns sprang up around mining locations, boomed, died, were sold, or moved away. The ore-hungry iron men scooped out an open pit at the Plymouth Mine so vast that it rivaled the yawning excavations on the Mesaba Range. Though most of the iron mining in Upper Michigan still is done underground in shaft mines and not in the open pits which resemble gravel quarries, copper men today scornfully refer to iron mining as "farming," an inexact analogy. They took so much ore out of the Norrie group that subsidence threatened to undermine the new million-dollar high school and pull it into the hole; the mine, therefore, was abandoned, though some old-timers still insist that a million tons of high-grade ore remain untouched. But, then, the old-timers always are telling of fabulous ore bodies they saw uncovered and then mysteriously walled up by the enigmatic companies.

As early as the nineties some of the companies were resented by the public or suspected of land frauds. Other evil portents appeared. The Democratic landslide in 1890 stunned the *News-Record*. Wailing: "What hope is there for the Republican party?" the Gogebic *Advocate* urged the nomination of a "western Garfield," General Russell A. Alger of Michigan, for the Presidency. But Alger, who had made a fortune in lumbering in the eastern end of the peninsula, never got to the White House, and in 1892 Grover Cleveland led another Democratic victory. Hard times in the early nineties hurt the range. And future trouble was foreshadowed: The Gogebic Miners Union was becoming powerful (though one of its officers absconded with the proceeds of the miners' ball), and the miners at Ishpeming went out on strike. More serious was competition from the west. Though Oliver's entry into the Gogebic Range was cheered, he symbolized the might of the Mesaba Range, which before long would produce ore so cheaply and abundantly that Upper Michigan would be nearly paralyzed.

But now the companies grew and prospered. They boomed the range and they ran the show. So great were their operations that, in 1890, 147 European iron and steel manufacturers came to view the wonders. Lake Superior iron ore was world-renowned.

~§ 14 §~

GOLD IN THE CHICKEN COOP

THE OLD MEN are preoccupied with death. They live out each day wondering if it will be their last. When one encounters another on Ishpeming's streets, each is astonished to find the other still alive. They sit in the sun on benches near the railroad station across the street from the new Mather Inn, they walk home past the twin shaft houses of the Cliffs Shaft Mine (they still call it the Barnum), they stop in at Hickey's, or Pete's, or Beanie's, or Jimmy Nardi's, Louie's, or one of the other old-time saloons. And they are comforted by these familiar things. They may know only vaguely that Mr. Mather was "one of the big men in the CCI," but they have heard his name all their lives; when a new hotel is named for Mr. Mather, who is an old-timer himself, they manage to partake, somehow, of Mr. Mather's own immortality.

Though the cocktail lounge has begun to invade Ishpeming and the other iron towns, the old men's saloons have not changed much. Some of them still have swinging doors. Beer still costs a nickel. The walls are painted dark. The bar is carved and backed by a decorated mirror. Clean-limbed calendar nudes have replaced the lush ladies of the dead days, but they're still nudes. There are no bar stools; men stand up and drink like men. The saloons are perhaps a little quieter than formerly. That is because the old men have quieted down, and the young miners don't come here much. They go to the cocktail lounges.

But here the old men meet and take nickels carefully from coin purses and talk about the old days and old companions, and about death.

189

"I can see him now, poor fellow, he's dead now."

"Yep," with a sigh and a shake of the head. "He's dead now, poor fellow."

And then a joke: "There's people dying now, Cal, that never died before."

"Guess so. And that's the *last* thing I'm going to do."

Always the same jokes, most of them wry and not very funny. Or maybe a poem recited with gestures:

> *When we're dead and in our grave*
> *No more liquor will we crave,*
> *But on our tombstones we can have wrote*
> *A lot of liquor went down our throat.*

Cal says: "That's right, Cap. But say, now—they oughta take us out and shoot us. Too gol-darn old for any good. Ain't that right? I guess they'll be puttin' us in that box pretty soon, eh, Pat?"

And the fat little bartender says vigorously: "I ain't gettin' in no box. They take me out naked in the woods and bury me where I come from. No son of bitch sayin' prayers over me—bunch o' loafers."

They all agree. It is a valiant gesture.

Remember the old days? The days when Dan Spencer tended bar for the Simon brothers after he come here from Nova Scotia. Old Dan—I hear he's all caught up out at Silver Lake. Hear the Cleveland-Cliffs is takin' over up there at Peter Moore's old camp. Poor Peter, he's dead now, poor fellow; I can see him now.

And Swen—remember the time, night before Christmas it was. Swen and his partner were moochin' around, hunting a quarter to buy a half pint. They'd been askin' all day and hadn't had no luck and along about dark, Swen went out to try once more and old Cap—what was his name? Well, 't don't matter, some old Cousin Jack mining captain, he was walkin' down Cleveland Avenue ahead of Swen and he pulled his gloves out of his pocket and a roll of money come out so big you'd of thought it was all the money in the world. Swen chased it to hell-and-gone up Cleveland Avenue; seventy-six dollars it added up to, and Swen and his partner bought seven pints and a quart of gin.

That Swen—he's a corker. Another time he took his saw and his ax and went out to cut some stove-wood, and right at the butt of the first tree he found a fifty-dollar bill. As God's my judge and I hope to sink right down to hell. Swen went back to the cabin so fast he looked like a deer white-flaggin' it through the slashings, and he put away his saw and ax and went into town and didn't come out for a week.

And remember Johnny Larson? Johnny and Pete, they was brothers. Worked in the Lake Angeline Mine. One time the railroad called up, all the way from Escanaba, and said what was the idea of puttin' such a big chunk o' ore in one o' the cars that it wouldn't go through the trap; the minin' company knew it oughtn't to load any chunk bigger'n one man could heft. Well, the company said they'd stuck to the rule—one man *had* lifted that chunk. The railroad didn't believe it. So the minin' company, the Lake Angeline, they sent Johnny Larson down to Escanaba and he took that chunk outta that ore car by himself. He'd put her in there, so he took her out. Must o' weighed six, eight hundred pounds. Johnny, he had shoulders on him like a railroad boxcar. But not a fightin' man neither.

Yep, them were the days. Remember the time the Salvation Army come to town, the first time? That was in '85. Wasn't either, 'twas about '80, 'cause they hadn't started minin' gold out at the Ropes location out north of town yet. Well, anyway, the boys heard that the Salvation Army was coming and the word got around that the Salvation Army was a kind of a whorehouse outfit. You see, none of us Swedes, nor the Finlanders and Irish neither, had ever heard tell of the Salvation Army. The Cousin Jacks, they stuck up for the ladies. Anything the Cousin Jacks was for, the rest o' the boys was against. Most o' the time they'd 'a' been glad enough to have a bunch o' new girls come into town, you can be damn sure. But now all at once they made up their minds they was going to stick up for their wives an' mothers, they wasn't lettin' no whorehouse outfit in black skirts come into Ishpeming. So the Salvation Army come, an' they had their parade, and everybody quit work in the mines an' come down to Main Street, must of been coupla thousand of the boys lined up just waitin'. So along comes the Army, band and all, and Buckeroo, he yells: "Leave the ladies be, boys, but give it to the whore-masters," so everybody makes a grand rush an' you never saw such a scrap, with the Cousin Jacks against everybody else an' the poor Salvation Army not knowin' what it was all about. Well, the marshal, he hustled the Army off and locked 'em up, and that satisfied the boys because they all thought he'd locked 'em up for runnin' a whorehouse. (Course, later on it turned out he did it to protect 'em, or for paradin' without they had a permit, or somethin'.) But anyway the mayor, he got 'em out, an' they held a meetin' in the hall up on Division Street, an' when the boys in Voelker's saloon heard about it, they went around to the other saloons and rounded up two, three hundred men and marched up to the hall and broke up the meeting and smashed all the furniture, you never saw the like of it. Or was it before the parade that they broke up the meeting? Anyway, 't don't matter; it was all over in a coupla days anyway when the boys found out it weren't no whore outfit, and the Army's still here and I guess it's all right. Give us a little more of that would-be-joyful, eh, Beanie?

Cal Olson was born in '73, and his life spans those great days. His father and mother came over from Sweden in the sixties, when Ishpeming was not much more than a collection of log cabins in the wilderness, a mining location huddled around the Jackson and Cleveland and the other earliest mines on this, the first iron range. By the time Cal was born, in '73, pioneering was done and the great days were dawning. Tilden's Iron Cliffs Company and Mather's Cleveland Company were booming; soon they would combine. The great Barnum Mine was opened and Longyear was here, and Oliver was coming, and Pickands and Mather would get together soon. Mines were opening everywhere, all the way west to Republic and Michigamme. Ishpeming was mushrooming from a mining camp into a city.

Hogs ran wild in the muddy streets, for some citizens believed the beasts destroyed offal. Each spring a new coating of earth, red with iron ore, was applied to the streets; almost immediately this became churned into a sticky paste; later, drying, it sent clouds of red ore dust billowing everywhere, coating bars and church pews alike. The year after Cal was born, 1,500 citizens fought a disastrous night fire in April, cursing the man who had left the cap off the fireplug, flinging household goods hysterically into the trampled red ore slough and snow of the streets, praying that the new steam fire engine from rival Negaunee, three miles away, would arrive in time to save the town. (It overturned, but the boys got the fire out anyway.) Ishpeming's more than fifty saloons flourished in the face of periodic crusades by temperance people; the saloonkeepers, led by Nicholas Voelker and Charles Anderson and John Gylling, ignored their preachments and demanded, unsuccessfully, free liquor licenses.

> *A man may chin*
> *And a man may work*
> *For the temperance cause all day,*
> *But he can't go fishin'*
> *And observe prohibition*
> *Because he ain't built that way.*

Money was plentiful, even though sometimes it was only company money. A miner's trunk containing five hundred dollars was stolen from his boarding house. There was more where that came from.

The Barnum House was going up, and before long the Nelson House was built, mining headquarters for years to come. The railroads had arrived, and the first Pullman palace car pulled into town about the time of the fire; now Chicago was only twenty-two hours away (today less than eight hours on the fastest run). Stage service also connected the range with down below. Circuses like "The Only James Robinson" came to town regularly, and at Austin's new Opera House on the corner of Division and Pine the leading lady "won every heart by her admirable acting" in Bulwer-Lytton's *The Lady of Lyons* and theatergoers could look forward to seeing Tom Taylor's celebrated *Ticket-of-Leave Man*. Holiday crowds trooped out to Lake Michigamme that summer, for Michigamme was a resort as well as a booming mining location. A wedding was celebrated with a parade through the streets in mid-afternoon. At the crowded roller-skating rink each girl wore a distinctive apron; neckties made of the same material were placed in a grab-bag and the lads drew them out and then sought the lady who wore the matching apron, thus winning her hand for the grand march, or grand skate. After due deliberation the city fathers granted a burial permit for a pair of "Finlander's legs which were run over by a street car"; street cars were new in those days.

The Swedes were on the range in force; now came the Finns, despised and belabored by all. The Irish came too, and the Cousin Jacks and some Italians. They all collided head-on. Cal Olson lived out at the Nebraska Location with the other Swedes. This was in the eastern part of Ishpeming, toward Negaunee, as were the New York and Cleveland Locations, also Swedish havens. The various sections of town were named for the mine shafts around which the homes were huddled. The French Canadians lived out of town, in the woods. The Irish lived west of Ishpeming, around the Barnum and the Burt and the Lake Angeline and the Salisbury Locations. Division Street was theirs. Main Street was the downtown dividing line; if a Swede went west of Main Street, he was hunting trouble. Invariably he found it. Men fought for the glory of the old country, for the glory of their home location, for the hell of it. A Swedish bartender shot an Irishman dead and the saloonkeeper, a prominent Swede, took the blame; subsequently he was elevated to high office. The *Svenska Posten* was established at Ishpeming in 1882 and attained a large circulation; its editor was a nobleman, Nathanael Mortonson, who also was organist in the Swedish Lutheran Church at Ishpeming. (Many of the Swedes were deeply religious.) A gang of Swedish railroad laborers sent one of their number out for a bucket of beer; they found him dead in the street, and, without inquiring into the cause of his demise, they set out to avenge themselves on all the Irish in town, an action which led to something resembling civil war. As an educational measure, the mining captains split national cliques and forced Swedes and Irish and Finns to work side by side in the mines, a practice still common today. This was not as perilous as the grumbling immigrant miners anticipated: a warning cry sounds much the same in any language. The Swedes made good iron miners just as the Cornishmen made good copper miners. The Cousin Jacks weren't so much for scrapping, but everybody else was. The miners earned fifty to seventy-five dollars a month. Once a month, when they'd get paid, they'd stay drunk for a week. Sometimes the super would make the rounds, up and down Cleveland Avenue and Division Street and Main Street—pronounced, uniquely, Main *Street*—trying to lure the men back to the mines. Few went as long as the money lasted. Fifty dollars was more money than most of them had seen in all their lives in the old country. Cal says: "Over here they had a glorious Fourth of July every day." It is as good an explanation of the fighting as any.

Their children fought, too. As a boy, Cal and the other Swedish youngsters constantly engaged the Irish in location wars. Sometimes after school when you were a kid you walked past Strawberry Hill, where the swells lived, and on across the rim of the hill, with the town spread out in winking lights below, and just about the time you got to the Barnum Location, your gang was ambushed by a mob of tough Irish kids. You grabbed up rocks and sticks, and if there were too many of the enemy, you headed for the railroad tracks, where you could fortify yourself behind ore cars, where ammunition was plentiful. There the battle raged long past dark, long past a boy's bedtime, and when you got home, your shirt stained from your bloody nose, your father was waiting with the hairbrush. But if you had licked the damned Irish, maybe there wouldn't be much of a thrashing after all.

Cal's mother took boarders into their home, mostly men who worked in the mines with her husband. He had come to America when he still was in his teens, bringing his bride with him and coming straight to Marquette by boat from New York. He worked underground in the iron mines near Ishpeming all the rest of his life, except for a brief period when he mined gold in the Ropes Mine.

Julius Ropes, Ishpeming's postmaster, was an amateur explorer, geologist, and chemist. In 1880, during the silver-lead and gold fever, he opened a laboratory. Presently making assays and analyses occupied most of his time. Prospectors were bringing mineral samples into town from all over Marquette County. Most of the interest centered in the silver-lead "range" near Silver Lake, some twenty-one miles northwest of Ishpeming; here men had found silver as early as the sixties and—who knew?—perhaps they had struck it as rich as the prospectors farther west in the Porcupines. (As it turned out, they had. Neither strike amounted to much.) And now in the eighties, they found gold in the gravel of the Dead River. That was the golden region, a remote area of rugged country, stretching northward up beyond the Dead and the Barnhardt and the Mulligan and the Connors, up beyond Silver Lake to the foothills of the Huron Mountains where the Yellow Dog rises. Into this wild region went the prospectors, scrambling up and down the cliffs, crossing the pine plains, fingering the yellow sand in the cold rushing mountain streams. They amused the lumberjacks, the men like Peter Moore who were driving pine on the Big Dead, but they did not care: they had seen the glint of gold in the streams, and they were out to find the mother lode in the hills. They brought their mineral specimens to Julius Ropes, and he prepared analyses until, in 1881, he deserted his laboratory and opened the Ropes Mine near the Dead, just a few miles northwest of Ishpeming. It was Michigan's first gold mine and probably the only one ever developed sufficiently to be called a mine.

A shaft was put down and a stamp mill erected, and soon they were taking out rock which averaged around $7.50 in gold per ton of rock milled. When a brick of bullion was molded and brought into Ishpeming, it passed from hand to hand all over town. After that, men from the iron mines who had been skeptical flocked to the gold fields. But the tiny shaft—and the company's inadequate bank account—could only accommodate twelve miners. These, questioned eagerly, all told of seeing gold in the rock everywhere, especially in the lower workings, which indicated that the richest point of the vein had not yet been reached. When he was a boy, Cal Olson would go out to the Ropes Mine to watch his father mine gold. It set him apart among the other boys at Nebraska Location, and he was disappointed when his father went back to the iron mines.

The Ropes Mine was developed by fits and starts. One month they were sinking shaft down to the seventh level and milling $4,457 worth of gold; a few months later the mine was idle and the directors were out hunting new capital. For some ten years after 1886 the future of the Ropes Mine looked brilliant indeed. Gold worth more than half a million dollars was produced. Approximately $20,000 worth of gold was taken out of near-by property by various other companies, the largest of which were the Michigan Gold Company (its president was Peter White) and the Fire Center Gold Mine Company. But in July 1897 the Ropes ceased operations. The old workings had been exhausted and the company lacked the $20,000 needed to sink the shaft to new levels. Other mines fared similarly. A few desultory and unsuccessful attempts were made to reopen the Ropes Mine, and it changed hands a number of times, until its machinery was dismantled and sold for scrap and its galvanized tin washing tanks were put to use as chicken coops by several families. Years later some $40,000 in gold was recovered by two operators using modern scientific methods. Immediately the chicken-raisers scurried out to the chicken yards and, ousting the squawking fowls from their homes, scraped diligently at the sides of the chicken coops, salvaging, legend says, thousands of dollars in gold which had clung to the sides of the tanks.

In the 1930's the Calumet & Hecla copper-mining company leased the Ropes property, but it has not yet worked it, and a Canadian company bought some land farther north, not far from Silver Lake, and spent a summer prospecting for gold with diamond-drill rigs. By these methods, says Buck Anderson, one of the drillers, they found numerous gold stringers, but they never found the mother lode, and the project was abandoned. The bonanza still lay locked in the hills just as it was when closemouthed Silver Jack Driscoll took his secret with him to his grave at L'Anse. Today around Ishpeming men—and not just bearded old-timers, but younger men of education, too—still whisper that one day the mother lode will be found, and they say that in years to come, Ishpeming will be known not so much as an iron town as a gold town, that the real rich strike is yet to be made somewhere in the wild rocky timbered hills and plains stretching northward from town. They may be right at that.

Cal's father went back to the iron mines and he stayed there till he died, Cal says, of "miner's consumption;" probably silicosis. He had been ill for some time and the captain told him: "You better work on surface." The old man tried it, but he only lasted a couple of days. Then he went back underground. He was a miner, not a laborer; a miner he had lived and a miner he died.

Not every man who works at an iron mine, not even every man who works underground, is a miner. The miner is at the top of the heap. A boy starting out in the mine usually works on surface first. Then he is permitted to work underground. Here he may be a trammer, or a timber man, or he may be apprenticed to a miner. Before becoming a miner, sometimes after years of apprenticeship, he is an expert craftsman. "Put a greenhorn in here," says the old captain, "and you'd kill him in a day."

Although boys frequently follow their fathers underground, Cal didn't. He was a printer's devil, a teamster, a bartender, and a diamond driller. Only once did he go to work in the mines. In the soft-ore Lake shaft of the Cleveland-Cliffs Company it was, and two days were enough for Cal. His first trip underground was terrifying despite his long familiarity with mining talk. After donning his protective "digging clothes" and miner's lamp in the locker room of the change-house, he walked to the shaft house and, at the shaft, stepped into the men's cage with a group of other miners. Even when the cage was idle you knew with certainty that it was suspended in space by only a slender cable. Already earthy smells were strong in his nostrils, and he could hear the incessant drip of water, and his boots squashed wetly in slime. Suddenly bells clanged raucously, were echoed from the control room; without other warning, the cage dropped from beneath him—dropped through space like an elevator out of control, and the walls of the shaft were only wet darkness broken intermittently by flashes of light as the cage plummeted past the upper levels of the underground workings. Abruptly the pace of the cage slowed, and Cal's breath came back, but his ears ached with a great ringing. Then the cage stopped, bounced high, fell again, bounced, repeated the springy motion until finally it came to rest. The men stepped out into the station room, a large lighted subterranean cavern surrounding the shaft.

Cal's job was to load cars. At the bottom of a chute was a stopper-board. When a car was moved into place beneath the mouth of the chute, Cal had to remove the stopper-board, permitting the ore to rush crashing into the car. Sometimes the ore got stuck in the chute and Cal had to ram his long iron bar up the chute and loosen the ore. And when the stuff did come loose, it roared down the steep incline before he could get his pole out of the way. Once as he struggled to remove his iron pole, it struck the electric trolley wire behind and over him, and he got the shock of his life.

But the thing that really bothered him was the constant creaking of the huge timbers which supported the walls and roof of the workings. These timbers were enormous, perhaps two feet thick, and hewn from the toughest tamarack. Yet the terrific pressure snapped them constantly as though they were match sticks. Each time one broke, Cal stood rigid and ready to run for his life, certain that this time the whole mountain of earth and rock and iron above him was coming in on his head. It wasn't, of course; the timbers work and snap constantly, and old-timers say complacently: "When she's workin', she's holdin', but when she's quiet, look out." But Cal didn't know it, or couldn't believe it, and, indeed, few men can believe it on their first trip into the weird dark world underground. He kept thinking of stories of disasters he had heard since he was a boy, and when something moved at his feet, he was terribly certain that it was one of the rats which he had heard were kept and fed underground to warn by their flight of a coming cave-in. Distraught, Cal was able to load only two cars in a shift instead of the normal twenty or thirty. He worked two shifts, and then he quit; he never went underground again except a few times with a diamond-drill crew, and he didn't like that much better.

In some mines the shaft is sunk on an incline, in others vertically. Years ago the miners located ore by compass, then quarried it in open pits or mined it in open stopes. But the ore was deep, the ore was pockety; open-pit mining was unprofitable. In the seventies shaft mining started. Charles H. Hall, who pulled the Lake Superior Iron Company out of the depression of 1874, was credited by some authorities with introducing underground shaft mining, power drills, the caving system of mining soft hematite, the loading of ore with steam shovels, and the widespread use of the diamond drill.

At first the miners sank their shafts directly into the ore formation, which might be rock called jasper. This proved impractical. It was near Ishpeming that diamond drilling was developed in the early eighties. Today diamond-drill crews, operating on the surface, sample the rock and mineral with holes bored deep into the earth. Geologists then map the area. Then the shaft is sunk, usually not into the iron formation itself but outside it, perhaps back of the quartzite footwall. The iron formation usually is tipped at an angle between two non-bearing belts of rock, which may be quartzite or granite; the upper edge of the belt beneath the iron formation is called the footwall, while the edge of the belt above the iron formation is called the hanging wall. The first task in opening a mine is to sink the shaft through the surface soil, or overburden, which may be sandy or swampy; shaft-sinking under these conditions sometimes is so difficult, dangerous, or expensive that a mine must be abandoned, for the earth caves constantly. Once the rock ledge is reached, shaft-sinking becomes easier but perhaps no less expensive. At one new hard-ore mine near Ishpeming shaft-sinking in quartzite cost about $100 a foot, and since the shaft is some 1,700 feet deep, it can be seen that it "takes a gold mine to make an iron mine" just as truly as it does to mine copper, as was said before. The shaft may have but a single compartment, like an elevator shaft, or it may be divided into several compartments; in one runs the skip which carries ore to the surface, in another runs the cage which hauls the men, in a third is a system of emergency escape ladders. There are other variations.

As the shaft is sunk into the quartzite, every hundred or two hundred feet a drift, or horizontal tunnel, is driven off through the quartzite and perhaps through hard diorite dikes that intersect the formation and on through the footwall and into the iron formation. But much iron formation is totally barren of iron ore; the "iron formation" is simply the kind of rock (such as jasper) where iron ore occurs. Frequently the ore itself is pockety, clustering in isolated pockets along the footwall or hanging wall or along a dike. True, some of these pockets are enormous and may not be exhausted after years of mining; but others are tiny and, though they may look promising when first encountered, they peter out abruptly after a few days. It is the business of the engineers and the mining captain to judge where these pockets will be found, how extensive they will be, and so on. Successful mining requires thousands of precise calculations, years of experience.

When, along the horizontal drift, a pocket of ore is located, the miners drive a pair of raises upward. These are tunnels, perhaps four feet square, which angle upward toward the drift, or level, a hundred feet above. When the raises have been pushed sixty feet up into the rock, they are connected by a short horizontal tunnel called a sublevel. Here the actual mining is done; this is the working place, or contract. To get to it, the miners climb ladders in one raise, the "men's raise"; the other, the "ore raise," is used as a chute down which they throw the ore they mine. If they are working in a hard-ore mine, the men may use the sublevel stoping method of mining. That is, at the working place they blast loose successive bodies of rock and ore, which is scraped into the ore raise, and continue this process until they have enlarged around themselves a huge cavern, or stope, in the rock. In hard ore no timber is used to support the roof and walls of this stope; the miners know how to blast away treacherous rock that might cave in and kill them, leaving rock which is solid and not weakened by faults, or fissures. Some of these stopes are enormous, reaching upward through level after level perhaps four hundred feet, so high that a powerful searchlight's glare is diffused and smothered in the dust and blackness long before it picks out the actual roof of the cavern. Even a tiny piece of rock falling from so great a height and striking a miner on the head might kill him instantly. A pair of men in one mine spent twenty-five years of their lives, it is said, working day after day, year after year, in the same immense gallery. Pillars are left to support the roof of the stope; when all other ore has been removed, the men "rob the pillar," getting out every pound of ore which can be removed without bringing the whole formation down on their heads.

In soft-ore mines, where the ore is sandy or muddy and will not support itself, the ore may be taken out by one of several methods, such as the sublevel caving method or the top-slicing method. The nature of the formation determines the method employed. In general, mining soft ore involves pushing raises upward under protective timber covering, slicing down ore overhead, and, as the pocket becomes exhausted, building in the cavity a matting of timbers and tamarack poles and then permitting— indeed, encouraging—the walls and roof to cave in until the cavity is filled solidly.

Wherever possible, the ore is sent roaring down the ore raise to the level or drift below; here it tumbles into cars and is hauled along the drift out to the station, where it is dumped into the skip and hoisted to the surface to be graded, treated, and dumped on mountainous stockpiles or shipped direct to the ore ports to be loaded on freighters and carried down below to the steel mills.

Long and vigorous are the arguments: is it safer and better to work in a hard-ore mine, where a chunk may fall on you, or in a soft-ore mine, where the timbers are cracking all the time and some day may catch fire or give way completely? Men who have worked in one kind of mine never would leave it, considering anybody who works in the other kind a foolhardy adventurer.

With modern scientific methods much of the guesswork has been taken out of iron mining, but the danger can't be taken out of it. Death is always at a miner's elbow. A single misstep in the murky gloom may send him plummeting sixty or seventy feet down a raise; he may overlook, in the constant choking dust and smoke after a blast, a chunk of treacherous rotten-stone or slick-and-slide still hanging from the roof of the stope and a moment later its tenuous hold may be snapped by somebody's mere voice; gas from a blast may suffocate him as he works alone high up in a raise, his voice unheard by his fellow workers below. And there are other ways that a man can die underground, as we shall see.

❧ 15 ❧

HEMATITE IN MY HAIR

༄

THE SOFT ORE at the Blueberry Mine near Ishpeming comes almost up to the surface and, from underground, they robbed it until the gravel started coming in. The engineers got worried about an air blast—if the surface came in, compressed air might smash its way down to the lowest level, into every cranny of the mine, gathering momentum as it went until its terrific pressure killed everyone. So, with the miners out of the mine, men blasted the surface to make it come in. It refused. Even deep diamond-drill holes filled with powder failed. So the engineers concluded it must be safe. Then one day the whole surface came in without warning, trees and all. Fortunately, the air found a way out and no one was injured.

In the Blueberry, "a wet hole of a mine," during the summer of 1943 a miner and his partner, pulling timber in a stope that was to be abandoned, had an experience not unlike that of a man with a ringside seat at an earthquake. They were on the twelfth level, some twelve hundred feet underground. They would hitch a cable to a timber and, with a stationary engine, pull the timber from under the roof of the worked-out stope, dragging it some sixty feet across the floor of the stope toward the mouth of the drift. As they worked with the cable, suddenly, without warning, a crack appeared in the earth at their heels. From all about them in the darkness came a deep-throated rumbling. The crack widened to a yawning chasm. The man's partner tried to leap forward, but his feet became entangled in the cable. The miner seized him by the neck as he started to topple backward into the crack, hauled him forward, and dragged him toward the drift. The timbers at the mouth of the drift were coming in; by the time the men reached it, the opening, normally big enough for a man to walk through, was but an eighteen-inch hole. They squeezed through this on their bellies. Scarcely had they stood upright and begun to run on down the drift when they heard the whole stope cave in behind them, and the air blast knocked them flat. But they emerged unhurt. The next day they went back and started calmly scraping out the ore which had completely filled the stope. So much ore had fallen in that they still were removing it five weeks after the accident. The significant thing is that they did not mention the accident to a friend who had been working in the same mine on a different level. When, weeks later, he chanced to hear about it, he said: "Oh sure, that happens all the time."

Driving drift requires much knowledge of geology and engineering. If the ore is hard to find, a diamond-drill outfit is brought down and put to work. But sometimes a particularly hard seam will deflect the drill as much as two hundred feet, thus leading to serious inaccuracy. To ensure accurate drilling, George Maas, of Negaunee, a pioneer diamond-drill and mining man, invented his celebrated Maas compass, used the world over. Even so, the diamond drill is not infallible, and sometimes the drifts run wild underground as the harassed captains hunt the elusive pockety ore.

Blasting requires expert knowledge. In extremely hard rock it may take day after day of ceaseless drilling to prepare the blast holes. When the job is done, the face to be blasted looks something like a punchboard. The holes are filled with powder, and fuse and primer are prepared. The fuse must be timed carefully. Sometimes the charge is set off with an electric battery outfit by remote control, or it may be done on the spot simply by lighting the fuse with a "scratcher" (Finnish miners call it a "ratcher"). Then the miners turn their backs and stroll away along the drift, and presently the blast lets go with a muffled roar heard in distant levels. On returning after the deadly gases have disappeared, the miners must study the results carefully to determine if any of the shots have missed—that is, have failed to explode. Many men have been maimed by missed shots.

Following intrepid John Mabbs's rather fantastic introduction of nitroglycerine to the Marquette Range, plants were built to manufacture it on the spot. Accidents and fatalities were common in the early days. Nobody knew a great deal about the dangerous stuff. The dynamite-makers, laboring in their little sheds on the edge of town, came to be regarded, not without reason, as sorcerers who concocted mysterious and terrible potions. They made their nitroglycerine in stoneware crocks set in a trough of running water, and one of the nonchalant conjurers had the habit of placing his lighted cigar on a board over the washing tank as he worked. Everybody thought nitroglycerine was safe to handle under water, a belief that was dissipated in a cloud of smoke one day. In wintertime at one plant tubs of mixed dynamite were placed around a hot pot-bellied stove to prevent the dynamite from freezing. Smoking was permitted. Packed cartridges of dynamite were held in a pair of pliers and dipped into a pot of stearic acid, which was melted on a common kitchen stove. Nitroglycerine was packed in fifty-pound cans, frozen, and delivered by team in jolting wagons to the mines. Some of it went by boat to the copper mines of the Keweenaw Peninsula, and one time the *Tom Boy*, a small schooner, split wide open on a rock without damage to the crew or the explosive cargo. But more than once a team and driver disappeared in a flashing blast along a rutted road, taking trees and rocks with them.

So casual were the men on the range that companies were forced to issue educational pamphlets, adjuring the men not to smoke or wear open-flame lights in their hats while making primers, not to thaw frozen dynamite by warming it in Mamma's pasty tin atop a hot stove. Moralistic stories were circulated, like the one about the poker-playing Italians who steadied their card table by placing a stick of dynamite under one leg and then, forgetting it, became excited when somebody caught a straight flush and hammered the table top, with disastrous results. Or the story about the man who tied a sick dog to a tree, fastened a dynamite cartridge to his collar, lighted the fuse, and ran, a sensible procedure except that, being penurious, the man had used a worn-out piece of rope and thus the dog was able to free himself; playfully the dog chased his master while the spitting fuse burned closer and closer to the scruff of his neck; the man fled into the house and flung boots, flatirons, and stove lids at the dog, whereupon the dog sought shelter under the house and blew it up.

The most serious explosion on the range occurred on January 2, 1878, when 4,800 pounds of canned nitroglycerine were being loaded into a railroad car at Negaunee for shipment to Republic. Theories that a spark from the engine ignited the stuff or that the handlers treated it too roughly were purely speculative. All seven men closely involved were killed instantly. The blast rocked buildings all over Negaunee. This accident caused the city fathers to pass ordinances regulating the transportation of nitroglycerine and hastened the general use of dynamite, a less volatile substance. Today dynamite is manufactured in plants isolated from the city under rigid safety regulations. Serious accidents are rare.

Whenever a fatal accident occurred in a mine, the victim's fellow workers abandoned their jobs until after the funeral. This was expensive. The companies began safety promotion. Accidents were reduced greatly. Yet the worst disaster in the history of the range occurred as late as 1926. At 11.20 a.m. on November 3 the men on the day shift in the Cleveland-Cliffs Barnes-Hecker Mine five miles west of Ishpeming were about ready to go on surface for lunch. Captain William Tippett and County Mine Inspector William E. Hill were signaling for the cage from the third level, 1,000 feet underground. Five men were working near them on this, the bottom of the mine's three levels. The other forty-six miners and helpers were busy on the two upper levels, at 600 and 800 feet underground, or in sublevels. Wilfred Wills, twenty-three, was running the motor on the second level, 800 feet down. From above him, from all about him in the deep wet earth, came ominous rumblings. He was accustomed to the constant creak and snap of mine timbers. This was different. The earth itself was shifting. Shouting to three men near him, he ran for the shaft, 200 feet away. There was no time to signal for the cage and wait for it; besides, it might be already wrecked. Wills started climbing. He was 800 feet from daylight. Below him on the ladders he could hear his companions scrambling after him. Then suddenly he heard another sound—the distant roar, far below and all about him, of rushing quicksand and water. First the roar, then a hissing sound, as though a giant were sucking breath through his teeth. Wills climbed faster, his headlamp the only light in the narrow blackness of the ladder road. Beneath him he heard sudden cries for help. Then nothing more except the louder roar of the upsurging flood. He was the only man who reached the gray sunlight on surface alive.

A quarter of a mile southeast of the shaft, 300 square feet of surface had caved in. The mine had been wet and troublesome all along. Now suddenly quicksand had come into the lowest level and surged toward the shaft, a terrible hydraulic ram carrying everything with it, filling every corner of the workings within fifteen minutes and rising up the shaft to the upper levels.

The bodies of Captain Tippett and Inspector Hill and five workers were found late that evening on the bottom level; apparently, hearing the approaching flood, they ran for a raise which connected with the Morris-Lloyd Mine, more than a mile away. They were among the fifty-one who died in the Barnes-Hecker. All that night widows and orphans and the curious from the little locations stood mute near the shaft while rescuers worked by searchlight. None of the bodies but those seven was recovered from beneath the tons of muck. The shaft was sealed, and the shaft house those miners had venerated became their tombstone. For weeks Ishpeming was different. In the saloons men were quiet. This was a mining town, not boisterous now, but mourning its dead. Death always is close at Ishpeming; it becomes real but rarely, as on that day, and then it becomes real with enormous impact. When a mine kills men, it is almost as though their best friend had betrayed them.

When Cal Olson was in his teens he started working for Braastad the merchant, and now when Cal speaks of Ishpeming's great days, he means the days of Braastad the merchant. "You could buy anything in that store," Cal recalls, and his enumeration of Braastad's merchandise is like a triumphal fanfare: "Flour, straw, hay, salt, furniture, toys, fruit, butter, watermelons, carpets, clothes, shoes—one whole side of the building was shoes up to the ceiling, and the ceiling was twenty feet high—grapes, pins, needles, I guess you could buy a mine in that store if you wanted to."

Braastad had worked in the New York Mine, where he had one horse running around a drum to pull the bucket up the skip road; then he went into business, and was he a plunger! "He bought flour by the carload, oats loose in the car, corn loose in the car, carloads of bananas. Everything." He kept seven teams and a dozen heavy wagons—"My wagon weighed nineteen hundred pounds empty when I was drivin' for him"—and he sent his catalogues all over the range and defied anybody to match his prices. Cal delivered for him to the locations outside of Ishpeming and to the logging camps, and sometimes in the winter the teams would have to pull the loaded wagons through snowdrifts six feet deep, but they always made it; they're better for pullin' than any truck is today. And Cal learned to speak French because he delivered to some French Canadians out in the woods, people that peeled the bark off maple trees and boiled it and made syrup. And to lots of others who spoke no English.

He was a volunteer fireman for a long time. He had a firebell up over his bed at home, and sometimes at four a.m. in midwinter it would clang and he'd have to get up and run seven blocks on the ice to the firehouse. "When you got to the fire you felt more like goin' to bed than like pullin' hose." But it was worth it on Christmas, because the fire boys got a free turkey and a free bottle. (And Christmas seems to belong peculiarly to the north country.) And it was worth it, too, on the Fourth of July, for then you went, expenses paid, to tournaments—pronounced "torn-aments"—in other towns of Upper Michigan. These theoretically involved contests among the various fire departments—hose-laying, hose-breaking, footraces, and so on—but usually they were simply like any other convention spree. Visiting firemen, the phrase goes; and nowhere is the Fourth of July celebrated more enthusiastically than in Upper Michigan. And remember the time we were up at a tournament at Laurium, you know, up on the copper range, and we was all in a saloon and I stood on my hands on the bar, like this, just standing up at the bar having a drink, then put your two hands on the top of the bar and hoist yourself up till you're standing on your hands; and one of the copper miners, a Cousin Jack he was, said 'tweren't nothin', he could do it, so he tried it and he fell and hurt hisself; wasn't he the same gol-darn mulligan caught the greasy pig that afternoon?

Yep, them were the days. All the mines were goin' full blast. The Cleveland-Cliffs built a town out southeast of Ishpeming in the Cascade district and named it Gwinn, after Mr. Mather's mother, I think it was, and out that way was the Palmer Location, too. Remember the time they blew forty thousand pounds of powder at one time out by Palmer and busted windows in Negaunee, three miles away? She was a corker in them days. They was openin' new mines everywhere, and the three-legged diamond-drill rigs was everywhere, right in your back yard, maybe. The Barnum was workin' three shifts—it's got fifty-two miles of drift and crosscut under Ishpeming now, they say, the whole ground under Ishpeming's all honeycombed anyway. And the mines out west toward Humboldt and Champion and Republic and Michi-gamme and Spurr, they was goin' full blast too. And George Maas claimed they was a billion tons of ore out that way. Ishpeming had fifteen, sixteen thousand people, 'twas biggern Marquette in them days, you never saw such a place.

That was 'long in the nineties maybe, or nineteen-hunerd or so, I don't remember for sure. It was after the strike, when all the miners went out and the soldiers come and a big hardwood tree blew down on the soldiers' tents up on Burt Hill and killed one of 'em, poor fellow, and everybody went up and sawed off souvenirs-like from the big hardwood tree.

Cal, you was tending bar then, wasn't you? Yes, but say, saloons was different in them days, the places like Tim Cooney's and The Rag and The Stinkpotter and The Hump where the boys used to stop for a facemaker after Mass of a Sunday morning, and Toutloff's Jump-on-Top saloon. But you never saw no women, none o' these girls in the saloons, 'less, of course, they was you know, whores like. The Irish and the Swedes, they're the worst drinkin' people goin'. They was a few Finlander saloons on Pearl Street and one time a fellow got stabbed to death, but there weren't much of that. Sometimes one o' the miners wouldn't show up for work after he'd had an elegant sufficiency down at

Hickey's or some place like that; the capn, o' course, wouldn't let him go underground if he caught him, 'tweren't safe, but he didn't always catch him and sometimes one o' the boys'd work a whole shift down in that wet hole when it was all he could do to stand up.

Everybody was feelin' his oats in them days. Remember that time old George Newett put it in his paper, in the *Iron Ore*, that Teddy Roosevelt liked his liquor pretty good an' Teddy sued him for libel and collected six cents? There was work for everybody that wanted it. The boys took out so much iron ore they like to sank the boats on the Big Lake. Remember old Gust? He usta say: "I broke so much rock that I got hematite in my hair an' my ears an' my nose an' every other damn place." He usta take a Finnish steam bath every night when he come up from underground, an' fifteen years after he quit workin', hematite come outa his ears. Poor fellow, he's dead now; died like my dad, miner's consumption.

Remember John Brynteson? There was one Swede done something. I can see him now, big and tall and red-haired; he was a miner at the Lake Shaft, and the church here was sending a man up to the coal mines in Alaska, and Johnny, he went along. When he got there, he got split up from the man from the church, got mixed up with a coupla mulligans, one was a Laplander or some such and the other one was a tailor who got drunk in San Francisco and went down to the docks and then somebody yelled: "Sailors wanted," and this tailor, he thought they'd hollered: "Tailors wanted," so the next thing he knew, there he was, a day out at sea bound for Alaska. So he met Johnny Brynteson up there, and them and this Laplander started moochin' round and what do you think? They made the strike that started the city of Nome, Alaska. Ain't that a corker? I hear Johnny went back to Sweden and bought himself a king's palace or some such in Värmland, in Sweden.

One day when Buck Anderson asked Cal how he'd like to go to China with a diamond-drill crew, Cal said sure, might's well. He'd been tending bar and when "it went dry" in 1919, selling pop got on his nerves. Buck was (and is) a veteran driller, with experience all over the world. He and Cal and the rest of the crew sailed from Brooklyn in an old tub that wallowed like a wounded porpoise. Halfway round the world they went, to India, then up the Irrawaddy to Rangoon, and from there they struck out overland across Burma on a trail that must have been the trail which became the Burma Road. After spending several weeks covering 200-odd miles on the trail, they started prospecting in China with their diamond drills. They found nearly everything. "China is very rich," Cal says. "Very rich." When they had finished they came back by way of Japan and the Hawaiian Islands and San Francisco, and on the way they drank the boat dry.

Cal is not a big man—indeed, he is short of stature—but he must have been powerful in his prime. He is so soft-spoken that most people think him timid, and, indeed, he is sentimental and sometimes even fearful. But he has also a hard core that gives him a stiff-backed independence so that today, seventy years old and living alone in a camp at Three Lakes, he will walk the five miles to Michigamme for a glass of beer rather than accept a ride from someone who, even unintentionally, appears patronizing. He still goes into the woods alone and cuts trees and drags them back to camp and chops and saws them up for firewood; he still would rather walk in the woods than in town, though he knows almost nothing of hunting or fishing; he gets lonesome sometimes, and now and then he must go into town to "visit my friends," but, by and large, he likes living alone. He partakes of the great tradition of the dam-keepers at Silver Lake—Peter Moore, Neil Steffans, Dan Spencer. Neil and Dan were his friends, and though he has not their knowledge of the woods, he has their independence and their feel for this hard lonely country, this Upper Michigan. He belongs to it, and it to him.

ᵔᵔᵔ 16 ᵔᵔᵔ

A FACEMAKER FOR THE BOYS

ᵔ

IN THE NINETIES the iron kings were the heroes, and the people worshipped noisily. In 1890 they shipped for the first time more than three million tons of ore from the Marquette Range alone, nearly four times the amount moved twenty years earlier. The ore never would be exhausted; some of it from the Republic Mine glistened like diamonds in sunlight, it looked good enough to eat; that soft red stuff from the Mesaba didn't amount to much. And who said there wasn't much timber left? How about the pine around the headwaters of the Peshekee, and in the Porcupines? Anyway, new mines were opening everywhere, and if they worked out the ore around Ishpeming and Negaunee, they still had the western end of the range, didn't they, the stuff around Michigamme, and who knew how much farther west the range went? This country would never die.

Would it not? Consider the case of Michigamme.

Lake Michigamme is large, deep, rock-walled; it is dotted with timbered islands and its shoreline is cut up by many deep bays and jutting rock points. It lies roughly in the middle of "the hump" of the western end of Upper Michigan, about halfway between Marquette and L'Anse, which squats at the foot of Keweenaw Bay. In its greatest length it stretches some six miles west from the town of Champion to the town of Michigamme. A long

narrow southern arm extends some four miles down to the outlet, the gorge-locked Michigamme River. Among the numerous
streams coming into Lake Michigamme from the north is the
Peshekee River, an Indian word pronounced Peh-*shee*-kee. It
rises below the Huron Mountain foothills in the pine plains; a
divide separates its headwaters from those of the Yellow Dog.

Along the north side of Lake Michigamme lies a long high rock
ridge. It contains iron. So do the hills and knobs to the west, in
Spurr Township of Baraga County. (The dividing line between
Baraga and Marquette Counties passes through the western edge
of the village of Michigamme.) Numerous other minerals are
present in the rock formation around Lake Michigamme: asbestos,
quartz, copper, mica, iron pyrites, feldspar, and, some say, gold,
lead, and silver.

All these natural factors combined to make Lake Michigamme
a focal point, from the earliest days. Indian trails led to it, for so
large a body of water meant a long unobstructed stretch of speedy
paddling. *Voyageurs* used it for the same reason. The mail sleds
en route from Green Bay to L'Anse, Ontonagon and the copper
country followed the Indian trails near Lake Michigamme. The
geologists and explorers included Lake Michigamme and Michigamme River in their well-traveled network of river highways.
The Welsh Brothers stagecoaches carried mail, express, and
passengers over the old mail route toward the copper country.
The Marquette, Houghton & Ontonagon Railroad pursued the
same course. When the lumbermen came, following the pine,
they drove their timber down the Peshekee into Lake Michigamme. It was inevitable that a town should grow on the shores
of Lake Michigamme. But a mine made the town.

Foster and Whitney as early as the fifties, had remarked on
the iron-bearing formation here. But not until 1872 was the Michigamme Mine discovered by Jacob Houghton. Brother of Douglass
Houghton and aide to William Austin Burt, he had managed
mines without notable success and had failed in a tool business at
Detroit by 1870, when he undertook to survey and build the
M. H. & O., now part of the Duluth, South Shore & Atlantic.
Its roadbed followed water level valleys and thus it passed along
the northern shore of Lake Michigamme on the narrow strip of

flatland beneath the frowning rock bluffs. Atop these bluffs near the western end of the lake Houghton located the Michigamme Mine. He sank test pits and began stripping in 1872, and that year the mine shipped 141 tons of the hard gray hematite ore that was to become a symbol of hope and despair to the townspeople.

The town's first building was a log cabin erected on the lake shore to shelter the mining engineers. They laid out the town site on a gently-sloping ridge between the tracks and the lake. During that fall and winter of 1872 buildings sprouted everywhere. To supply mine timbers and harvest the virgin timber north up the Peshekee, F. W. Read & Co. built a sawmill on the lake shore between town and mine. A. F. Newnert opened the first store on Railroad Avenue. In a few months Michigamme was a boom town, with 300 men at work opening the stopes of the mine. Times were good that spring of '73 (when Cal Olson was born), and the men were working from sunup to dark, tramming ore out of the open stope and down the hill to the lake, loading it on barges and towing it with a steam tug to Champion, the railhead at the eastern end of the lake.

June 19 of that year a forest fire swept into town, and when the smoke had cleared, nothing remained but one business house and two or three dwellings. But what of it? The men built her up again almost overnight, and by September she was bigger than ever. But a month later the nationwide panic of '73 had penetrated to this boom town in the wilderness. The price of ore fell. The mine laid off all but seventeen men. Nobody had any money; the mining company issued scrip. And for a year Michigamme knew poverty. Thus was the pattern set. When the mine was booming, so was the town; when the mine went dead, so did the town. Forever after Michigamme's fortunes would soar and crash like an ore skip out of control.

That first depression lasted a year. Then the town boomed for three years, until 1876, when the price of ore slumped again. The second bust-up lasted three years. From 1879 to 1883 was another period of prosperity, and the Michigamme Mine expanded under the guidance of its bearded heavy-set Cousin Jack captain, John P. Christopher. He located further ore bodies and opened new stopes and sank new shafts until, by 1883, the State Commissioner of Mineral Statistics reported: "Few mines in Marquette County show greater recent improvement in their prospect for the present and the future than does the Michigamme."

Captain Christopher arrived from England in 1863. After a year in the copper region he was hired by the Jackson Iron Company's famed Captain Henry Merry. He worked for Merry eight years, served a year in the Missouri lead mines, returned to the Marquette Range, and became foreman of the Barnum Mine and captain of the Pioneer Mine, which was under lease from Sam Tilden's Iron Cliffs Company. William H. Barnum, of Lyme Rock, Connecticut, one of the great men of the range, was Iron Cliffs' president by that time. He gained control of the Michigamme Mine, and Captain Christopher was sent, in 1877, to Michigamme as captain of the mine. Thenceforward, he was one of the town's foremost oracles.

The Michigamme Mine—local residents still call it "the *hard-ore* mine"—possessed two distinctions: the extremely pockety nature of its ore, and its engine house atop the bluff, which was so fine that mining men came all the way from England to marvel at its brick walls, four feet thick, and its expensive machinery.

Although the hard-ore mine was the most famed and beloved, it was by no means the only mine in the vicinity of Michigamme. Indeed, this whole western end of the Marquette Range was booming in the seventies and eighties. Back at the rival town of Humboldt they took 38,014 tons of ore out of the Baron-Humboldt in 1873 (although even by then this mine was on the downgrade), and out of the Lincoln-Edwards-Argyle group, 39,023 tons, a peak figure. The Champion, near the town of Champion, shipped a whopping 72,782 tons that same year. The Jim Pascoe was not yet opened, but it would be, eight years later, and so rich did it appear that enthusiasts predicted it would eclipse all other mines in the nation. (Actually, it operated only four years.) The Republic, a few miles down the Michigamme River, was the real bonanza of '73: in that, its second year of shipping, it got rid of 105,453 tons of its famous glittering specular hematite, and its captain, Peter Pascoe, conducted visitors about it proudly, like a country gentleman exhibiting his estate.

Michigamme's own mines were booming, not only Cap

Christopher's hard-ore mine but the other mines to the west, in Baraga County: the Spurr, the Stewart (or Iron King), the Steward (or Orleans), the Wetmore (or the Farm, and later the Imperial), the Webster, the Portland, the Ohio, the Norwood, the Titan, and the Beaufort. Ten in all, and they were strung on a winding thread of road through the woods along the banks of the Beaufort River, five miles west from Michigamme to a chain of three dark-water lakes called Beaufort and George and Ruth; at night, if you drove out there in a carriage, you would see the lights of the ten locations gleaming in the dark below the bluffs. Houses, rough lonely houses out here in the woods, huddled around the shafts; people in them, rough lonely people, hoping that the vein wouldn't peter out. "I heard they're going to put down another shaft at the Beaufort." Or "Cap told me that the Spurr's a bad one, all pockety, but she'll pay out *yet;* he told me so hisself, he did." Or "The clerk says the ore runs up to sixty-eight per cent." Sitting and hoping beside oil lamps. It was new country; even in the 1870's nobody knew much about it; no proper geological study had been made. The formation out here differed from that immediately on the shores of Lake Michigamme. The whole surface was loose and decomposed, making it difficult to determine the probable extent of the ore bed underneath. But a writer in 1883 said of the Wetmore, which shipped 2,777 tons of soft brownish-yellow hematite in that, its second year: "From the present outlook, 'there are millions in it.' " Ten years later it was idle (though its operation was resumed three times, last by Henry Ford).

This, then, was the hinterland of the boom-town Michigamme. Of course, some of the ore from these mines five miles west of town in Baraga County was shipped on westward to L'Anse, historic fur-trading post and now blossoming with a brand-new wooden ore dock and high hopes of rivaling Marquette. But Michigamme was the real hub; to it on Saturday night came the miners from the locations in the woods all around, and to it came the lumberjacks from the camps up north, roaring down the Peshekee driving pine in the spring. First stop were the saloons, maybe Dick Brown's Parlor Saloon, or John Murray's, or the barroom in the Northwestern Hotel or the Michigamme House. On the floor was sawdust from the mill and a protective eighteen-inch steel mat in front of the bar, and on Saturday nights the saloon-keepers passed out a free lunch, hot dogs usually. Some say that Michigamme once had sixty saloons (it now has one), and this may be true if you include the cozy blind pigs, for in this frontier town pitchers of beer were sold in the parlors of many private homes. Estimates of the peak population of Michigamme range from 1,000 to 3,000, depending on whether you include the lumberjacks and the miners from near-by locations.

But certainly this was a boom town, its muddy streets jammed on Saturday night with brawling jacks and miners, its storekeepers working furiously night and day, its carpenters hammering from dawn to dark at the new squat square-fronted homes and boarding houses.

Frank Brown, Sr., born in England, came here in '73 from Negaunee and went to work in the Michigamme Mine while his wife ran a hotel and saloon beside the firehouse. The saloon occupied one 26-by-40-foot room and next door were twelve bedrooms above the Brown living quarters. They charged twenty-five cents for a bed and twenty-five cents for a good meal, which was cheap enough, for the miners were making around two dollars a day and some of the mill hands up to five dollars. Their clientele included mainly miners, millmen, and mine mechanics, and the Browns, unlike their rivals, did not need to send porters to meet the trains and grab the traveling salesmen. Sometimes the lumberjacks would arrive from the woods with fistfuls of tickets good for a meal in the Brown hotel; they'd have one meal and "put the rest of the tickets over the bar."

One night after Brown locked the saloon and went to bed, he scarcely had put out the lamp when his wife said she could hear someone breathing in the bedroom. Brown climbed out of bed in his long flannel nightgown and there was a Cousin Jack miner, all cut up and bruised and with a smashed-in nose, lying between the safe and the bed. He had crawled through a window to escape a brawl between Cousin Jacks and Irish in the pool hall next door.

Running a boarding house in Michigamme was no job for a woman. Once Mrs. Brown had to subdue a drunken lumberjack with a potato-masher. That same day occurred the long-remembered big jack fight. It was a Sunday, and thirteen of J. C.

Brown's lumberjacks came into town by sleigh from Stevens's camp on the West Branch of the Peshekee; they landed in Frank Brown's saloon and before long a fight had started. Two bullet holes appeared in the ceiling, and when the bartender protested, the boys heaved him through the wooden door to the dining-room without opening the door. These pleasures palled toward evening and the jacks drove around town in their sleigh, hunting trouble and finding it, until, long past midnight, they headed for camp to begin the day's work. On the way they passed one of Read's camps, where the men were just getting breakfast. Brown's men figured they might as well end the night in a blaze of glory, so they stopped their sleigh and invaded the Read cook camp. When the battle was over, the invaders' team was in the Read barn, their sleigh was in the river, and they were straggling homeward through the brush on foot.

Billy Lamour had helped Read's boys stem the onslaught. He is remembered as the greatest fighter of them all. He was a trapper and a lumberjack and, some claimed, a constant violator. (A violator is a man who violates the fish and game conservation laws; cheating the game warden is so common in remote regions of Upper Michigan like Michigamme that it has almost become a sport in itself.) Billy Lamour weighed only about 160 pounds, but he had a neck like a bull's; he usually won his innumerable fights by butting his adversary. He never lost a fight, they say, but once he fought to a draw. He and a huge powerful jack locked horns in the alley behind Sundstrom's store. They fought in silence a half block north up the alley, two big men clubbing at each other's bodies, and then they fought their way out between two buildings and started battling down the middle of the main street back toward Sundstrom's. By this time they were wheezing and snorting and chewing up the mud like a pair of enraged bulls, and they had attracted a huge crowd. In front of Frank Brown's saloon they stood still and, toe to toe, slugged it out, and the thud of their blows and their grunts of pain were the only sound in the town; business had ceased, the crowd was mute in wonder: Billy Lamour, the Michigamme golden boy, had met his equal. The townsfolk began to worry. Would their boy get licked? Surely not Billy Lamour. But look at his face, like steak in a meat-grinder.

And were his legs quivering with fatigue? How long could he last? From his saloon Scotch Gordon Murray, a cousin of Lamour, strode to the gladiators and stepped between them. Everybody was relieved: Murray would call it a draw, saving Lamour's honor. But no—Murray wanted the visiting challenger arrested for using obscene language. Apparently he felt in some obscure manner that this would win victory for Lamour. It was a bold stroke. But he reckoned without Frank Brown, who stepped now from his saloon in the role of champion of fair play. If they were going to arrest the jack, he wanted Lamour pinched too for using obscene language. The crowd was stunned, as much at the legal erudition of Murray and Brown as at the novelty of the situation. Was there really such a law? After a moment loud arguments began. Curbstone lawyers screamed for attention. The crowd milled about, splitting into factions. In their midst, forgotten in the excitement, stood the two stupefied warriors, bloody and uncomprehending. Just as a general melee seemed imminent, some forgotten hero laughed. The quarrelers paused—and somebody said into the silence: "Let's call it a draw and have a drink," and the toasts to Billy Lamour and his worthy opponent bulged the walls of the town saloons far into the night.

Another of Michigamme's legendary warriors was Bum Busch, who ran a logging camp up on Busch Lake beyond Busch rapids on the East Branch of the Peshekee. (Many of the place names hereabouts stem from half-forgotten nobodies rather than from mining company big shots.) Bum Busch was a pretty good man in a scrap, but he encountered a valiant halfbreed and every time they met, whether on a trail in the woods or in town, they fought. All together they battled forty-nine times, and who won that last rubber brawl is forgotten, so evenly were they matched. "Bum Busch and the halfbreed had it again," was heard often in the saloons.

Sometimes the jacks in from the drive down the Peshekee would come to sit in Murray's or Brown's day after day, waiting for the time to begin driving the pine on down the Michigamme. There was a sorting boom at the mouth of the Peshekee; here the logs were trapped in the boom, sorted, and made up into rafts. Some of these were towed up the lake to the Read mill at the foot of town; others were towed all the way down the lake to the outlet, to be driven on down to the Paint and the Menominee Rivers. The towing was done by steam tugs, first the *Jim Hayes*, brought from the copper country, and then the *Rose*, and a stern-wheeler houseboat, the *Michigamme*. There also were motorless scows; to propel these, the anchor was carried three or four hundred yards ahead in a smaller boat and dropped, then the anchor rope was hitched to a team of mules on board the scow, which walked in a circle and wrapped the rope around a capstan, thus pulling the scow and its trailing raft of logs up to the anchor. In this manner it used to take a week to get from the sorting boom up to the sawmill, four or five miles away, and some of the river-hogs would ride up to town on the houseboat, lolling in the cook camp on board and taking things easy with a jug to pass around. The others sat in Murray's on the hill, listening to the whistle of the puffing tugs on the lake below, and when the time came to resume the drive at the foot of the lake, some of the boys could scarcely stand on Michigamme's board sidewalks let alone on plunging thundering logs in white water.

A dozen or more lumbering camps were active in the woods in those days, and there might be as many as a hundred men in one camp. The logging companies had headquarters in Michigamme—F. W. Read, J. C. Brown, Silverthorn, Bay Shore. In Read's sawmill two hundred men were running two or three shifts, and J. C. Brown's shingle mill was furiously busy at the mouth of the Peshekee. Captain Christopher was not the only hero on the board sidewalks. There was I. C. Fowle, the elegant mine superintendent, who almost never went underground. And Captain George Orr, of the Michigamme. And there was Bob Bruce, who came down from Keweenaw Point in '93 to run camp for Read; they took him out to Camp Nine Lake and he gazed at the enormous stands of timber there and said: "Boys, there's enough here to last for twenty years." (By 1906 it was all gone.) And there was Joe Comer, the walking boss who used to live in town and inspect the logging camps from a carriage. And Antoine Dishnow, born in Canada and married to a Lamour; he was one of Michigamme's earliest pioneers. Jack Treado was a timber cruiser and a jobber; he learned the woods around Michigamme as few men have

known them, and his family is today one of the town's most prominent. And Ben Fritz, the jam foreman; he almost died in a jam
at Levine's flats on the East Branch of the Peshekee; there were
a million feet of timber in that jam.

Fourth of July everybody in and near Michigamme knocked
off work. The saloons bulged. The town's "good people" watched
the children's footraces in the main street in front of the saloons,
or they went on the houseboat far down the lake to the picnic
islands, keeping sharp lookout for the sea serpent of many claws
and tails supposed to inhabit the deep water near the islands.
People on the range came all the way from Ishpeming and even
Marquette to ride on the tug *Michigamme*. Every Labor Day
Read took his mill employees down the lake for an outing, always
a gay affair. (On one of these islands some prospectors reported
a silver strike and excitement ran high until the vein turned out
to be nothing but fine crystallized quartz, mica, and iron pyrites.)
In the evening the holiday picnic party would attend a big dance
at the hall on the second floor of the Michigamme House, above
the saloon and dining-room. The dances were usually staid affairs,
except for the antics of the children whom the old folks brought.
Sometimes the fire department gave a dance as often as twice a
month. When there was no dance, the hall was used as a roller
rink, for skating was a local craze in those days. One night the
Good Templars gave a program that included speeches by gentlemen, readings by ladies, and songs by the choir. The Good Templars still were congratulating themselves upon the success of this
enterprise when they discovered that the treasurer had skipped
town with the treasury, containing $6.25, leaving behind him a
four months' board bill which the organization was asked to pay.

About this same time the Michigamme scene was further enlivened by the business visit of Wau-ben-ess and his friend
Nob-i-na-osh, both Chippewa chiefs who formerly had lived here.
Having raised a lot of potatoes at their present home on the
Menominee, they brought their produce back up here to sell,
making the trip by water and passing the Republic and Kloman
mine locations by night for fear of being robbed. They sold out
for cash, got gloriously drunk, and departed for L'Anse on the
afternoon train.

John Dolan, brakeman of Number 18, caused a stir in town when, en route to church one Sunday, he was detained in a saloon, went home, smashed furniture and threw crockery about, and frightened his family for two days, finally going downtown with a club. Here, unfortunately, he paused in front of Ryan and Gallagher's saloon and, seeing his reflection in the window, thought he had come upon an enemy and so fell to with his club, smashing the window and generally wreaking havoc until Deputy Sheriff Dolf picked him up.

About the same time four Scandinavian couples were married, and the wedding celebration lasted till dawn. A Spurr Mountain girl from west of town was incensed because, when she inadvertently put her foot into a two-bushel basket of eggs, the Michigamme smart alecs spread a rumor that her peasant's feet were so big she had broken all the eggs but six. J. O. Camph opened a drug store near the First National Bank, adjoining B. S. Bigelow & Company's large store. The barber bragged that he could jump eleven feet six inches and did so, on slight provocation. The town's more lettered citizens tittered at the new sign proudly emblazoned over a saloon door: "Milwake lacker behr," but noted approvingly that farmers hereabouts would raise nearly 3,000 bushels of potatoes this year, no small item come next winter when the town might be snowbound. The Michigamme *Bee* was founded (its life would be short), and its editor, Colonel B. F. H. Lynn, promptly disappeared into the woods to hunt ore. Lawyers in frock coats arrived to conduct solemn inquiry into litigation involving one of the district's more promising mines. Thomas Edison paid a visit to this end of the range about 1888. He was experimenting with a method of extracting ore by magnetism, which failed.

Even the theoretically innocent amusements of the boys were performed in the lusty tradition. One Sunday some of them started out for Republic, where they were scheduled to play a baseball game against a team representing the rival town. On the way they had to change horses, and they whiled away the delay drinking beer in a whorehouse between Champion and Humboldt; on the way back from the game at Republic, they paid another call on the girls, this one more lengthy. This bagnio enjoyed no little renown; men came all the way from Ishpeming and Negaunee to savor its charms.

It appears that no bawdy house ever flourished in Michigamme itself, although old-timers refer to various free-lance cuties. However, the boys did not have to go far from town for pleasure. There was a house out near the Webster Mine, in Spurr Township, and another out in the woods south of there. Today, a saloon or a bawdy house stuck way out in the woods seems strange. Not then. Business was where the ore was, and the ore might be anywhere.

Except among the lumbermen, all the talk was mining talk. Every evening the mining men came in to E. G. Muck's general store and talked till the lamp wicks burned low. Mr. Muck—he still runs his store, a small bright-eyed, white-haired man, and it is impossible, somehow, to think of him simply as Muck: he must be *Mr.* Muck—was brought to Michigamme by his parents in 1882, taken back to Wisconsin for schooling, and then allowed to return to take a job in the biggest store in town, Hirschman & Johnston's. He never left Michigamme for long. Mr. Muck soon opened his own store, and he had an ice box custom-built for him in Chicago. It was fourteen feet by sixteen feet, the biggest in all Marquette County, and it cost him $1,080. He installed great meat-chopping blocks, he stocked his shelves to the ceiling with enormous quantities of merchandise, he had eleven clerks scurrying about the store.

This was headquarters for the mining men, this little office at the rear of the store with its high slanting desk and its high stool, its heavy safe red-lettered boldly: "E. G. Muck," and its clutter of documents and its thick-bellied stove. The Michigamme Mine shipped 80,777 tons, the greatest amount ever, in 1890, and the Wetmore (Imperial), 38,460. Who knew how vast the ore beds really were? Take out west, out by the Wetmore and the Beaufort, they don't really know what they got out there. Enough ore to last forever, maybe. And high-grade ore, too. Lots of it's that funny yellow powdery stuff, or reddish-yellow. Looks funny, but it'll run as high as sixty per cent iron, almost as good as Republic or the Cleveland Lake. It's shallow, too; cheap to mine.

But the real mine's the hard-ore mine, the Michigamme. Cap's got her down pret' near five hundred feet now, they say. He's goin' right out under Mill Bay, right out under the lake. He'll chase that vein to hell. An' she's a corker to follow, too.

What do you think of that Huron Bay Grade proposition? Runnin' a railroad right up the Peshekee to Lake Superior, to the Huron Bay. Might be all right. Sure would cut out Marquette and Ishpeming. Then we wouldn't be tied to them towns. Best thing could happen to Michigamme. Sure, it'd help Champion too, and I hate to see anything good happen to Champion, but it'd help us as much as it would them—more, after we get those soft yellow hematites goin' out west by Spurr. It'd kill L'Anse too, prob'ly. I dunno, though; it's a hell of an upgrade, up the Peshekee. Dunno whether they can make it or not. Sure they can make it. Well, there's lots of folks think they can anyway; I never seen so much stock sold in anything.

That's right. But this is only the starter. This town'll be biggern Ishpeming or Marquette either one some day. You wait. This town's got a future. I don't care if property does come high these days; I'm gettin' me some more, and I'm stayin' right here. This town's got a future.

ALL CAUGHT UP

A TOWN DOES NOT DIE all at once. A town dies slowly. Sometimes you can't even see that it's dying (especially if you've lived in it all your life). Then suddenly it is dead.

Just past the turn of the century, word started around Michigamme that the loggers were about all cut out on the East Branch and the West Branch of the Peshekee, on Baraga Creek, on Dishnow Creek. It was puzzling. Everybody'd thought there was plenty of timber up there.

Well, probably there was. Probably just a rumor.

Then, all at once, in 1906, Read drove the Peshekee for the last time, ran the cut through his mill, and tore down the mill and sold it for scrap. Bang! Just like that.

Michigamme wasn't a lumbering town any more.

The jacks moved on. The good people might say: "Good riddance," but—well, the town did look empty on Saturday night without them.

Still, there were the mines. There'd always be the mines.

Always? Well, sure. What the billy hell? Just because the Michigamme Mine hadn't made such a good showing in the last few years didn't mean anything. The hell it don't—look at the records; here's the shipments, right here in Mr. Muck's papers, right here on his desk; look here and see how good that wonderful hard-ore mine is. Here—tons shipped:

1889	56,999	1895	3,214	1901	24,483
1890	80,777	1896	none	1902	10,684
1891	23,169	1897	none	1903	1,104
1892	1,894	1898	none	1904	none
1893	935	1899	none	1905	153
1894	1,610	1900	19,094	1906	none

Now what do you think? I tell you, the Michigamme's through.

'T'ain't neither. Hell, look at the figures yourself. She was boomin' in the eighties, weren't she? Then she went dead in '96 and stayed that way, and remember how everybody said she was all caught up? All right. What happened? She was dead four years, then she come back, an' in 1900 she shipped more'n nineteen thousand tons o' damn good ore. Sure she went dead year before last, an' last year she only got out a hunert 'n' fifty-three tons. An' none this year. But I'll betcha—let's see—this is 1906—I'll betcha a drink that by 1910, she'll have shipped fifty thousand tons. Bet?

Well, I dunno. You may be right. She's been dead before, like you say, and she's always come back.

Sure she has. An' what if she don't? Ain't we got the stuff out west, out at Spurr an' on out toward Three Lakes?

Ah, whatta we got out there? The Beaufort ain't shipped a pound o' ore this year, an' from what I hear tell, they ain't likely to. The Wetmore only got out somethin' like fifteen hunert tons last year. The others've been dead for ten years or more, just about.

Sure, but ain't you heard o' the Ohio?

Well, now, maybe at that. . . .

The Ohio was the next big bonanza. The town leaped from its doldrums the very next year, 1907, when the Ohio Mine out in Spurr Township shipped a whopping 78,029 tons its first year of operation. That was more than the great Michigamme ever shipped in any single year save one. And that same year the Wetmore shipped 55,756 tons. The boys in Murray's and the boys at Mr. Muck's were jubilant. What did it matter if the hard-ore mine was all caught up? The soft-ore mines to the west would keep this town booming for a long time. Lamps burned late once more in Mr. Muck's office. To it one evening went Mr. Wood, the general manager of the Ohio Mine, out from the East and now a town hero. Well, everybody looked pleased and self-conscious when he came in and waited for him to say something. But he told old George, his captain: "George, we're already down four levels and we've spent a lot of money. Maybe we better not go ahead with that new drift. It doesn't look so good to me anyway; it doesn't look like it should."

Well sir, old George, he stood up and everybody knew what

he was goin' to say; he'd been tellin' the boys about it all evening, and they hoped he wouldn't say it now to the chief, to Mr. Wood; but they knew he would, and he did: "Mr. Wood, I'm gonna drive that drift as long as I'm on the job. You can fire me if you want to, Mr. Wood, but you're a god-damn book miner."

And he stomped out of Mr. Muck's store. But Mr. Wood didn't fire him, and old George went ahead and drove that drift, and as a result they opened up the fifth level and hit a vein of the prettiest blue ore you ever saw, ore that was almost sixty per cent pure iron. Mr. Wood went back east.

So it looked for a time like the town was good for another twenty years, maybe forever. But then the Wetmore, the Imperial that is, shut down in 1914—shut down, it looked like, for keeps. The Ohio gave up in 1912 for three years, then reopened during the war, but shut down for good in 1920. The Portland opened in 1914 out in Spurr Township, but it only ran two years.

And that was all. The Michigamme, the great, worshipped hard-ore mine, never did reopen. Some say they quit working it when a blast blew air bubbles up through the waters of the lake. Some claim they just quit because they wanted to, that there's plenty of ore in that hole yet. But the authoritative handbook, Lake Superior Iron Ores, says the Michigamme was exhausted in 1905.

And all at once, about the time of the 1914–18 war, the town of Michigamme was dead. The timber was gone. The mines were shut down. People who remembered the boom days wandered in the deserted streets, unable to comprehend what had happened. Where had everybody gone? Once there had been 3,000 people hereabouts. Now only a few hundred. The saloons were boarded up. The hotels were empty. The trains didn't stop very often any more. Even the tracks had been torn up, all but a single track. (Remember when there were three or four sidings at Read's mill?) On Saturday night no more check-shirted lumberjacks on the sidewalks, no more miners with hematite red in their clothes and skin, hematite in their hair. No more crowds in Mr. Muck's store, in Sundstrom's or Christianson's or Simonen's or Majhannu's. No more whistling steamboats on the lake; they had been taken away bodily or junked; the lake was strangely quiet. No more noonday whistles from the mine shafts and the sawmill, no more deafening buzz of saws, no more picnics on the Fourth. The bank and even the piles of sawdust by the mill site were gone. So were the dreams. The Huron Bay Grade was an aching memory. They had built it all right, but something went wrong and it was not used. Mr. Muck lost $10,000 in it and he was only one of hundreds. After a time they tore up the tracks and built a logger's road atop the grade, burying the dream forever.

It was the same story at Humboldt, at Champion. The mines were down, the towns were dead. Humboldt disappeared almost entirely except on road maps. Champion looked like Michigamme, empty homes clustered about a tumble-down shaft house. The blight killed even Republic, though not quite so thoroughly or so soon as it killed Michigamme.

By 1920 Michigamme was all caught up. Realists were saying that in ten years it would be nothing but a heap of crumbling building foundations.

Then suddenly the unpredictable magic lightning struck: Henry Ford was coming to town. Henry Ford was going to re-open the Imperial Mine. Henry Ford was buying out the old railroad grant lands. Henry Ford was going to buy into some Ishpeming mines. Henry Ford was going to commence large-scale logging operations in the Huron Mountain foothills. Henry Ford might build a modern sawmill on the shores of Lake Michigamme. Henry Ford, reaching swiftly for Upper Michigan empire, might make of Michigamme a new River Rouge.

Michigamme was busting its corset to be seduced by the motor wizard. Its grovelings—and it was by no means alone—became almost embarrassing. But one should not condemn the citizens of Michigamme for welcoming a sugar daddy. They had suffered much. Many of them had lived here all their lives; they had poured their lives into making this town great; they had seen it soar to the heights and they had seen it flattened. They had stuck by it, for they loved this town, these hills, these lakes and mines and forests.

First Ford sent his timber cruisers into town, twenty of them, and they made their headquarters at Mr. Muck's store. It was like old times, Mr. Muck's store had been deserted so long, and now suddenly it rang again with mining talk, lumbering talk, with the rustle of maps and the plans for grub for the explorers. Mr. Muck, he put 'em right on their sections. One of 'em wanted to go up the Huron Bay Grade, and it was not painful memory that led Mr. Muck to deter him; it was minute knowledge of every inch of the hinterland: You don't want to go up the Grade, you want to go up the Section 16 road and you can stay overnight in an old logging camp; then you've only got a mile and a quarter to snowshoe next morning before you hit the section you want. But, Mr. Muck, are you a landlooker? No, my boy, I'm a map looker, and, what's more, I've been collecting taxes in this township more years than you've been cruising timber, and I know what I'm talking about. He did, too.

So the timber cruisers looked the land and departed and Michigamme held its breath. Everybody knew that Ford already had extensive holdings near Iron Mountain, on the Wisconsin line south of Michigamme; indeed, Kingsford, Michigan, Iron Mountain's twin city, was named for a top Ford executive, E. G. Kingsford, a brother of Ford's wife. But would the great man actually move into Michigamme? The town, nervous as a bride, talked of nothing else. And then one day the word became official: Henry Ford had bought out the holdings of the Michigan Land & Iron Company, Ltd., an English company which had taken over the lands granted to the old Marquette, Houghton & Ontonagon Railroad, every odd-numbered section for six miles on each side of its right-of-way roughly between Sidnaw and Marquette, L'Anse and Floodwood. All together, some 440,000 acres, enough to take a man's breath away. All that Ford bought, and he also bought out the whole Hebard lumbering outfit around L'Anse and Pequaming, and the Stearns & Culver Lumber Co. there; and he bought other pieces of land until, in the end, his Upper Michigan empire comprised perhaps a million acres, probably the largest single holding in the Upper Peninsula.

And of this, more than 30,000 acres was in Michigamme Township. Mr. Muck was Township Supervisor and a member of the County Board, and, though he had not had the pleasure of meeting Mr. Ford, he composed, not without trepidation, a letter welcoming Mr. Ford to Michigamme and expressing hope that a committee from the town could meet with the Ford people when they arrived to take over.

Then one morning a private railroad car pulled into the little Michigamme station—about the size of an outdoor privy—and Mr. Muck led a welcoming committee down to meet it. They could see that it was the Fair Lane, Mr. Ford's private car. From it emerged Mrs. Ford and Edsel Ford and Mrs. Edsel Ford and Harry Bennett and that Mr. Sorenson, and some others, Henry's private physicians probably. But Mr. Ford wasn't there, nor was Mr. Kingsford. They, Mrs. Ford explained, were driving up from Iron Mountain, in a Ford, of course. They arrived presently. That was quite a day in Michigamme. School was dismissed, and all the kids lined up and greeted Mr. Ford. Led, or followed, by the eager committee, he inspected the town, and he inspected the Imperial Mine, the old Wetmore which Cleveland-Cliffs had sold to him, and he declined to buy the old Read mill site—"It's rather small for our purposes"—and besides he'd need a new road into town. Oh, we'll build you a road, Mr. Ford. And they did, too. But he never took over the mill site. He said that he would rearrange Michigamme's electric lighting system, which he did (even today the town by night looks like a good-sized city). Mr. Muck invited him to take a boat ride on the lake and Mr. Ford accepted—"That'd suit the ladies; they've been sitting in the car or walking in the woods all day; we'll be at your store at eight a.m." They were, too, for you know Mr. Ford, he's an early riser. The only boat available was the launch *Annette*, which would carry only twenty-five persons—damn it, wouldn't you know we'd of scrapped the *Rose*, that used to carry a hundred and fifty?—but they all piled into it and cruised around the islands and all the way down to the dam at the outlet. Here Mr. Ford took off his shoes and socks and went wading. He also asked about the waterfall which he had bought, but Mr. Muck told him it wasn't here, wasn't on Lake Michigamme at all; it was up north on the Peshekee. Up the southeast corner of Section 10 is where the old slide dam is, and your dam site would be on Section 12. Mr. Ford was impressed with the accuracy of this information when they went up the Huron Bay Grade (for once, the Grade seemed good: it got Mr. Ford where he wanted to go) and inspected the dam site. Mr. Muck gave Mr. Ford a rare map of this, his empire, and Mr. Ford was mighty pleased.

There was more to the love feast, and then Mr. Ford departed. And Michigamme kept on wearing its Sunday best. It would yet be great. In Mr. Muck's store the dreams were dreamed again. All you had to do was look at a map to see that Mr. Ford would center his vast Upper Michigan operations right here. The watershed lay this way from the northwest. There was everything here— water, timber (the loggers had taken only the prime stuff), ore (everybody always knew there was plenty of *that* left). Michigamme was all set.

For a time it looked that way. Of course, Mr. Ford decided to erect his huge sawmill at L'Anse and Pequaming (the L'Anse *Sentinel* headlined in seventy-two-point type "L'ANSE GETS BIGGEST GIFT OF ITS CAREER" the day Ford's entry into L'Anse was announced). Of course Mr. Ford built his private summer home at Pequaming, outside L'Anse, and visited there more frequently than he visited at Michigamme. Of course, Mr. Ford built his "model" lumber town of Alberta, named for Kingsford's daughter, closer to L'Anse than to Michigamme and he built his logging railroad into the Huron Mountains from L'Anse, not from Michigamme.

But he operated the Imperial Mine, and he sent drill crews into the Michigamme hinterland, and he opened the Blueberry Mine, between Michigamme and Ishpeming, thereby giving employment to many Michigamme men. And in 1922, after eight long years of idleness, the Imperial shipped 73,083 tons of that brownish-yellow hematite, and the following year it shipped an enormous 211,302 tons, nearly three times as much as even the sacred Michigamme had shipped in its best year. Over and over the townspeople told one another the little inevitable jokes. About the time Henry and that Kingsford fellow walked into the Imperial location during a snowstorm and Mr. Muck called up and offered to send his team for them, but Henry, he said no at first; then he said: "Wait a minute—you better send it for Mr. Kingsford," so Mr. Muck did, and Kingsford rode in with the team; but Henry, he grabbed a freight at the Spurr crossing and walked across the tops of twenty-two cars on the way into town. Or about the time that Henry was supposed to visit here with Edison and Harvey Firestone and the whole town turned out to meet them at nine o'clock but couldn't find them; finally somebody found Henry down on Birch Point wading in the lake with about forty kids; he said that Firestone and Edison couldn't make it or were still asleep or something, I forget which. Little jokes about genial Henry Ford, the people's choice. The town was booming, the town was his.

But before long the honeymoon ended. Ford sent a drill man in to put a drill on Section 27 near the old Ohio Mine and then ordered him to pull his drill when he was only 800 feet down. The drill man remonstrated; he felt confident he'd hit ore at 1,400. But, the story goes, Ford's man replied loftily: "We're not looking for ore; we're looking for formation." And the town answered: "Book miners, all of 'em. Formation be damned; the ore is where you find it."

That wasn't the worst. Henry Ford paid his taxes—he still pays some $8,000—and he furnished Michigamme with cheap electricity and he did a lot of other things. But somehow he seemed remote, foreign, an outsider, a cold absentee landlord. It wasn't that Mr. Ford was stand-offish; look at how he waded barefoot in Lake Michigamme. But—well, hell, the townsfolk were accustomed to drink with the mining captains and to see the superintendent at church and to have their kids play with the kids of the company owners. Cleveland-Cliffs seemed like it belonged here; even its big shots could sit on the edge of a meat block in Mr. Muck's store. Cleveland-Cliffs seemed, well, solid; Henry Ford seemed flighty, impermanent. The old-timers here had seen these mines, the Imperial among them, develop from nothing but rock ledges in the woods; they had a personal feeling about these mines; some of them had died in these mines; suddenly a stranger said: "These belong to me." Stories began to appear, stories of a different sort. Like the one about Henry Ford's muscling into the exclusive Huron Mountain Club, the private club hated by common people from Marquette to L'Anse, and about how armed guards patrolled the boundaries of the club grounds in the beautiful Huron Mountains. Like the story about how Ford brought hundreds of men to L'Anse—so many that some of them lived in tents for a while—then capriciously laid off six or seven hundred of them just before Christmas, turning them out for the town to care for. About his chauffeurs and his private yacht when he arrived at L'Anse to visit his home, a fantastic place which he spent thousands of dollars on but only occupied for a few hours at a time. About the close-mouthed arrogance of his lieutenants. True or not, the stories demonstrated the death of respect for Henry Ford among many persons in Michigamme and L'Anse. When he visited L'Anse, the mill hands threw into the pond big virgin pine logs that they'd been saving all summer for his arrival, then joked about it afterward.

True, his sawmill was a model of safety. True, the Blueberry Mine's surface layout was "a delight," with concrete, brick, and glass buildings. And true, he spent a lot of money in this region, and he built a school at Pequaming, and he had to buck the notorious clannishness of small communities.

But Ford never built the new ore dock which he had hinted he would build at L'Anse. He held his land tightly. He did not develop it to anything approaching the extent which enthusiasts had hoped. And in 1933 he abandoned the Imperial Mine.

Some people at Michigamme never will forgive him for that. One resident said: "He says the Imperial's all worked out. But he don't know, he didn't go deep enough. Henry Ford just can't mine ore." Today the skip road is clogged with sawdust, the shaft is boarded over, weeds grow where the shaft house rose. The Imperial shipped a total of 2,057,781 tons, more than twice as much as the Michigamme's 935,880 tons. It was the last mine to operate near Michigamme.

Today Michigamme is not a ghost town in the sense that it is utterly deserted. But it is a tatterdemalion memory of great dreams. Three hundred people inhabit it. It has a magnificent high school and a new town hall, little else. The WPA built a seaplane dock on the lake at the foot of the hill below the town, but it never was used. There is a movie once a week. The streets are unpaved and quiet; cows wander in them, and sometimes deer. Now and then in the spring a bear comes into town. The town is across the tracks from the new concrete U. S. 41; little traffic is diverted to the town. Tourists are not big business as they are in some Upper Michigan towns; there are few facilities for them, though the fishing and hunting near by are excellent. The town has no modern hotel. The townspeople do not seem to encourage tourists, nor do they mingle with the people from the rich girls' camp or the religious institute on the shores of the lake. Though the townsfolk are extremely hospitable and friendly with those whom they accept, they are cool to outsiders. This always has been a lumbering and a mining town; its residents, among them the pioneers who still remember, respect this heritage and have a stiff-backed independence. Why cater to a lot of fat women in shorts from down below, a lot of fishermen with hundred-dollar outfits? The town has pride, and dignity.

One saloon survives from the old days, Clarence Murray's. It belonged to his father before him, and it is little changed from the brave days when fighting Billy Lamour was a regular customer. Four sets of moth-eaten antlers are on the wall behind the bar; in the horns of one rests a sign urging the purchase of war bonds and displaying a picture, captioned "For All We Hold Dear," of a young woman at a picket fence. A plaque on the back bar portrays a number of penniless drunks in a saloon: "Waiting for a Live One." It is appropriate; usually several of the boys are stacked up in the "snake room," the back room at Murray's where the boys collapse after they have had one too many. Fourth of July and, indeed, any Saturday night, are something to behold at Murray's. The customers are mostly lumberjacks—they still are cutting pulpwood and second growth around Michigamme—and miners. These men drink a lot. They shake dice for drinks, and when they win and are caught up on drinks, they take chips worth a nickel in trade, which old John Murray used to pass out to Billy Lamour and his pals. A round-bellied wood stove stands near the battered poker table. The bar itself is old, its edge worn into wavy depressions by many elbows. The Coca-Cola cooler is full of beer. Beer is still a nickel a glass, as by God it should be, says Clarence, the proprietor. The lineoleum on the floor is worn, the sanitary facilities somewhat primitive. Calendar nudes adorn the smoke-begrimed walls. There are two entrances, one for ladies; this opens into a room separated from the bar by an ineffectual partition.

Curled flypapers dangle from the ceiling beside the unshaded electric light bulbs, though in the last year or two Clarence has added some newfangled fancy lights that seem oddly anachronistic. Likewise, the weatherbeaten frame front of the building recently has been covered with a composition material designed, unsuccessfully, to imitate brick. The only sign on the window says simply "Beer," with two pictures of sudsy steins flanking it. To Murray's come the boys for their Saturday night bats, and here they come on Sunday for their facemakers. Through Clarence's front window you can see the range of hills beyond the tracks, the Michigamme Mine. Today the famous Michigamme is an ice mine: all summer long ice stays frozen in one of its open stopes behind Maurice Ball's "Mt. Shasta Lodge," and the townsfolk turn to it when they run out of ice in August, as they almost invariably do (they never seem to cut enough from the frozen lakes in the winter, somehow).

Mr. Muck's store is nearly always deserted. His shelves are almost empty. His magnificent refrigerator, the town's marvel not so many years ago, now is a dumping place for rolls of tar-paper roofing and assorted bottles and mattresses and golf clubs and blown-out inner tubes, all the debris of housekeeping and storekeeping. But Mr. Muck himself has not given up. Not by a long shot. Old man though he was, in the summer of 1943 he went out into the woods south of the Imperial location and from a strip four miles long he took two hundred pounds of ore and crushed it and sent it to R. S. Archibald, vice-president and manager of the North Range Mining Company, which was operating the Blueberry on a lease. Analysis of this ore showed 60.90 per cent iron, a very high percentage, Mr. Muck claims. He pointed this out to Archibald, who admitted: "That's pretty good ore, Muck."

"Well?" demanded Mr. Muck, his eyes gleaming.

Archibald shrugged. "Outcroppings."

Mr. Muck denies it. These are no isolated chancy outcroppings. This is a real range, richer, perhaps, than any heretofore discovered. To prove it—and the old man's eyes glisten—there's an old geologist's map, maybe almost a hundred years old, and if you could take a look at that, you'd see that *they* knew there was a range out there in the woods.

His maps and his bag of yellow ore Mr. Muck keeps locked always in the safe in his office. Periodically he argues with Archibald, trying to convince him that the Michigamme Mine never was properly explored, that "the main body of ore here is still untapped—this range has a future and Michigamme *will* come back."

A few years ago Mr. Muck had a caller. His was a great name, Christopher. He was Will Christopher, son of old Captain John Christopher, and he had come back to Michigamme to look into the possibilities of reopening the Spurr Mine. But he stayed only briefly, his project did not materialize. Nor has anything come as yet of other plans to reopen the old Portland Mine.

Mr. Muck—and he is not alone—has kept the faith. He is convinced that the ore is still here, that the great days will dawn again as surely as skips run up and down. He may be right.

܍§ 18 §܊

"AT A MEETING
OF THE BOARD . . ."

WHAT HAPPENED to Michigamme is, in little, what happened to much of Upper Michigan. Who is to blame? The giant corporations, those villains of the soap-box orators? Or the very nature of mining country, timber country? Or simply human greed, human stupidity?

As a problem child, Upper Michigan has engaged the attention of numerous Government experts and other professional viewers with alarm. Well it may. At the bottom of the depression in the early thirties, seventy-five per cent of the population of Keweenaw County was "on relief." Nor was that atypical; in December 1934, thirty-four per cent of the population of all the Upper Peninsula was receiving relief, as compared to only 17.8 per cent for the state of Michigan as a whole. The Upper Peninsula has been termed a rural slum, another Dust Bowl; its people have been compared to the Okies.

The problems here are, in general, common to the whole "Northern Lakes States Cutover Region," an area which, with Upper Michigan as its heart, embraces the northern portion of Lower Michigan, northern Wisconsin, and Northeastern Minnesota. Of this cutover country the National Resources Committee reported in 1939: "Woodsmen, miners, farmers, and others once made a good living in this Region; some even prospered, but with the turn of the century the trend of opportunity declined. Even

237

before 1929 there were more workers than jobs. Today the Region holds a stranded population. But there are bright spots."

Why did opportunity decline? We have seen, in little, the reasons. Loggers took the timber, and fire destroyed what little they left. Copper mining declined because the veins grew thinner, thus forcing up the cost of production. Technological advances threw men out of work in the iron mines; moreover, open-pit iron mining always was seasonal, and a shortsighted taxation policy tended to make underground iron mining seasonal also. Commercial fishing, once a major industry, declined because the fish grew scarce, owing to unwise or inadequate conservation laws. The people were saddled with a heavy financial burden because government itself cost too much money, chiefly the result of overlapping taxation districts and the overabundance of widely scattered small communities. Making a farmer out of a miner or a lumberjack would be difficult anywhere; it is nearly impossible in Upper Michigan, where, with few exceptions, the land is rocky or is forest land which should be rebuilt as forest land and not converted to agriculture; while parts of the peninsula have been farmed successfully for many years, elsewhere attempts at farming have led to heartbreak and personal disaster, to abandoned farms and rotting log-cabin farmhouses which the wilderness is reclaiming. Nor, despite almost unsurpassed natural assets, has the tourist trade on a big-business scale yet replaced mining and logging as a source of revenue in Upper Michigan as it has elsewhere, notably in northern Wisconsin.

Curiously, the war has not brought a boom to Upper Michigan. This is no San Diego shipyard region, no Detroit. True, the armed services and logging and mining have taken up the unemployment slack. But the workers, though busy, are not on a boom-time spree. It is as though this country has seen so many boom-and-bust periods that it views wartime prosperity with a jaundiced eye. There are also more material reasons why no boom exists here. The copper range is quiet because the Government has pegged the price of copper at a figure below the cost of production in all but the richest mines. (Great Calumet & Hecla was operating but one shaft in the summer of 1943.) Sawmills like those of the IXL at Hermansville were idle; no men were available to cut the few trees still standing, for many men had gone into the armed services or down below to work in war plants. Despite the increased wartime demand for lumber, the I. Stephenson Company, whose name had had a ring of greatness in Escanaba since the Seney days, closed its mill. It seemed apparent that the days of the giant logging companies were over. To take their place came scores of small operators with portable saw rigs; traveling light, they moved in, bought a few forties which were isolated timbered islands in cutover regions, logged them, and packed up and moved on. Most of what they were cutting was small timber for paper pulp or chemical manufacture. One operator began hot-logging at Ontonagon, in one of the peninsula's few remaining stands of virgin timber. But none of this added up to a lumbering boom. A pulp mill at Munising rafted wood from Canada, and a resort keeper imported knotty pine from the South to build his "cabins in the virgin forests."

Some of the iron mines were working three shifts a day; in some cases old explorations, long abandoned, were reopened. But it is hard to have a boom in an underground iron mine. Capacity is limited to the number of times a skip can go up and down; production simply cannot be increased again and again. Nor was it advisable to sink many new shafts in the ore reserves; before they could be put into production, the ore from the vast open-pit mines of the Minnesota ranges, untrammeled by the skip limitation, would have met the wartime demand and the Michigan companies would have been stranded in postwar days with overexpanded plants.

Similarly the shipment of ore on the Great Lakes is limited by the short navigation season. True, the long low ships carried a record-breaking 92,076,781 tons down to the war-hungry steel furnaces in 1942, and this was reflected at all the lake ports, from Duluth and Superior to Marquette and Escanaba. Valiant efforts in 1943 to beat this tonnage were defeated by a late spring which delayed the opening date a full month. The car ferry *Sainte Marie* smashed a lane through floe-locked Whitefish Bay before the ice was "ripe." Nearly all the boats sailed shorthanded. One reached the head of the Lakes without deckhands. Beardless youths manned the boats beside veterans retired since sailing days. Fog did not halt the ships, nor did storms. Some sank in collisions; all took a merciless beating and so did their crews, who frequently were too exhausted to go ashore even during the brief loading hours. Even the new MacArthur lock (named for General Douglas MacArthur) at the Soo did not overcome the handicap of the late opening. None the less, tonnage was far above normal. But this meant less to Upper Michigan than to the steel towns down below. Escanaba went through a typical Upper Peninsula experience when the Government abandoned a dock project which might have restored the town's position as the biggest ore port on the upper Lakes, a position it had not held for years.

Lakes shipping has come a long way since the sailing days. Now the ships are the familiar hog-backed ore boats, floating holds with a blunt jutting house at either end for cramped crewmen and engines and instruments. They are enormous boats, larger than many salt-water vessels, some of them more than a block long and of more than 18,000 tons. The largest carry crews of more than thirty. They can make the 1,000-odd mile run from Duluth to Buffalo in ninety-six hours or less, for they are capable of fifteen miles an hour. Few go beyond Buffalo. The chief lower Lakes ports near the steel centers are Cleveland, Ashtabula, Conneaut, Lorain, Toledo, Erie, Fairport, Huron, Detroit, Indiana Harbor, South Chicago. The boats are loaded in about four hours at massive docks which may reach nearly half a mile out into the lake, rising perhaps a hundred feet above the water, and at night the hard ore thunders down steep metal chutes into the ship's hold, striking blue sparks and shaking mightily the silent dark giant settling in the water. In 1943 nearly three hundred boats were in the Lakes ore trade, owned chiefly by five companies: Pittsburgh Steamship Company, Interlake Steamship Company, Hutchinson & Company, Cleveland-Cliffs, and M. A. Hanna Company. They were sailed by about 11,000 officers and men. Many of the men held war-industry jobs in the winter, their customary vacation time. Some had homes at Sault Ste. Marie or Detroit, and when their ships passed through the narrow channels of the St. Mary's River or the St. Clair River, they seized megaphones and hurried to the rails to carry on shouted conversation with their wives who paced the shore.

In short, the war lifted Upper Michigan from the paralyzing depression of the thirties. But the country was only busy, not booming. It may be safe to say that the war of the 1940's has meant less to Upper Michigan than any other war since the Civil War.

Perhaps it had had enough of booms. Actually, that attitude may well be a healthy symptom. Upper Michigan has a future, uncertain though it may be. It is not dead. Probably the worst already has happened.

The first shock of the disappearance of timber has passed. Now the U. S. Forestry Service is restocking the timberland, maintaining huge tree plantations, supervising, wherever possible, logging operations so that, in accordance with "selective logging" principles, only full-grown or defective trees will be cut and the sound small trees left to replenish the forest. Fires have done their worst. The Michigan Conservation Department, one of the nation's best, has developed a highly efficient system of fighting fire, involving a network of high steel fire towers, a close-knit organization of wardens and citizens, and the use of modern apparatus. These agencies have something worth saving: Upper Michigan contains more merchantable timber today than any other comparable area in the cutover country, and 88.3 per cent of its total acreage is in forest land.

A more realistic approach to the farm problem has been achieved. The mad scramble to convert cutover country to farmland has ended; no longer is farming encouraged on land unsuited to agriculture, but the small areas of high-grade soil are being farmed intensively and scientifically. Happily, the ill-advised attempts to publicize Upper Michigan as "Cloverland" have been abandoned.

Copper mining may not have reached bottom, for the veins are not completely worked out, but it is hard to see how the situation could become a great deal worse. Before and during the 1914–18 war copper supported some 16,000 workers in Houghton County alone; by 1933 this number had dropped to 2,000, and even in 1940, as rearmament broke the depression's grip, only about 2,600 men were employed in copper mining. In 1849 Michigan produced 96 per cent of the nation's copper; in 1943 only about 4 per cent. It appears obvious that, barring technological advances or relaxation of economic controls that would make profitable the mining of low-grade deep-lying veins, the Upper Peninsula will not be able to count copper a major industry. In the past the copper miners and their families have refused to recognize this and have stayed in the copper country even though it could not support them. This refusal to leave a land they love has intensified economic problems all over Upper Michigan; few people are more loyal to their homeland. Perhaps now they have been scraping bottom in the copper country so long that their sons will find employment either in new areas or in new home industries, such as the tourist trade.

Iron ore remains. Here again the worst probably has happened to the Upper Peninsula. For a long time Michigan had iron-ore production all to itself. But after the vast Mesaba Range was opened up in Minnesota, Upper Michigan held its own for only a few years, and in 1900 Minnesota took and kept the lead in ore production. In the boom year of 1937 the Mesaba alone produced 45,824,000 tons of ore, more than three times the 14,058,000 tons from all three Michigan ranges; and to the Minnesota total for that year must be added 1,453,000 tons from the Vermilion Range and 1,775,000 tons from the Cuyuna Range. The reason for Mesaba's supremacy lies not only in its vastness but in the accessibility of its ore, which makes possible low production costs with which the pockety ore of Michigan cannot compete. Other physical factors have militated against Michigan ore. Thus some of the ore on the Menominee Range was so high in silica or phosphorus content that when penalties for these impurities were deducted by modern blast-furnace operators, the mines became unprofitable. Time was, in the eighties, when mining men in Michigan scorned the Mesaba mud. When this turned out to be unjustified and Mesaba forged ahead, Michigan mining men thought the great Michigan ranges would be abandoned. This has proved equally untrue. A place, solid and probably permanent, has been made in steel economy for Michigan ore. It can no longer be the ore leader; neither can it be discarded. Curiously, the very inaccessibility of Michigan's ore during the rush for ore in the war of the 1940's has worked to the advantage of the region's future. That is, while production has been pushed up to astronomical figures in Minnesota, thus seriously depleting ore reserves, Michigan's reserves probably have not been tapped to a much greater extent than during any normal period of exploration and development. As a consequence, it is conceivable that, years from now when Minnesota's ore reserves may be nearing exhaustion, Michigan's will remain, despite an extra fifty-odd years of mining. Estimates of Lake Superior ore reserves, largely guesswork because the mining companies which hold them are close-mouthed, range all the way from a fifteen years' supply to an "unlimited" supply. These will be greatly modified if, as may be reasonably expected, technological advances make profitable the mining of low-grade ores not now included in estimates. Ore men say "there is no conservation problem" here. A new ore field opened up in Canada during the present war may affect the future of the ranges on the south shore of Lake Superior. The major wartime development on the iron ranges is the sinking of the shaft of the new Mather Mine at Ishpeming. CCI and Bethlehem Steel, its joint owners, expected to pour into it two million dollars and to make it the nation's largest underground producer. Ishpeming also was talking about the scientists' wartime search, by night with ultraviolet rays, for tungsten in the hills of the Dead River country where the old-time prospectors found gold.

In general, it may be said with justification that out of a past made hysterical by boom-and-bust development, iron ore has emerged as the solid backbone of Upper Michigan's economy. (The picture, of course, may change.) It may be well to inquire into the position of the big iron companies in Michigan's affairs, into the complicated question of whether big companies in general have ruined Upper Michigan or made it great. You can hear both opinions expressed.

The opinion of one qualified observer in an iron region runs: "The big companies never did a thing for this country. Every once in a while one of the big shots will come out from the East to see where all his money came from and maybe to get a street named after him. But that's all; they never stay and build up the country; they strip it and get out."

On the other hand, another equally well-informed man says: "This country wouldn't be anything if it wasn't for Cleveland-

Cliffs and the other big outfits. During the depression they kept their mines running a few days a week just to help out on employment—not because they could make any money mining ore. They pay the taxes and they built the towns and they did everything."

The copper companies have been similarly reviled and lauded.

Virtual unanimity is achieved only in the lumbering regions, where nearly everyone agrees that the big companies' greed in the early days contributed to the rapid decline of forest resources.

This diversity of opinion is perhaps inevitable, depending upon the individual experience of the man talking. But a few generalities emerge from the welter of contradictions.

Few major industrial regions have experienced less serious labor trouble than the Michigan iron ranges. However, so many factors enter here—the non-volatile temper of the workers, the long history of common struggle in the wilderness, the policy of appeasement by management, and so on—that this is an unreliable index. Copper's labor history has been more stormy; here again the single tragic strike of 1913 may cloud perspective.

Management has claimed that the influence of "outside agitators" has been almost wholly responsible for the major strikes in Upper Michigan industry. By "outside agitators" usually is meant the leaders of various Western unions connected with the I. W. W., which unquestionably had a hand in both the tragic copper-country strike of 1913 and the unrest among timber workers shortly thereafter. But unionization would have occurred without the encouragement of the Wobblies. As early as 1890 the workmen struck in the mines around Ishpeming. Even before that, unrest had occurred from time to time.

The copper-country strike was by all odds Upper Michigan's bloodiest. It began on July 23, 1913 after Charles W. Moyer, president of the Western Federation of Miners, had climaxed four years of proselytizing by unsuccessfully demanding that two men be employed to operate the new one-man air drill. About 16,000 workers left the copper mines and stamp mills, virtually paralyzing copper production for nearly a year. Rioting and violence drew out the militia. On Christmas Eve disaster occurred. The strikers' families gathered in a hall at Red Jacket for a children's party. Some never identified person in or behind the crowd cried: "Fire." In the rush to escape, more than seventy persons, most of them children, perished. The alarm was false. To this day men in the region dispute the blame. Moyer charged the Citizens' Alliance, an organization formed during the strike, with responsibility for the panic. One version today claims that the companies had imported strike-breakers who gave the false alarm. Another version claims that the "outside agitators," endeavoring to mislead the workers into believing the strike-breakers guilty, gave the alarm. Though a great hue and cry was raised at the time and a considerable investigation ensued, no one was punished. Moyer was mobbed and run out of town. A Congressional committee reported that the companies discriminated against union men and confessed itself helpless to stop the strike. The stalemate ended when the strikers, long unemployed and hungry, straggled back to work. Before long they went on an eight-hour day and received wage increases and other concessions. But they lost their demand which had precipitated the strike.

In general, no one can deny that Upper Michigan industry has experienced fewer strikes and less labor unrest than many other regions. A number of factors may have caused this. For one, the workers simply are phlegmatic. Many of them came direct to this region from the old country; workers and bosses have grown up side by side and there has been less time for a gulf to widen between them than in older industrial areas. Fathers—not grandfathers or great-grandfathers—of some of today's young workers can speak little English; they feel they owe their comfortable circumstances and their imperfect but advantageous Americanization to the companies. A loyalty has grown and persisted.

Yet all is not completely serene. For one reason or another, some company officials today decline to discuss labor relations for publication. "Let sleeping dogs lie" seems a rather common attitude. Whether this indicates trouble ahead—or a fear of it—is impossible to determine. That the paternal craftsman-employer relationship may be breaking down may be indicated by the rapidity with which unionization has spread in recent years. Today nearly all the workers in the iron and copper mines are organized. So are the men on the ore boats, and in the lumber industry, mainly in the sawmills. Especially is this true among the younger workers, the second-generation Americans. The C. I. O. gave unionization great impetus here as elsewhere in heavy industry, and probably can claim as members most of the union men. This apparent trend toward unionization may account for the circumspect silence of management on labor questions. Nevertheless, strikes here have not impeded the war effort. But future labor-management relations are uncertain. They will be affected by the peculiarly strong position of the few great companies which dominate much of Upper Michigan and the odd pioneer characteristics of the region.

But many other factors impinge on the question of the benevolence of the big companies.

They have paid enormous taxes. But they have made a great deal of money.

The companies have built towns and have maintained some well, some poorly. They charge low rents—five dollars a month in 1943 in Gwinn, near Ishpeming, for a six-room house without indoor plumbing or fresh paint—and this gives them a handle on their employees. They have built Y. M. C. A.'s and community houses and have furthered the education and Americanization of their immigrant employees.

The companies have furnished the huge capital required to develop the country. In the process, they have acquired great land holdings; much of these they do not develop, thus standing in the way of progress by individual enterprise. For example, why should a lone prospector hunt gold in the foothills of the Huron Mountains today knowing that, if he found it, he would only find it for one of the big companies which owns the land? Similarly, one of the larger sawmills is near collapse because it cannot get logs, although a mile or so to the north lies a vast tract of forest which a mining company holds and refuses to sell. Minerals are taxed when they have been "discovered"—that is, explored and mapped; land thus is permitted to lie fallow until its particular large owner needs its mineral resources, and thus, while conservation results, normal development may be halted. Similarly, the big companies frequently refuse to sell land to persons who might build a resort that would encourage tourist trade, a necessary item.

Absentee ownership or operation tends to produce indifference.

This is perhaps more prevalent on the Gogebic Range, where most mines are operated under lease by non-owners, than on the Marquette Range, where Cleveland-Cliffs, the dominant power, operates its own mines.

Big companies exercise almost life-and-death control over their people. Remove one such company and the town collapses, the people starve. To varying degrees the companies have recognized their responsibility. All profess a vital concern over the welfare of their communities; some have demonstrated this, others have not. Some, whether through intelligent handling of public relations or through true benevolence, enjoy the goodwill of their communities; others are resented bitterly.

Only a few, like IXL with Blaney Park and Cleveland-Cliffs with Grand Island, appear to have made efforts toward building up the resort industry as a substitute for vanishing resources.

Other powerful industrialists have roused resentment with private clubs, like the Huron Mountain Club. And like the vast wooded private tract near one of the iron ranges where, vicious saloon rumor says, fat nude steel magnates have pursued naked countesses and opera divas on horseback through the wooded glens.

All this resentment is sometimes exploited by local politicians who promise vociferously to drive the magnates from the temples if elected. This is called impossible by the same bitter man who says the iron kings care nothing for the range: "The companies could quit here on a motion by the board of directors and they'd get along all right, but the country would be killed for keeps."

The power of the ore companies came under the scrutiny of the Temporary National Economic Committee, which in 1939 inquired into the question of monopoly and the concentration of economic power. This power was important, not only to Upper Michigan but to the United States as a whole. To supply the nation's steel industry, one of its largest enterprises, the United States produced more iron ore than any other nation in the world, accounting in 1936 for 28.8 per cent of world production. The Lake Superior district produced 85.6 per cent of all United States ore in 1937—63,110,000 tons. Of this amount, 49,052,000 tons, or about three fourths, came from Minnesota, 12,640,000 tons, or one fifth, from Upper Michigan, and the balance from Wisconsin. Put another way, the mines of Upper Michigan alone produced that year more iron ore than any foreign nation except France, nearly one and a half times as much as Germany (exclusive of ore carrying 12 to 30 per cent manganese). And Minnesota produced more than France, which was the largest producer outside the United States.

Obviously, therefore, the companies which lead in the ore fields of Lake Superior wield enormous power in national and world affairs. What are these companies which grew to such greatness from the makeshift beginnings of the pioneers?

Oliver Iron Mining Company ranks first. It is a subsidiary of the United States Steel Corporation, and in 1937 it produced 26,648,159 tons, or 42.2 per cent of the Lake Superior total. It sold its ore only to its parent company. Though active on the three Michigan ranges, it obtained the bulk of its ore from Minnesota.

Behind Oliver came the independents, who sold their ore in the open market. The leader in this group was Pickands, Mather & Company, with 13,816,332 tons, or 21.9 per cent of the total. P-M was an operating company—that is, it operated mining properties owned by others, including the Bethlehem Steel Corporation, and one of its officers described it to the TNEC as "a personal service corporation."

Second largest of the independents was the Cleveland-Cliffs Iron Company, with shipments of 5,733,879 tons, or 9.1 per cent of the total. This $69,000,000 corporation sold more of its own ore than any other company in the district; it maintained the fourth largest fleet of ore-carrying vessels on the Great Lakes, it owned a 75 per cent interest in the Lake Superior & Ishpeming Railroad, and it was engaged in numerous other enterprises. This was Samuel L. Mather's boy grown up.

The third big independent outside the United States Steel Corporation was the M. A. Hanna Company, with 2,239,442 tons, or 3.5 per cent; and the last of the "Big Four," as Patrick Butler called it, was Oglebay, Norton & Company, with 1,636,577 tons, or 2.6 per cent. Butler's own company, Butler Brothers, shipped more than Oglebay, Norton: 1,817,779 tons, or 2.9 per cent.

Seven scattered small producers shipped that year only 1,816,291 tons, or 2.9 per cent, and steel companies other than U. S. Steel shipped 9,401,541 tons, or 14.9 per cent of the total, from their own mines.

Obviously, this was a big fellow's game. All these vast ore resources—greatest in the world—were controlled by perhaps a dozen companies, and of those, the three leaders, Oliver, Cleveland-Cliffs, and Pickands, Mather, shipped nearly three fourths of the total.

The mines were owned or operated by these few companies, in the main. Sometimes several steel companies owned pieces of a mine, much as gamblers own pieces of a prize fighter, and hired an operating company like P-M to work it for them.

Broadly speaking, the competitor of the five independents was Oliver, much as its parent company, U. S. Steel, was the competitor of other steel companies like Bethlehem, Republic, Jones & Laughlin, Youngstown, National, Inland. But the independent ore-producers testified that they also competed with each other. The TNEC was interested in the fact that the basic price of iron ore—no matter which one of these competitors was selling it—had remained the same from 1925 to 1928, had risen then twenty-five cents and stayed at that level for eight years despite the depression of the thirties, and then had risen again and remained on even keel from 1937 till the Committee met late in 1939. The explanations which the leading ore-producers made were highly involved, and at one point Leon Henderson, who sat with the Committee as a representative of the Securities and Exchange Commission, said of this base price: "I still haven't got a satisfactory explanation of . . . why it came out for all of the sellers and all of the buyers at this particular base point." Testimony indicated that the sellers consulted on the price, that the few larger independents took the leadership in these discussions, that one outside customer charged that prices were maintained at "fictitiously high levels" (an allegation denied by Crispin Oglebay, president of Oglebay, Norton), that the base price was maintained through the terrible early thirties by renegotiation of individual contracts with the steel companies.

A letter by President Edward B. Greene of CCI read, in part:

"I am glad that the iron ore business is so largely in the hands of a small group of men who all work on a close and friendly basis." He testified that this was only an offhand note to a friend and did not imply impropriety. A letter written in 1930 by William G. Mather, then president of CCI, discussed his company's acquisition of control of Oglebay, Norton (this was not a true merger) thus: "I think it is an excellent move and will have a stabilizing effect on the conduct of the iron ore industry, but you can see that it is a relationship which we do not want to talk about as such publicity might result in opposition on the part of the public or the consumers to a move which they may construe as tending toward an undue control of prices." President Greene was at a loss to explain this fully.

This whole question of the urge toward combination of ore-producers occupied much of the Committee's attention. Led by U. S. Steel, the steelmakers were becoming integrated—that is, were acquiring blast furnaces, open-hearth furnaces, access to or ownership of ore and other natural resources, and manufacture of a variety of numerous finished steel products. Concomitantly, as President Greene testified, ". . . as the steel people grew in size why maybe the ore companies if they grew in size would be better able to hold their own." By 1939 it was estimated that U. S. Steel owned about 50 per cent of Lake Superior ore reserves and that other integrated steel companies owned perhaps two thirds of the balance, and nearly every steel company obtained from 50 to 100 per cent of its ore from its own mines. This greatly narrowed the market for the independent ore men, and the process was fairly well along by 1930, when the CCI-Oglebay, Norton combination occurred. At that same time other great events were in the making. A powerful financier, Cyrus S. Eaton, through his investment companies, had acquired large blocks of stock in several steel companies. He planned to form the Midwestern Steel Company which would challenge gigantic U. S. Steel for world leadership. He wanted to know whether CCI wanted to become the raw-material company for his combine. CCI thought his chances for success looked very good. But the "big plan" never materialized, although its first unit, Republic Steel Corporation, was formed by merger and Tom Girdler became its head. With him CCI's President

Greene discussed the mutual relationships of their companies, "calling attention to the very large holding in Cliffs Corporation and the possibility that matters of investment in steel companies might be arranged to further the growth and prosperity of Republic as well as Cleveland-Cliffs."

President Greene testified: "I think greater efficiency is generally brought about by large integrated companies, and I think greater efficiency brings about a lower price." He denied any attempt at monopoly and declared there was "very keen competition" among the ore-producers—to compete, "you had to work from Monday morning till Saturday noon." He expressed strong opposition to "a Government-controlled economy" and said: "I believe thoroughly in the competitive system of business." He believed the anti-trust laws should be enforced.

The only other salient point brought out by the Committee concerned interlocking directorates. Testimony and a Government-prepared chart showed that CCI, considered as a unit, held stock in Wheeling, Otis, Republic, Inland, and Youngstown and had at least one director on the board of each. Pickands, Mather and its partners had "financial connections" with Interlake Iron, Dalton Ore, the Steel Company of Canada, Youngstown, and the National City Bank of Cleveland, and directors in the latter two. Similarly the M. A. Hanna Company had two directors on the board of the National City Bank of Cleveland and three directors in National Steel Corporation; the Cleveland Trust Company had a director in Otis Steel Company and Youngstown and exchanged a director with CCI; Oglebay, Norton had a director of Wheeling Steel Corporation and CCI.

All this, then, was the end result of the pioneering. This was where the followers of Burt and Everett arrived. These were the companies that made the iron ranges of Upper Michigan great. It was inevitable, probably, that they should become so powerful. What—if anything—to do toward regulating them is a problem which has baffled economists and administrations for years, a problem which is beyond the scope of this book. Problems aside, these are the companies, as a Congressional committee views them, that employ the miners who spend their money in the saloons of Ishpeming and Ironwood and Crystal Falls and Michigamme.

None of this necessarily means the companies are evil; the Committee's purpose, its chairman said, was not to search out criminal intent, but to promote the welfare of consumers—that is, Cal and Clarence—and companies alike. This is simply another facet of the shaft houses that dot the Ishpeming locations, of the revered names like Mather and Barnum and Pickands, of the company towns and the ghost towns and the safety measures underground in the deep black mines. It rounds out the picture. These goings-on in board rooms and Washington inquiry chambers seem a long way off from the hills and lakes of Upper Michigan, from Clarence Murray's saloon and Mr. Muck's store at Michigamme and Peter Moore's camp up at Silver Lake. Actually they are not. They impinge themselves on the little people in the woods inevitably, whether for good or evil it is impossible to say with finality.

◆§ 19 §◆

TOUGH COUNTRY

𝕿

UPPER MICHIGAN is still tough country. It is one of the few remaining wild and remote regions of the United States. Off the highways which connect the towns there is nothing but wilderness, just as fifty or seventy years ago. Only a comparatively few trunk highways crisscross the peninsula, and vast areas have no roads at all except impassable tote roads abandoned by the loggers. The Soo canal may be the busiest canal in the world and a vital strategic factor in wartime, guarded by the far-away bastion of Iceland and a huge military establishment at Sault Ste. Marie, but the townspeople of Marquette greet the first boat up in the spring with all the enthusiasm of their half-starved winterbound grandparents. L' Anse, with numerous logging camps toward the Huron Mountains, with its tough waterfront saloons thronged with lumberjacks and illegally drunken Indians, has changed little from the hell-roaring days. In other towns you see jacks and miners brawling on Saturday night, see drunken squaws clawing one another in the center of the street. A curious anomaly during Prohibition was a lumberjack in a speakeasy. A posse with bloodhounds hunted an escaped convict for days in a wilderness area he knew like the back of his hand. Two soldiers froze to death on maneuvers near Sidnaw in the winter of 1942–3. A favorite racket a few years ago was shipping coyote hides from neighboring states into Upper Michigan, where the bounty was higher. Bears are fair game the year round in about half of the Upper Peninsula's counties; in the summer of 1943 they were a major problem in the

253

Keweenaw Peninsula, where, having been protected for several years, they were destroying crops and upsetting garbage pails nightly. So much wild territory remains that, periodically, police are called to form a citizens' searching party to hunt for somebody lost in the woods. One woman got lost on the Yellow Dog and walked for three days and three nights, alone but for a dog, through forty miles of uninhabited wilderness all the way to Skanee, a Swedish settlement across the Hump on Huron Bay. Periodically some bearded prospector shows up with hints of a gold strike in the hills. Game wardens have been murdered by violators who, reared in the woods, resent state interference in what they consider their own private domain. When a warden came into a tavern on a summer afternoon, the boys ribbed him by saying loudly: "I'm not going to shoot any more deer this summer [that is, out of season] because that last one didn't taste right," and the warden knows they are not entirely facetious. Trappers still come into town in the spring with piles of beaver hides, not all of them bearing the license tag. In 1942 a deer ran through the Northwestern Café on the main street of Ironwood. Trappers earned $1,930 in bounties during May 1943, taking 102 coyotes, fifteen bobcats, and a lone timber wolf. More than 20,000 deer and elk hides went to the leather trade from Michigan during the 1942–3 hunting season.

Just living is difficult sometimes in Upper Michigan, away from the towns. Danger is always at hand, down-to-earth hardship, not only such perils of modern civilization as unemployment, but the same natural perils the pioneers faced. Upper Michigan is still tough country. It is fifty years behind the times.

Sunday morning, March 16, 1941, was cold—ten below zero— and clear. (But men with barometers stayed home.) The ice on Huron Bay of Lake Superior, northeast of L'Anse, was more than a foot thick and by ten o'clock more than sixty fishermen moved about on it, chopping holes in the ice, erecting three-cornered tents over the holes, building fires in stoves inside the tents, and bobbing for lake trout. Suddenly the wind shifted to the north, the leaden sky turned a brilliant orange, and, without other warning, an enormous piece of ice a mile square at the mouth of the bay broke off. One ice veteran heard the floe cracking and yelled a warning to five men near him; then he leaped for safety. By the time the other five realized what was happening, the blizzard had struck. The howling wind bore snow that stung men's faces like gravel. This was not soft friendly white snow, but blizzard snow, so thick and hard-driving that it looked black, not white.

Everywhere on the shifting, crumbling ice men raced frantically for shore. Five escaped from the big floe and picked their way to land over rough broken ice. Not until nearly midnight did they reach home. Others were less fortunate. The huge floe whirled out into Lake Superior and kept breaking up. The men were forced to leap from cake to crumbling cake. One large chunk carrying seven men was dashed against the Huron Islands; five of the men managed to leap ashore on rocky MacIntyre Island, but the other two were swept away from the island and eastward in the Big Lake on the floe. It crumbled. Wet and numb with cold, the two men reached more solid cakes. Finally, after being carried twenty-eight miles, they were able to get ashore near the Huron River, where they met another party of five refugees, including a man and his wife. They all built a fire to keep from freezing—the temperature by now was perhaps twenty below zero—and spent the night huddled behind a windbreak they built of ice.

Another fisherman had to swim the open water. Two men without a compass became separated and lost in the blizzard. One old Swede—most of the fishermen were either Finns or Swedes— hopped from cake to cake as the disaster struck, salvaging abandoned fishing lines.

So mountainous were the waves that the Coast Guard could not launch a rescue boat. The sheriff and state police sent doctors to treat frostbitten feet, hands, or faces of the refugees who reached lumbering camps. The blizzard ended next morning. The last men to be saved were those marooned on tiny MacIntyre Island; they had spent thirty hours there, five men huddled in a fishing shanty with nothing to eat but a pound of beans and a little candy. Luckily, none died in this near-disaster. The following Sunday four men who escaped were back fishing again.

People wait through the holidays for the ice to come in; usually L'Anse Bay is frozen solid by January, and then as many as three hundred little tents may dot its surface. Similarly, summertime mid-continent deep-sea fishing for lake trout is a popular sport at L'Anse, Baraga, Copper Harbor, Munising, Marquette, and elsewhere, attracting many tourists, who, to the amusement of the natives, usually go after lake trout in the hottest part of the summer although the fishing is not at its best until September or October.

The tourist trade is not yet big business in Upper Michigan. The eastern half of the state, its forests gone and without other economic base, has wakened more to the possibilities of the tourist trade than the western portion, where mining still flourishes. Typically, in the western area impatient public opinion squelched the howl of outside proponents of recreation that damming a stream to provide a mining company with hydroelectric power would destroy a lovely waterfall.

In recent years organizations like the Upper Peninsula Development Bureau have attempted to encourage tourists with elaborate brochures and ambitious promotion stunts like the election of "Smelt Queens," young ladies who shiver in bathing suits at the annual spring run up the rivers of the smelt, which are small fish. Northern Wisconsin is highly commercialized and publicized. So is the Lower Peninsula; so are portions of Minnesota. Upper Michigan has all the natural advantages of these. Why has it not the tourists?

To begin with, it is an obscure out-of-the-way region, as it has been since the days when the Western emigrants passed it by. (A current story concerns a Washington official who telephoned Ishpeming and peremptorily asked for the town's snowplow; when the local authorities wanted to know how the miners would go to work through ten-foot snowdrifts, the Washington man asked in amazement: "Do you have mines up there?") Indeed, comparatively few tourists realize such a place exists, and those who do know little about it. To most Midwest sportsmen, the north woods mean Wisconsin or Minnesota.

Until recently highways and rail service were inadequate. This is no longer true.

But facilities for tourists are still inadequate, though the resort keepers would deny it vigorously. Wealthy tourists do not find here the elegant accommodations to which they are accustomed. True, inexpensive long auto trips with only overnight stops are possible, for sufficient state-cleared camp sites and roadside cabins exist (though the cabins are, in general, far from elaborate). But with a few exceptions, such as the establishments at Mackinac Island, remote Isle Royale, Blaney Park, Grand Island, the Keweenaw Club near Copper Harbor, and Cardinal's Lodge on Lake Michigamme, top-notch resorts for long vacations are far from plentiful. In northern Wisconsin the tourist has a choice of perhaps a dozen or more lodges on one lake, priced from $3 to $15 a day, American plan, or he can rent a housekeeping cabin. In Upper Michigan he may find one first-class lodge in two or three counties. Similarly, a really first-class meal is hard to buy in Upper Michigan. Houghton's storied Douglass House, with copper medallions in the barroom floor, still serves excellent meals, and so does the new Mather Inn at Ishpeming. They are unusual. Certain sections, like the Au Train region and the Watersmeet area, are well supplied with housekeeping cottages; but in other vast remote areas, such as the Porcupine and Huron Mountains, the Whitefish Bay and Two-Hearted River regions, little but tarpaper shacks is available, and few of them.

Still the people come, lured by magnificent waterfalls, great forests, high rough hills, long stretches of uninhabited country, abundant fish and game. They are reminded everywhere that this is north country. The gravel in the roads is red with iron ore. Roadside signs enjoin tourists to avoid forest fires, warn them of logging trucks and deer crossings in the vicinity. So numerous are deer in some areas that they constitute a positive highway menace at night. Only the main highways are open throughout the winter. In remote areas of poor farmland all food must be imported, and sometimes, even in summer, it becomes scarce. Along the highways rumble heavy trucks with towering loads of logs. Lakeside cottages frequently are called "camps," probably after the old-time lumbering camps. Hotel lobbies are filled with salesmen of mining equipment, not tourists. Outside the cities, modern plumbing and, in some places, electric lights are rare. So are many other conveniences the tourist expects.

Upper Michigan sports include some of the best fishing and

hunting in the Midwest and, at Ironwood, Iron Mountain, and Ishpeming, skiing and tobogganing. Winter sports are comparatively new tourist attractions, though long popular among the Scandinavian immigrants. During the deer season, November 15 to 30, a hunter is allowed one bear and one male deer with antlers not less than three inches long. In some counties bears are protected the year round. Fish and game regulations are highly complicated. In general, the trout season opens the last Saturday in April and the season on other fish June 25, although certain lakes may be fished for pike after May 15. One should study carefully the regulations issued with each license and consult conservation officers locally. Contrary to popular opinion, the laws are based on conservation necessities and are not simply designed to confuse the sportsman. Fishing license fees for non-residents are only $2 for the season or $1 for ten days, and in either case the spouse of the licensee may buy a license for an additional fifty cents. A non-resident deer-bear license costs $25, a small-game license $5. Probably the most popular small game is ruffed grouse, called partridge; the two-week season usually opens October 1, and a good place to hunt is in the flatlands around Covington or on the Burnt Plains north of there, a vast strange area burned out hundreds of years ago by Indians driving deer into traps. Deer are plentiful in the vicinity of the Tahquamenon swamp, between Seney and Shingleton, between Channing and Republic, east of L'Anse, and in many other regions; deer prefer swampy or cutover land to virgin timber. The woods are not crowded enough with hunters to be dangerous, as they are elsewhere.

Many natives indulge in illegal "headlighting," driving a truck down a logging road at night and hypnotizing deer with a spotlight; since deer hold still only when but a single beam of light is focused on them, they are protected by nailing to trees at breast height shiny pieces of tin which reflect the headlight beam. Other game found in Upper Michigan includes rabbits, squirrels, pheasants, prairie chickens, woodcock, geese, and ducks.

The principal game fish are brook trout and rainbows and the less common German browns; wall-eyed pike; small- and large-mouth black bass; and northern pike. Upper Michigan has no true muskellunge except in its half of Lac Vieux Desert, where they were planted by Wisconsin, which has concentrated on muskies to the neglect of other species. With similar effects, Michigan has emphasized panfish, such as bluegills, probably to please the numerous cane-pole fishing farmers and workers from Lower Michigan. Furthermore, since Upper Michigan is so far from the state capital and since its sparse population carries so little political weight in relation to its area, it has been neglected to some extent in fish stocking as in other ways. Recently, however, the tendency has been to correct this.

Trout are found in most of the smaller streams throughout Upper Michigan. Among the better known are the Two-Hearted, the tributaries of the Dead and the Manistique system, the upper Escanaba, the Sturgeon, the western Presque Isle, the upper Ontonagon. Many of the natives use live bait, chiefly worms; outsiders use artificial flies. Bass and pike are found chiefly in lakes, though a few rivers, like the Paint, are good. Of the numerous lake regions, those near Manistique, Munising, Gwinn, Michigamme, Watersmeet, and Crystal Falls are among the best. Oddly, the most remote lakes do not always provide the best fishing. Only the more accessible lakes are stocked. Some lakes miles from any highway are said to be entirely without bass or pike; never stocked, they contained no native fish because they were drained by long rivers too broken by steep falls to permit the entry of fish from the Great Lakes.

A fisherman or hunter may have a hard time in Upper Michigan. A city dweller does not want to spend half his short vacation in hunting a boat and information on where to fish, in performing for himself all the countless tasks which are performed for him at better-organized resort centers. There are absolutely no boats on some of the best lakes, and if you carry one in—no task for a soft city man—the natives may burn it. You will find few professional guides in the Maine or Wisconsin sense. The ignorance of the natives about their own hills and lakes and streams is often appalling; they scorn all fish but trout and frequently they won't tell you where the trout are. They know more, in general, about hunting than fishing, but they are too busy getting their own buck to help the tourist. These generalities apply more to the western than the eastern end of the Upper Peninsula.

All of this is not to say that a pleasant vacation cannot be spent in Upper Michigan. Quite the contrary. But the tourist should be forewarned that he will find no Sea Island, Georgia, resorts, few entrepreneurs catering desperately to his wants during the short season. You can get fish and game, lots of them, but you will have to work for them, and chances are you will have to find them yourself. You will have to do nearly everything for yourself. The region is not geared to make your visit painless. Sometimes the absence of conveniences and the clannishness of the people are maddening to an outsider. If you fight it, you are lost. If you slide into the system, you can find no better vacation spot. A tourist should know what to expect in Upper Michigan. The truth is that the Upper Peninsula is poised uneasily between past and future. Its destiny lies somewhere between the eager but inept efforts of the eastern portion to encourage tourists and the haughty poverty and the memories of the western portion.

As a general rule, the tourist cannot do better than to hunt up the nearest conservation officer. Most conservation officers are courteous and fairly well informed. Their chief duties are not, as the majority of tourists and nearly all the natives appear to believe, to annoy and arrest sportsmen. Their job is to conserve the game and fish and timber and other natural resources. It is not an easy job. The conservation officer is on call twenty-four hours a day, he must endure the resentment of many of his local acquaintances and the hauteur of some tourists, he must make arrests that are always unpleasant and frequently downright danger-ous, he must spend long days in the woods at common labor, he must expect sleepless days and nights of the hardest kind of work when a forest fire is raging. He must combat the ignorance of natives, one of whom blames the tourists for the disappearance of trout which "I used to catch by the barrel at night with a lantern and a net." He is underpaid, reviled, unappreciated. He would be the last to say so.

His chief duty is fire-fighting. Upper Michigan has had no forest fires as disastrous to life and property as the Hinckley, Minnesota, fire or the fire just south of the Michigan line at Pesh-tigo, Wisconsin, where in 1871, on the night of the great Chicago fire, hundreds burned to death. Nevertheless, Upper Peninsula wardens can recall some humdingers. One in 1890 leaped from ridge to ridge as it burned north from the Dead River all the way to Lake Superior, leaving the hardwood in the valleys nearly untouched. Others, during the period between 1884 and 1890, burned over much of the territory between Wetmore and St. Ignace. In 1913 a stand of jackpine a hundred feet tall was burned in a great swath nine miles long and three miles wide near the Yellow Dog and Salmon Trout Rivers. In the autumn of 1923 a fire started near Silver City, in the Porcupines, and burned at least 50,000 acres of woodland and numerous lumbering camps. A stubborn fire near Escanaba burned from August 5 to September 29 in 1933, despite the efforts of more than 600 men, including 225 CCC workers. In 1919 the Whorl Fire started on the banks of the Two-Hearted River and burned into the outskirts of Newberry, devastating 30,000 acres. The Driggs and Fox River area, already cutover by the boys from Seney, was further ravished in 1930 by a fire which seared 40,000 acres of marsh and jackpine. Indeed, so common were large fires in the eastern end of Upper Michigan that a haze of smoke hung over the whole territory during July and August in 1912, 1918, 1920, 1925, 1930, and 1933.

Some years, of course, are worse than others, because of drought and other weather conditions. Following logging as it does, fire destroys fish and game as well as timber, and it may destroy whole towns as it razes isolated farm buildings or lumbering camps. No fire is small enough to be neglected. Sometimes wardens spend days in the roadless wilderness hunting a column of smoke which a watcher has spotted from a fire tower, only to discover that a trapper left a pair of worn-out rubber boots near a campfire.

On an afternoon in August 1931 Nels Crebassa, conservation officer of the Baraga district, was walking back from the wild Huron Mountains where a fire had been reported (without basis) when, still five miles from the end of the tote road where he had left his car, he saw so much smoke to the westward as he topped Bald Mountain that "I thought the world was on fire." There was not much he could do about it right then except make certain that he got out of there before, as seemed likely, the fire trapped him. By the time he reached his car, the setting sun was nearly hidden behind a dense black pall. At Skanee he saw that the fire was across Huron Bay, on Point Abbaye. The faces of scores of onlookers were garish in the red night light.

Crebassa drove down the bay to headquarters in the twin towns of Baraga and L'Anse below Dynamite Hill. Men had been fighting the fire nearly all that day. When the first alarm was turned in, the officers had collected hand pumps, shovels, axes, hoes, an outboard motor, and other tools and hastened up the long narrow point of land. They had no bulldozers, tractors, plows, booster units, trucks, or other heavy equipment such as is now in use. Everything had to be done by hand. Actually, not much of anything could be done with that fire. It had started about three miles northeast of L'Anse and, on the wings of a high southwest wind, had roared out on the point through the farming community of Aura. So high was the wind that chunks of flaming birch bark whirled through the air for sometimes three quarters of a mile. The fire moved so fast the men could not get ahead of it to cut it off. They followed it as closely as possible in the terrible heat, cutting converging trenches about two feet wide in an effort to pinch the fire in. They were not successful. The fire overleaped a vast area and started another fire on Point Abbaye, which quickly became a major conflagration. In the end, the workers could do nothing but throw water on buildings. Fortunately, the wind was blowing away from instead of toward the only sizable towns in the vicinity, L'Anse and Baraga. The fire burned about 12,000 acres before, at six p.m. on the second day, the wind abated and a light rain fell. Quickly the workers brought the fire under control by cutting a belt around it; this it could not overleap unaided by wind. One man who fought it says it wasn't the biggest fire ever in Upper Michigan, but it sure was one of the hottest.

Nels Crebassa was fighting on home ground here. His grandfather, Peter Crebassa, arrived at L'Anse in 1836 from Canada and became the fur company's agent. He was instrumental in getting the church to send Father, later Bishop, Frederic Baraga to L'Anse Bay, and divine services were held in the forties in the Crebassa house. From this beginning came the Assinins Mission, which still flourishes, a vital factor among the Indians of Catholic persuasion who live on the west side of L'Anse Bay. (The Methodist Indians live on the east side. All together, about a thousand live in the reservation at L'Anse.) Peter Crebassa's store account-book lists items charged to such men as Peter Courtariell (a famous muskie lake in northern Wisconsin is named Courtariell), Little Eagle, George Brown, and The Wolf, who spent $5 for two pairs of booties, 15 cents for fifteen flints, and, recklessly, $16 for eight yards of satin. Peter Crebassa fathered fifteen children and lived to be ninety-two; he was active in opening the Michigamme Mine. His grandson Nels, the conservation man, is stationed at Three Lakes, five miles west of Michigamme in Spurr Township, where the westernmost iron mines of the Marquette Range were located. The roots of these people today in Upper Michigan go deep as the mine shafts.

Three Lakes is on the map as a town. Actually it is nothing but a country store on U. S. 41. Once mining locations flourished near by. Today they have vanished. Not far off are summer cottages—camps—on Ruth and George and Beaufort Lakes, a few decrepit farms, some loggers' camps, nothing more. The cultural and commercial center of these is Numi's store. Earl Numinen is a cheerful short-legged, round-bellied man whose father came here from Finland and never quite learned to speak English. The old man, with his hollow cheeks and parchment skin, looks almost sinister by lamplight; he is in his seventies, but alone he cut and peeled logs in the woods and built the cluster of tourist cabins for Earl around the store. The Finns are wondrous log carpenters. The old man's chief pleasure outside of an occasional drink is attending movies with titles in Finnish, which are shown regularly in this region. When he first brought his family here he worked in the mines. Now he lives with Earl, perhaps the most progressive of the sons, who has studied at the excellent Michigan College of Mining and Technology at Houghton. Earl is a surveyor for the State Highway Department as well as the proprietor of the store at Three Lakes; this he calls Numi's Service Station because of its two gasoline pumps. (One is broken.) Earl's two brothers, who also live in this settlement, are miners.

Amusement is not readily available here. Michigamme offers only a movie in the town hall on Thursday nights and a single tourist-type tavern just outside town, that of Maurice Ball, who also is a miner and whose father was a miner. L'Anse, the nearest town westward, is thirty miles away and has little to offer. The alternative is Ishpeming or Negaunee, or, farther east, Marquette. Marquette seems more like a city than Ishpeming. It is bigger, has more modernistic taverns, more roadhouses, more unfriendly people—a small city trying to be big. Now and then Earl Numinen and his wife, Hilma, go to Marquette and meet Earl's sister, Lya, who is married to a man with the remarkable name of Uno Ollila. Close friends of this couple are Nina and Karlo Ketola, a miner who earns $300 a month in the new Mather Mine and pays $5 a month rent, and Helen and Waino Martonen. (Easy pronunciation of Finnish names and difficulty of reproducing Finnish dialect in print stem alike from the clear enunciation of each syllable. Many persons in Upper Michigan, particularly politicians, master rudimentary Finnish, and one veteran stump campaigner recalls the speech he learned by rote in Finnish which, translated, ran: "You vote for Mr. Roosevelt, you vote for me, thank you very much.") The Numinens and their friends go to Ollie's Barn outside of Marquette, where Swedes and Finns dance the Finnish waltz, the conventional waltz, the schottische, the polka, and the whistle dance, a march-like affair involving changing partners. Sometimes Earl and Hilma visit the Majhannus at their attractive apartment over their store in Michigamme for a Finnish feast on *silakka salattie* and *fillia;* sometimes they go to L'Anse, sometimes to Ishpeming. They never have been to Chicago, the nearest big city.

Of an evening, Earl's store becomes the gathering place, the social center. Frequently the Majhannus come out to play cribbage with the Numinens. Other residents congregate in the tiny store to buy slab bacon or a mosquito repellent called Lollacapop or the latest Finnish newspaper, or, once a week, fresh vegetables and fruit.

Sometimes they come to take a bath. One evening a week, and sometimes two, the Numinens fire up their *sauna*, or Finnish steam bath. The bath house, out behind the store, is a log cabin about the size of an ordinary tourist cabin in the woods. The building is divided into two rooms, one for dressing and resting and the other for the bath proper. A single kerosene lamp in a window between the two rooms lights both. The bathroom proper smells of pitch, its floor is wet and slippery, its air is hot and humid. To the right on the floor is a big iron boiler; in this a roaring fire is built. Atop the boiler are scores of boulders the size of cantaloupes. These become almost red-hot. Having first washed with soap and hot water from the tub near the boiler, you draw a pan of cold water from the pump beside the boiler and then cautiously mount the steps along the opposite wall until you are sitting naked on a bleacher-like bench with your head near the ceiling and your feet inches higher than the hot rocks in front of you. Onto the rocks you toss the pan of cold water. Immediately live steam billows up, almost invisible; as it surrounds you, perspiration drips from your body and your breath comes with difficulty unless you take the precaution of breathing through a moist washcloth. A few minutes of this at a time is all that a newcomer can endure. Two or more may take the bath together. Veterans at *sauna* jokingly overheat a newcomer. Men have fainted from too much steam. The Finns like to take *sauna* daily, even in below-zero weather; they can stand an unbelievable amount of steam and, to encourage perspiration, they beat their naked bodies with broom-like switches of balsam boughs while the steam billows around them. Miners take *sauna* to get the hematite out of their pores, something the modern shower baths in the mine change-houses never can accomplish. *Sauna* is almost a sure cure for a hangover. In any case, it is something not easily forgotten.

With hospitality characteristic of this tough country, inherited perhaps from earlier wilderness people who simply had to help each other to survive, the Numinens welcome tourists and natives alike to their *sauna*. After it, though drowsy, the people may sit in the little store and talk. Or they may go to one of the camps on a lake near by, a tar-paper shack with an outdoor privy, kerosene or gasoline lamps, a pump in the kitchen, a fireplace, and a glassed-in porch facing the lake. Sitting on the porch in the summer, you can look through the needles of the pine tree and see the northern lights shooting strange and high in the northern sky, and sometimes in the winter, when the atmosphere is right, you can see the weird sisters carrying their ghostly lanterns across the ice. Inside the camp the smoky pitchwood is burning out in the fireplace and the hardwood logs are beginning to catch.

"That's maple, that is," Cal says; "cut it myself last fall, and it's been seasoning all winter out in back; no better wood than maple for to keep a fire. Remember the time Johnny and Joe stayed overnight in the old logging camp while they was out deer-hunting? They filled the cook stove up tight with hardwood and let her go; 'bout midnight they woke up it was so hot in the camp, and when they come downstairs they saw the top of the stove was so white-hot you could see right through it, and they run out into the snow in their underwear; they thought the camp was going to burn down. It didn't though."

"You had any of that unrationed meat yet, Nels?"

And the warden looks the other way quickly.

Bill Numinen winks at his brother Earl and the others around the fire and says: "They tell me the deer meat is not very good this summer. But I would not know. Hey, Nels?"

Nels doesn't answer.

"Nels, remember that time you chased somebody up the Beaufort River? Somebody that had been netting fish in Beaufort Lake?"

Nels jumps at this; he remembers. "Was that you, Bill?"

"Maybe. My dad, he fell in the river that night anyway."

"We used to find a lot of nets in those days," Nels says.

"Sure," Bill says. "And we used to lose a lot."

It doesn't matter; the statute of limitations operates on game violations. Nels says he sure remembers one time when he and the judge, they went out on Point Abbaye with thirty-five blank warrants and they made twenty-nine arrests just hiding in the brush at the crossing of two trails and grabbing violators. They all got fined fifty dollars except one old man, and everybody felt sorry for him, but it turned out that he had a roll of bills in his pocket big as your hat.

"Not much headlighting this year yet," somebody says, and somebody else says: "No, but there will be. And say, did you hear that blasting the other night?"

They all had heard it. Someone had dynamited a lake deep in the woods. Nobody condones this; it isn't right, somehow.

For a moment it is quiet and the only sound is the soft hiss of the gasoline lamp, which you pump up and then hang by the hook of a coat-hanger from the ceiling. From near by, on the high bald rock bluffs, comes the bark of coyotes. But wasn't there a deeper howl in that, longer and deeper, like a timber wolf? There's lots of timber wolves out south, out toward Ned Lake, but you almost never see them. I heard one close by the other night, down by Petticoat Lake where I was fishin'; remember—just after the beaver slapped his tail? Yes, and didn't that make a racket, that beaver?

You know, beavers 'r' like people, kind of. They'll all get together to build theirselves a house and there'll be a foreman and everything, and any lazy beaver's chased away by the others. It's true; I hope to sink right down to hell if it ain't. Plenty of beaver round here yet. Not like there used to be though. I hear they raise beaver on a farm these days. Ain't that a corker? Did you know some man wrote a book about beavers, and he found it all out right around here? What's the name of that book? Wait a minute, it's out in the kitchen. And Cal gets it from behind the neat row of canned food: Lewis H. Morgan's definitive *The American Beaver and His Works*, written from observations made near Ishpeming.

Near Ishpeming, that was, and there used to be lots of beavers out north too, round Silver Lake. I remember old Peter Moore used to come into the Jump On Top saloon with a stack of hides that high. Poor fellow, he's dead now, old Peter; I can see him now. And old Dan Spencer used to trap lots of beavers out there too; Buck Anderson never could see how he did it. I went to China with Buck, you know. When we was in China—no, while we was still in Burma—well . . .

That beaver slappin' his tail and the coyotes and all, that's nothing compared to the way a lynx sounds in the woods. Specially at night. That's the worst. I heard one out north towards Camp Nine Lake, up by the old logging camp, and I ran halfway back to town. It sounds like a little baby crying.

Say, 'd you see where the bear chewed up the stump out in back of camp the other night? Grubbing for worms. Because it's spring, I guess. They always used to come down and upset the garbage can by the restaurant when I was runnin' it. One time I was playin' with the dog out in front of the place and the dog got his back all up and went around the corner and I heard a noise, so I went back there in the dark to the garbage can and there was a big black bear. He was standing up, he must of been nine feet tall. We just stood there a minute, him and me, and then he started coming towards me. I waited till he was about three or four feet away, then I turned around and run and so did he.

Wouldn't of done you no good to run, Cal, if he'd wanted to chase you. Any bear can outrun any man. They don't look it, but they can. Who was it, Earl, they tell that story about? About the time this, you know, this fellow was out picking berries back of Billy Manti's place, up by the waterfalls where they used to fish trout in the Nelligan Lake outlet, and he got into a thick tangle of brush and he saw a pit down below where there was a lots of blueberries, so he jumped down into the pit and almost jumped right on the back of a great big old she-bear. But she jumped out of the pit just as fast as he jumped in. Who was that anyway, Earl?

I don't remember his name, but wasn't that the same fellow that got chased by the bear? After his son'd shot it with a twenty-two, I mean. Anyway, the boy just wounded it, he didn't really hurt it, so the bear started after this fellow and he just had a shotgun. He was out after birds, you see. He fired and he hit the bear in the face and blinded him and that made the bear kind of crazy. The bear came after him and the man ran. All the time the bear was gaining. The man crawled through that fence by Billy's place and the bear didn't see the fence because he was blind; he came through that fence on his hind legs, standing up and roaring and swinging his arms and taking the fence with him. The man saw there wasn't use running any more and then he remembered he had a slug shell in his pocket, a solid slug like you use for deer. He put it in his gun and he waited till the bear was almost up to him, then he shot for the heart and the bear almost fell on top of him.

I guess Frank Brown killed one not so long ago that was eating apples in his orchard. And say, did you ever hear about the thing they used to see down by Gwinn? They'd see it at night, and it only had two legs and it always walked like a man, and for a long time everybody was scare' to death, everybody thought it was a big hairy man. But finally they trapped him, and it was a bear that had lost its two front legs in a trap.

Say, Cal, we could use some more wood on that fire. And another bottle of beer. We'll have to get some more at Clarence's tomorrow.

You want some more gas in the lamp?

No, let's let it go out. The fire makes enough light.

Sure. . . . You know, this country's about all caught up. You can always tell when the mines are about worked out and the timber's gone—the temperance people, they get strong. The saloons start to go away and there's nobody left but us old mulligans in the saloons any more, just a bunch of old drunks that nobody wants to talk to. I wonder if the old-timers, I mean a long time ago like during the pine days when you could drive a buggy through the pine out here the timber was so big—I wonder if maybe the old-timers wasn't just sort of old drunks, not, you know, sort of heroes like everybody thinks. I don't know.

But the old days was great. You take when the Michigamme Mine was runnin'. Them days. Just one glorious Fourth of July. Yep. And at Champion too. Last time anybody took any ore outta the old stockpiles couple of years ago. It ain't really been mined for twenty, thirty years. Just scrammin', that's all they is left around here now.

Yep, if they had a mine around here it'd sure help Michigamme a lot. They's plenty of ore around here. I guess they just don't need it bad enough. Plenty of ore yet around the Beaufort and the Ohio too. And the Imperial; remember when Ford had the Imperial goin' an' all the swells lived up on the hill there? They was the worst bunch for violatin' ever. Oh, they'll open her up again some day. Oh Chris', plenty o' ore around here.

They'll hit gold some day, too. Remember Silver Jack over at L'Anse? And Tappy what was his name? Anyways, Tappy, he usta go up into the Hurons an' come out with his pockets full o' dust. They'll hit her some day, prob'ly out by the Big Dead; they'll hit her all right. I hear they hit tin or tungsten or something out there now. There's lots o' mineral out that way in the jackpine country up toward Silver Lake. Lots o' mineral.

You'd think they'd hunt it more, with the war and all. But I guess they got all they need already. But say, ain't that war a corker? Ain't hardly nobody left around Michigamme any more —no young fellows anyhow. An' did you know they're goin' to have a funeral tomorrow morning, the first one? I remember when he went away, the night before, he was sayin' that Upper Michigan always did send good men to the wars, poor fellow. I hope they get them two drunk Indians outta town before the funeral; you should of seen 'em tonight out in front of Christianson's store. On their way to L'Anse, I guess. They'll probably get lost in the woods on the way.

Not Indians.

Hell, them Indians ain't as good in the woods as you or me.

Did you hear about that rum-dumb that got up outta Clarence's snake room an' went down by the station an' started to attackt the evening train with a knife? He thought it was a big animal. Somebody pulled him back in time so the train didn't kill him, an' he went after a telephone pole with the knife. Some rum-dumb.

No, but you ain't heard the best one. Last week it was. They was three of them sittin' round drinkin' out in camp up past the bridge, an' one o' 'em got a pain in his side, prob'ly from the rotten stuff they was drinkin'. Anyways, the other two, they decided he had an appendicitis and they'd better operate on him. So they put him on a table in the kitchen and looked around for a knife. They couldn't find a good sharp knife and that was lucky, but they did find a file, an old rusty file, and they took his shirt off an' started sawin' away at his side till it started to bleed. They figured he needed medicine on that wound bad, but they couldn't find no medicine in camp, so they poured a can of Flytox on it an' did he jump? He'd been just about all caught up, but he sure started hollerin' an' jumpin' when that Flytox took hold. But they sat on him and told him to be quiet or he'd die if they didn't get his appendicitis out. So they started sawin' away some more an' they'd of sawed right through to his gizzard if somebody sober hadn't come along, Waino Werginen I think it was, and stopped 'em. I guess he'll be in bed for a coupla weeks, poor fellow; they cut an awful gash in his side. Indtti Linimentti won't help that one.

The gasoline lamp flickered out. You could hardly see the deer head on the wall any longer, and all at once the silly paper flowers and pictures near it were gone; the fire was just glowing now, not blazing. Outside, the wind was springing up off the lake, and you could hear the waves lapping on the bottom of the boat on the shore. Far out in the lake a loon cried, long and mad.

Remember one Sunday afternoon, it was a long time ago, we was just kids, and we sneaked a ride on the ore train going up the grade to L'Anse and the train got stuck on the grade, it never could make that grade, and while they were backing up to get a run at it, us kids climbed off and caught six geese that was froze stiff there in the snow? That was near the old graphite pile. We used to do that a lot. It was in November month, real gray and cold like. Remember?

And remember the year the chickadees stayed all winter, it was so easy a winter? No snow at all. But then that summer—Holy O Jesus it was cold that summer, snow in July month. Weren't that the summer—sure it was—we was up on the Huron Bay Grade and we come to the lumber camp 'bout noon hungriern a coupla bears an' there weren't nobody in camp; all the boys had gone to town to get drunk. Remember? So we went on a little ways an' we come to a survey party an' they was fixin' dinner an' they give us some, an' afterwards you told the cookee that was the best mulligan stew you ever ate an' he told you it were made outta porcupines. Remember, Cal? You almost got sick to your stummick when you found that out.

No, but the squaw corn we used to make on fishin' trips, with a can o' corn an' a green pepper an' bacon cut up fine an' onion all fried up together. That used to be pretty nice. Some day let's see if we can't go out to Ned Lake; nobody's fished that lake ever, maybe, I guess, an' we can get some old cruiser to put us on the trail; course it's quite a walk, maybe ten, twelve miles, an' we'll have to build a raft 'cause there won't be no boat. I sure wish we could take a boat in with us an' float down from Ned to the Michigamme River and on down to the Paint, or down the other way over the portage and down the Deer River through Light Lake to the Paint. We'd get some fish I'm sure. Or maybe we'd ought to go up north of Ishpeming, up to Silver Lake, up to see old Dan Spencer. That's nice country up there in the jackpine, just like it always used to be, and it's nice walkin' through the hardwood, across the Mulligan and up the hill and then down to the lake, all blue and with whitecaps; it's tough country but it's nice country out that way. But I keep forgettin'. Pretty soon you won't have to walk any more. The Cleveland-Cliffs is buildin' a road right up to the lake, all the way up through the hardwood. An' I keep forgettin' too 'bout Dan. Dan's all caught up at Silver Lake. Yep, guess so. This country's changin'.

ACKNOWLEDGMENTS AND
BIBLIOGRAPHY

ٯ

SINCE THIS BOOK deals more with people than events, I have obtained my material more from people than documents. When resort to documents proved necessary, I have tried to consult contemporary newspapers and other writings by men "who had been there." Thus, the best account of a surveyor's problems is William Austin Burt's own.

I have obtained the great bulk of my information from miners, mining men, lumberjacks, trappers, newspapermen, saloon-keepers, local historians, police officers, retired fancy women, game wardens, tradesmen, and plain citizens, some of them old-timers with long memories. Many of these have made available to me valued family documents and photographs, and in their reminiscences and their everyday conversation lies the flavor of Upper Michigan.

These persons are too numerous to thank here individually. Moreover, because of the nature of some of the material, I would not embarrass the people who furnished it by acknowledging their aid publicly. And if I revealed the source of some of the frank opinions about, for example, the large companies, the persons who expressed them might be jeopardized. Perhaps the people who live in or near Michigamme helped me most to absorb the flavor of the region. They are my friends; I have spent much time pleasantly among them; I will not attempt to acknowledge formally their invaluable aid.

So far as I know, no one in recent years has written a book at-

274 ACKNOWLEDGMENTS AND BIBLIOGRAPHY

tempting to deal with Upper Michigan as a whole. In so doing, and especially in focusing attention on people rather than events, I have lacked sufficient space to treat fully each separate subject, or section of the region. These have been covered more completely by other writers. Among their more popular recent books are these:

On the Great Lakes, Norman Beasley's *Freighters of Fortune* (Harper & Brothers, 1930) and Walter Havighurst's *The Long Ships Passing* (The Macmillan Co., 1942).

On copper mining, Angus Murdoch's *Boom Copper* (The Macmillan Co., 1943).

On iron mining, Stewart Holbrook's *Iron Brew* (The Macmillan Co., 1939), Henry Oliver Evans's *Iron Pioneer* (a biography of Henry W. Oliver, published in 1942 by E. P. Dutton & Co.).

On lumbering, Holbrook's *Holy Old Mackinaw* (The Macmillan Co., 1938).

Robert Travers's *Troubleshooter* (Viking Press, 1943), written by a former Marquette County prosecutor, is a successful attempt to capture the feel of the region as a whole today. This is done for an earlier period with equal success on a more factual level by James K. Jamison in his too little known *This Ontonagon Country* (*Ontonagon Herald*, 1939).

Despite the exigencies of discretion and space, I am able to thank these persons for much valuable personal assistance in my research: John I. Bellaire, of Manistique; H. A. Keller of Philadelphia; Homer Guck, of Eagle Harbor and Chicago; Mr. and Mrs. M. S. Tucker, Evanston, Illinois; the Misses Isabel Jaehnig, Katherine Gillette, and May S. Jaehnig, Eagle Harbor; William Duchaine, the *Escanaba Daily Press*; G. Harold Earle, William J. Eisenzoph, David Downey, and Carl Schultz of the Wisconsin Land & Lumber Company at Hermansville; Thomas D. Conlin, of the Crystal Falls *Diamond Drill;* Professor James Fisher, of the Michigan College of Mining and Technology, at Houghton; Linwood I. Noyes and Edwin Johnson of the Ironwood *Globe;* Walter F. Gries of the Cleveland-Cliffs Iron Company, Ishpeming; John T. Burke, John Viking, John Voelker, all of Ishpeming; William L. Norton, of the Manistique *Pioneer-Tribune;* E. A.

Moore and James Trethewey, of the Marquette *Daily Mining Journal*; the staffs of the Peter White Library, Marquette, and the Ishpeming Public Library; Mrs. W. S. Wright of the Marquette County Historical Society; Lew Merwin, of the Munising *News*; Claude D. Riley, of the *Ontonagon Herald*; James K. Jamison, Ontonagon; Philip D. Pearson, superintendent of the Greenwood Mine, Ishpeming.

Above all in this category, I wish to thank Professor L. A. Chase, head of the Social Science Department of the Northern Michigan College of Education and Corresponding Secretary of the Marquette County Historical Society, and William H. Newett, editor of the Ishpeming *Iron Ore*. Both these gentlemen, in addition to furnishing a great amount of information and guidance, read the book in manuscript, enabling me to avoid numerous errors. Any errors which remain are mine. Mr. Newett has encouraged the writing of the book for three years, and has given me access to his extensive private library.

I am greatly indebted to Francis S. Nipp, long a personal friend of valued judgment, who has performed the prodigious labor of reading and criticizing the book in manuscript. His interest has been unflagging as we discussed and wrote the book. For secretarial assistance I am indebted to his wife, Mary Ellen Nipp and, for research assistance, to my own wife, Frances Rose Martin.

In a less personal but no less valuable way these persons assisted me: Oliver T. Burnham, of the Lake Carriers' Association; C. A. Paquin, of the Michigan Department of Conservation and his district supervisors; R. A. Smith, Michigan State Geologist; C. E. Randall, of the United States Department of Agriculture, Forest Service, Washington; Vico C. Isola, F. J. Champion, Raphael Zon, all of Forest Service's various Midwest stations; J. G. Wells, Jr., of the Michigan State College's Upper Peninsula Agricultural Experiment Station; Stanley Newton, of the Chippewa County Historical Society; T. J. Welsh, Chicago; Leon E. Truesdell, chief statistician for the Bureau of the Census.

I am indebted greatly to the Marquette County Historical Society and to the Michigan Historical Commission and George N. Fuller, its secretary and editor.

In my search for photographs, I have been aided, in addition to those persons or agencies already mentioned, by the Upper Peninsula Development Bureau, the United States Steel Corporation and its *News*, the United States Bureau of Mines, the United States Office of Indian Affairs, George K. North of Hancock, Nels Crebassa of L'Anse, Ralph Menge of the *L'Anse Sentinel*, and the Childs Art Gallery, Ishpeming.

For permission to reprint material or reproduce photographs still in copyright, I am indebted to the following: Random House (Gustavus Myers's *History of the Great American Fortunes*, 1937); Oxford University Press (Samuel Eliot Morison's and H. S. Commager's *The Growth of the American Republic*, 1942); Henry Holt and Company (Raphael Pumpelly's *My Reminiscences*, 1918); Sault News Publishing Company and Stanley Newton (Stanley Newton's *Mackinac Island and Sault Ste. Marie*, 1909); The Penton Publishing Company (Ralph D. Williams's *The Honorable Peter White*, 1905); Little, Brown & Company (Francis Parkman's *The Jesuits in North America*, 1880); Professor James Fisher (his *The History of the Michigan Copper Country*, 1924); the *Ontonagon Herald* and James K. Jamison (Mr. Jamison's *This Ontonagon Country*, 1939).

Some of those books were major sources in my research. I have examined literally hundreds of books, manuscripts, and magazine and newspaper articles. The proceedings of the Lake Superior Mining Institute, published on an annual basis since 1893 but with some years omitted, contain an enormous mass of material on the region, not only of a technical nature but also such valuable general papers as John Munro Longyear's "Reminiscences of Marquette and the Upper Peninsula of Michigan since 1873." In addition to those sources already mentioned, I found these most valuable:

BOOKS

ALLEN, R. C., Director: *Mineral Resources of Upper Michigan with Statistical Tables of Production and Value of Mineral Products for 1914 and Prior Years with a Treatise on Michigan Copper Deposits by R. E. Hore.* Lansing, Michigan: Wynkoop Hallenbeck Crawford Co., State Printers; 1915.

BROOKS, T. B., PUMPELLY, RAPHAEL, and ROMINGER, C.: *Geological Survey of Michigan. . . .* New York, 1873.

BURT, WILLIAM A.: *A Key to the Solar Compass, and Surveyor's Companion.* Philadelphia: William S. Young; 1855.

CARVER, JONATHAN: *Travels through the Interior Parts of North America, in the years 1766, 1767, and 1768.* Dublin, 1779.

CHASE, LEW ALLEN: *Rural Michigan.* New York: The Macmillan Company; 1921.

CHRISTY, BAYARD H., ed.: *The Book of Huron Mountain.* Huron Mountain Club; 1929.

FOSTER, JOHN WELLS, and WHITNEY, JOSIAH DWIGHT: *Report on the Geology and Topography of the Lake Superior Land District.* 2 vols. Washington, 1850-1.

FULLER, GEORGE N., ed.: *Geological Reports of Douglass Houghton, 1837-1845.* Lansing, Michigan: Michigan Historical Commission; 1928.

GOLD THWAITES, REUBEN, ed.: *The Jesuit Relations and Allied Documents. . . .* 73 vols. Cleveland, 1896.

History of the Upper Peninsula of Michigan. Chicago: Western Historical Company; 1883.

HOTCHKISS, GEORGE W.: *History of the Lumber and Forest Industry of the Northwest.* Chicago, 1898.

HOUGHTON, JACOB, JR.: *The Mineral Region of Lake Superior.* Buffalo, 1846.

HUBBARD, BELA: *Memorials of a Half Century in Michigan and the Lake Region.* New York: G. P. Putnam's Sons. (Reprinted in FULLER: *Geological Reports of Douglass Houghton;* see above.)

Lake Superior Iron Ores. Cleveland: The Lake Superior Iron Ore Association; 1938.

LEVERETT, FRANK: *Surface Geology of Michigan.* Lansing, 1917.

MARTIN, HELEN M.: *Ne-Saw-Je-Won.* Cleveland, 1939.

Michigan, A Guide to the Wolverine State Compiled by Workers of the Writers' Program of the Work Projects Administration in the State of Michigan. American Guide Series. New York: Oxford University Press; 1941.

Michigan Biographies. 2 vols. Lansing, Michigan: Michigan Historical Commission Publications; 1924.

OSBORN, CHASE S., and OSBORN, STELLANOVA: *Schoolcraft→Longfellow→Hiawatha.* Lancaster, Pennsylvania: The Jaques Cattell Press; 1942.

Proceedings of the Lake Superior Mining Institute. 30 vols. Ishpeming, Michigan: Lake Superior Mining Institute; First published 1893.

PUMPELLY, RAPHAEL: *Reminiscences of Raphael Pumpelly.* 2 vols. New York: Henry Holt & Co.; 1918.

RICKARD, T. A.: *A History of American Mining.* New York: McGraw-Hill Book Co.; 1932.

"Samuel Livingston Mather," *Dictionary of American Biography,* Dumas Malone, ed. New York: Charles Scribner's Sons; 1933.

SAWYER, A.: *A History of the Northern Peninsula of Michigan and Its People.* Chicago, 1911.

STEVENS, HORACE J.: *The Copper Handbook.* Houghton, Michigan, 1911.

SWINEFORD, A. P.: *Annual Review of the Iron Mining and Other Industries of the Upper Peninsula for the Year Ending Dec. 31, 1881.* Marquette, Michigan, *Mining Journal;* 1882.

——: *History and Review of the Copper, Iron, Silver, Slate, and other Material Interests of the South Shore of Lake Superior.* Marquette, Michigan, *Mining Journal;* 1876.

VAN HISE, C. R., and others: *The Marquette Iron-Bearing District of Michigan.* . . . Washington: Government Printing Office; 1897.

WILKINSON, THE REVEREND WILLIAM: *Memorials of the Minnesota Forest Fires in the Year 1894.* Minneapolis: Norman E. Wilkinson; 1895.

WRIGHT, CHARLES E.: *Annual Report of the Commissioner of Mineral Statistics of the State of Michigan, for 1882.* Lansing: W. S. George & Co., State Printers and Binders; 1883. (And other reports of a similar nature for other years.)

PAMPHLETS, MANUSCRIPTS, AND GOVERNMENT DOCUMENTS

BELLAIRE, JOHN I.: Scrapbooks and manuscripts published and unpublished.

BRUÈRE, MARTHA BENSLEY: *Taming Our Forests.* United States Department of Agriculture, 1939.

CASE, C. M.: *Hermansville Historiette* [unpublished manuscript]. 1925.

Characteristics of the Population of Michigan, Prepared under the Supervision of Dr. Leon E. Truesdell. Washington: Government Printing Office; 1942.

CHASE, LEW ALLEN: *Marquette, Its History, Industry, Natural Attractions.* Marquette, Michigan, 1924.

CONLIN, THOMAS: Untitled and unpublished manuscript on the history of Crystal Falls and Iron River [n.d.]. (In possession of his son, Thomas D. Conlin, Crystal Falls.)

Correspondence on Indian Affairs. Marquette Historical Society.

CUNNINGHAM, R. N., and WHITE, H. G.: *Forest Resources of the Upper Peninsula of Michigan.* United States Department of Agriculture Miscellaneous Publication No. 429. Washington: Government Printing Office; 1941.

CUNNINGHAM, WALTER: *Report of Mineral Lands on Lake Superior.* Senate Document 98. Washington, 1845.

FIELDER, R. H.: *Fishery Statistics of the United States 1940.* United States Department of the Interior Statistical Digest No. 4. Washington: Government Printing Office; 1943.

Forest Fire Fighting in Michigan. Department of Conservation, Field Administration Division [n.d.].

GUTHRIE, JOHN D.: *Great Forest Fires of America.* Washington: United States Department of Agriculture [n.d.].

HEADLEY, ROY: *Trends toward Mechanization of Forest Fire Control.* Bulletin of United States Department of Agriculture, 1940.

Historical Review of This Company's Development and Resources . . . , An. Cleveland: The Cleveland-Cliffs Iron Company; 1920.

Investigation of Concentration of Economic Power, Hearings before the Temporary National Economic Committee, Congress of the United States. . . . Part 18, *Iron and Steel Industry.* Washington: Government Printing Office; 1940.

JACKSON, CHARLES THOMAS: *Report on the Geological and Mineralogical Survey of the Mineral Lands of the United States in the State of Michigan,* Part 3. Washington, 1849.

Compo *vs.* Jackson Iron Mine Controversies. Photostats. Marquette Historical Society. United States Supreme Court Reports, 1886–7.

MARTIN, HELEN M., ed.: *They Need Not Vanish, A Discussion of the Natural Resources of Michigan.* Michigan Department of Conservation, 1942.

Michigan Forest Fire Fighters Service Manual, Prepared by Michigan Department of Conservation. Lansing: Office of Civilian Defense; 1943.

Michigan Log Marks, Their Function and Use during the Great Michigan Pine Harvest, Compiled by the Work Projects Administration. East Lansing: Michigan Agricultural Experiment Station; 1941.

Michigan State Department of Conservation, Eleventh Biennial Report; 1941–2.

Mother Tongue of the White Population for States and Large Cities: 1940, Series P-15, No. 10. Washington: United States Department of Commerce; March 3, 1943.

National Forests in Michigan. United States Department of Agriculture. Washington: Government Printing Office; 1941.

Regional Planning, Report of the Northern Lakes States Regional Committee to the National Resources Committee, Part VIII, *Northern Lakes States.* Washington: Government Printing Office; 1939.

Reports of various mining companies. Marquette Historical Society.

Statistical Supplement to the Annual Report of the Commissioner of Indian Affairs. . . . United States Department of the Interior, 1942.

Successful Farm Practices in the Upper Peninsula. Special Bulletin No. 215, Agricultural Experiment Station, Michigan State College. East Lansing: Michigan; October 1931.

Unpublished correspondence, field notes, and other documents relating to surveying. Marquette Historical Society.

PERIODICALS

Daily Mining Gazette; Houghton, Michigan.
Daily Mining Journal; Marquette, Michigan.
Diamond Drill; Crystal Falls, Michigan.
Escanaba Daily Press; Escanaba, Michigan.
Iron Ore (and predecessors under varying names); Ishpeming, Michigan.
Ironwood Globe (and predecessors under varying names); Ironwood, Michigan.
L'Anse Sentinel; L'Anse, Michigan.
Manistique Pioneer-Tribune; Manistique, Michigan
Merchants' Magazine and Commercial Review, Vol. XLIV. New York: William B. Dana; 1861.
Michigan History Magazine; Michigan Historical Commission, Lansing, Michigan.
Michigan Pioneer and Historical Collections; The Pioneer Society of the State of Michigan.
Munising News; Munising, Michigan.
Ontonagon Herald; Ontonagon, Michigan.
Skillings' Mining Review; Duluth, Minnesota.
Sunday Sentinel; Milwaukee, Wisconsin.

INDEX